BIBLE AND ECOLOGY

Also in the *Sarum Theological Lectures Series*

SARUM THEOLOGICAL LECTURES
°°°∞°°°

BIBLE AND ECOLOGY

Rediscovering the Community of Creation

Richard Bauckham

BAYLOR UNIVERSITY PRESS

This edition published in 2010 by
Baylor University Press
Waco, Texas 76798–7363

Cover Design by Jeremy Reiss

First published in 2010 by
Darton, Longman and Todd Ltd
1 Spencer Court
140 – 142 Wandsworth High Street
London SW18 4JJ

Library of Congress Cataloging-in-Publication Data

Bauckham, Richard.
  The Bible and ecology : rediscovering the community of creation / Richard Bauckham.
     p. cm.
  Includes bibliographical references (p.   ) and index.
  ISBN 978-1-60258-310-8 (pbk. : alk. paper)
  1. Human ecology–Biblical teaching. 2. Human ecology–Religious aspects–Christianity. I. Title.
  BS660.B38 2010
  261.8'8–dc22

                            2010015524

Phototypeset by Kerrypress Ltd, Luton, Bedfordshire

To Della

CONTENTS

PREFACE

This is a book about the Bible's understanding of the place of humans within the rest of God's creation. I use the word 'ecology', as is now common, in the rather general sense of the interconnectedness of all things, living and inanimate, on the planet. The biblical writers did not, of course, know what recent science has taught us about the ways in which these complex interrelationships work. (We ourselves are doubtless only near the beginning of this contemporary journey of scientific understanding, which is steadily revealing more and more aspects of the delicate web of creation within which we belong.) But the Bible does evince a strong sense of the interconnectedness of all creatures and relates this to their common dependence on God their Creator. The phrase 'community of creation' in the subtitle of the book refers to the kind of vision of creation that the Bible, read as a whole, offers us. It highlights our commonality with other creatures, our dependence on them as well as our significance for them, in a life in which all creatures exist for the glory of God.

Much recent reflection on the human relationship to the rest of the creation has focused on the notion of stewardship, which I take to refer to a vocation of caring responsibility for other creatures. This is part of the biblical picture. But I think that to be adequately understood it needs to be set within the wider vision of the community of creation. We need to realise more fully the biblical sense in which humans are fellow-creatures with other creatures. Stewardship (or 'dominion', the biblical term) is a role within the larger sphere of community relationships, which it does not exhaust. Major difficulties in the concept of stewardship can be overcome when we recognise this. We need to expand our biblical horizons beyond Genesis 1, important as that is, and begin to learn from the rich resources the rest of the Bible provides for understanding the place of humans within the rest of God's creation. We shall discover there other major themes that are just as important as dominion, such as the praise that all creatures, ourselves among them, offer to their Creator.

While writing this book I have, of course, been deeply aware of the massive ecological crisis in which we are all currently living. I have not, however, attempted even a brief summary of this contemporary context in which all Christian thinking about creation must be done. This is because it is well known and has been described and analysed by others much more adequately than I can do.[1] However, one point about it is worth making here. Recently, and understandably, the focus has been overwhelmingly on the issue of climate change. But this is only the most threatening aspect of a deep crisis in the human relationship to the rest of nature that stems from the modern technological project of mastering nature. While, despite the overwhelming evidence, some people are still sceptical about climate change, there can be no doubt about the extent to which humans have been thoughtlessly and rapidly exhausting the resources of the earth or about the extinction of species on a vast scale as a result of human destruction of their habitats. Modernity inculcated ways of thinking about the human relationship to nature that have proved disastrous. The debate about climate change, important as it is, has perhaps been in danger of deflecting attention from these other problems and their deep roots in fundamental attitudes. For Christians, it is imperative that we return to the biblical sources of our faith and rediscover the community of creation.

I have been working on the ideas in this book for many years. But the opportunity to develop them into the kind of shape they have in this book came when I was invited by Sarum College, Salisbury, to give the Sarum Theological Lectures in Salisbury Cathedral in 2006. I entitled them 'Beyond Stewardship: The Bible and the Community of Creation'. This book is a very much expanded version of them. I am grateful to David Catchpole and his colleagues at Sarum College for inviting me, for making my stay in Sarum enjoyable, and also for their patience over the period when I have taken so long to get them into publishable form. I am also grateful to many people, too many to name, who have discussed these issues with me and helped to clarify my thinking by responding to the presentations, in oral or printed form, in which I have developed my ideas over the years.

1 See, for example, Michael Northcott, *The Environment and Christian Ethics* (Cambridge: Cambridge University Press, 1996), chapters 1–2. See also the recent, interdisciplinary collection of essays: Robert S. White ed., *Creation in Crisis: Christian Perspectives on Sustainability* (London: SPCK, 2009), a product of a workshop organised by the Faraday Centre in Cambridge. In my judgement, Bill McKibben, *The End of Nature* (London: Viking (Penguin), 1990), remains a classic in its thoroughgoing revelation of the way the human relationship to the rest of 'nature' has changed in the last half-century.

STEWARDSHIP IN QUESTION

INTRODUCTION

How should Christians read the Bible in an age of ecological disaster? How does the Bible construct for us the relationship of humans to the rest of creation? The most popular current answer to these questions is the notion of stewardship. As Christopher Southgate puts it: 'That human beings are called to be stewards of creation tends to be the default position within ordinary Christian groups.'[1]

We are concerned here only with Christian theological use of the idea of stewardship. The term 'stewardship' is also now heard in purely secular discourse about environmental issues, but this secular use, because it leaves aside reference to God, in fact deprives the notion of stewardship of most of its Christian meaning. The main point of the term, in Christian usage, is the steward's responsibility to God. Secular use of the term deprives it of this essential theological content.

As a fairly representative, short statement of what human stewardship of the non-human creation is taken to mean, I have taken the following from a report published in 1991 by the Board for Social Responsibility of the General Synod of the Church of England:

> We all share and depend on the same world, with its finite and often non-renewable resources. Christians believe that this world belongs to God by creation, redemption and sustenance, and that he has entrusted it to humankind, made in his image and responsible to him; we are in the position

of stewards, tenants, curators, trustees or guardians, whether or not we acknowledge this responsibility. Stewardship implies caring management, not selfish exploitation; it involves a concern for both present and future as well as self, and a recognition that the world we manage has an interest in its own survival and wellbeing independent of its value to us ... Good stewardship requires justice, truthfulness, sensitivity, and compassion.[2]

The main value of the stewardship model of humanity's relation to the rest of creation has been to provide a strong alternative to the idea of the human role in creation as domination and exploitation. Rather, this human role, when defined as stewardship, is one of care and service, exercised on behalf of God and with accountability to God.[3] It can hardly be contested that the stewardship model has had an enormous influence for good in giving Christians a framework within which to approach ecological issues with concern and responsibility.

However, in my view, the stewardship model also has distinct limitations that consist more in what it does not say than in what it does, or in what it suggests without necessarily requiring. A review of criticisms of stewardship may appropriately begin with James Lovelock, famous for his Gaia hypothesis, who has dismissed the idea of stewardship as 'sheer hubris'.[4]

CRITICISMS OF STEWARDSHIP: (1) STEWARDSHIP AS HUBRIS

Lovelock makes this point most fully in his recent book, *The Revenge of Gaia: Why the Earth is Fighting Back – and How We Can Still Save Humanity*.[5] It is not surprising that his criticism of stewardship relates closely to his idea of Gaia, and so it will be helpful first briefly to explain that idea. Lovelock's Gaia hypothesis is a scientific theory, and he rejects responsibility for the way it has been adopted into New Age religious contexts.[6] On the other hand, he does encourage a more than merely scientific, dispassionate attitude to Gaia, arguably amounting to a religious approach ('there is a deep need in all of us for trust in something larger than ourselves, and I put my trust in Gaia'[7]). But Christian suspicion of the idea of Gaia on the grounds that it entails some form of nature religion exaggerates the problem. Simply as a scientific theory, it requires no particular form of religious stance, any more than the Darwinian theory of evolution does. However the natural world is understood, in scientific terms, to work, it is possible to elevate natural processes to divine status and ethical normativity, but it is also possible to treat them as aspects of the way the transcendent God has created the natural world.

Lovelock's theory is that the whole Earth system, which Lovelock calls Gaia – comprising both all life on Earth and the material environment – behaves as a single system, *like* a living organism.[8] It is a self-regulating system that automatically controls such things as the global climate and the composition of the atmosphere in such a way as to maximise their capacity to form a comfortable environment for life. Gaia is a self-regulating system that operates to sustain the habitability of the Earth. Lovelock admits that he is far from a full understanding of how it works, but the theory has accumulated evidence and adherents since he first propounded it, even if most conventional scientists remain sceptical. We cannot enter scientific debate about the validity of the theory here.[9]

Lovelock takes the Christian idea of stewardship to mean that humans are in charge of the whole Earth and its destiny. He fully takes the point that this human role is understood to be not exploitative, but responsible and caring. But he claims that it is 'flawed by unconscious hubris'. Humans have 'neither the knowledge nor the capacity to achieve' the goals envisaged by this notion. 'We are no more qualified to be stewards or developers of the Earth than are goats to be gardeners'.[10]

Stewardship, he concedes, might make some sense if Gaia turned out not to be true. Then we should have to do our best to manage the Earth. But if Gaia is the case – if the Earth is a self-regulating system – then stewardship is a hubristic attempt to do what Gaia is designed to do, what Gaia has been doing for millions of years before humans came on the scene, and what Gaia can do very much better than we can.[11]

One does not have to adopt the Gaia hypothesis to find this kind of criticism cogent. The claim that humans simply do not have the knowledge or the power to be stewards of the Earth, i.e. to manage it for the best, is also made by Clare Palmer, along with other criticisms, in a devastatingly critical attack on the idea of stewardship in environmental ethics:

> To be a successful steward, either in the feudal or the financial sense, it is necessary to understand that which is being controlled. But the natural world is not like an estate, nor like money in this respect. It is composed of complex ecosystems and atmospheric conditions that we do not understand and cannot predict.

She does not mean we can do nothing about, for example, climate change, but that the control we have is partial and 'we must see it in the context of the many things we do not know and perhaps will never know'.[12]

This kind of criticism of the notion of stewardship makes a strong case.[13] It can be very dangerous to overestimate one's power to achieve or to control things. Arguably, the ecological crisis of the last few decades has its roots in generally well-meaning scientific and technological projects whose benefits seemed obvious but whose catastrophic effects were not foreseen. The whole of the modern scientific-technological project of dominating nature and exploiting its resources for the good of humanity presumed that total mastery of the Earth's natural processes was within human grasp. It exaggerated what was known and turned a blind eye to what was not. On a small scale, this need not be disastrous: one can learn from mistakes and nature has the resources to repair the damage. But the bigger the scale, the more dangerous it becomes. And in the face of all the examples that should have taught humans this lesson, the optimistic progressivism that stakes everything on achieving total control survives. It is alive and well among the technophiliacs who assume that we shall be able to create a technological fix for climate change and every other danger that comes along, as well as the biotechnologists and the artificial intelligence people who dream of a world in which technology has taken over from evolution.

Lovelock appropriately refers to the idea of a 'technological fix' for climate change as 'breathtaking hubris'.[14] Even if it were possible, do we really want to be in charge of such things as climate change? Lovelock says:

> The more we meddle with the Earth's composition and try to fix its climate, the more we take on the responsibility for keeping the Earth a fit place for life, until eventually our whole lives may be spent in drudgery doing the tasks that Gaia had freely done for over three billion years. This would be the worst of fates for us and [would] reduce us to a truly miserable state, where we were forever wondering whether anyone, any nation [the USA? China?] or any international body could be trusted to regulate the climate and the atmospheric composition. The idea that humans are yet intelligent enough to serve as stewards of the Earth is among the most hubristic ever.[15]

Others would point to an even worse danger: that developing technology in this direction, technology so smart and so powerful it could manage tasks as formidable as the global climate, will lead to the point where technology in the form of artificial intelligence will take over from us, either replacing us or modifying human nature itself to the extent of creating a new species. This is the posthuman future envisaged by the technological futurists (many of them actually working in bioengineering or in the development of artificial intelligence). It may seem odd to find it in the vicinity of the notion of stewardship, but there is a real connection. If stewardship requires total control of the Earth's processes, only posthumans will be equal to the task.

Thus one major problem about the modern Christian idea of stewardship of creation is this: if it means that humans consider themselves to have controlling charge over the Earth, then it is indeed hubristic, consciously or not, since the facts of human knowledge and power do not measure up to such a role. The concept of stewardship is usually represented as an interpretation of the human dominion over other creatures granted to humans by God in Genesis (1:26 and 28). It is, we should remember, an interpretation, which says more than the text indisputably does. In order to discuss the text without pre-judging issues of interpretation, and since there is no doubt that it uses the notion of 'rule', I shall call what God gives to humans in Genesis 1 the human dominion. Does this dominion, as presented in Genesis 1, entail total control over the rest of creation on Earth, or mandate a project to achieve such control?

For a start, it is well worth observing that this 'totalising' reading of the dominion is a peculiarly modern one. No one before the early modern period read it in that way. Medieval western Christians, for example, supposed it to refer to the kinds of use of other creatures and the environment that were normal in their time: farming, hunting, building, mining and so forth. They did not suppose that Genesis 1 set humanity a task of achieving total control over the Earth. Total control obviously belonged to God alone. The totalising interpretation of the Genesis dominion is typically modern in its aspiration to reject all limits on human power and activity, to throw off all the constraints of nature, to remake the world according to human design, to become in fact some kind of god over the world. It was Francis Bacon, in the seventeenth century, who hijacked the Genesis text to authorise the project of scientific knowledge and technological exploitation whose excesses have given us the ecological crisis. The modern project of domination is indeed hubristic in that it aspired (and for technophiliac progressivists still aspires) to the kind of control that had always been thought to belong to God alone.[16]

Christian thought about the world, drawing on its biblical sources, has normally supposed that all human action takes place within the larger framework of divine providence, which may work to limit the effects of our evil or to prosper the effects of our good actions. It has also supposed that there are structures of order inherent in creation as God has made it that humans violate at their peril. Whatever dominion or stewardship might mean it must belong within those limits. If James Lovelock is right about Gaia, I see no difficulty at all in seeing the self-regulating Earth system as part of the order of creation within which humans must live.[17] *Of course* it can do the job better than we can: God has designed it to do so. So science and good theology may combine to require a more modest, more limited understanding of the human dominion than the hubristic and dangerously exaggerated notion that has been with us for the last four centuries. We need to cut the dominion down to size. In the present chapter, we shall attempt that by observing carefully the limits on dominion that the Bible itself sets and the qualifications of dominion that the Bible itself gives it. Interpretation of the dominion has gone wrong when Genesis 1:26 and 28 has been isolated as the only part of Scripture used to define the God-given relationship of humans to the rest of creation. We need to put it back into a much larger context of the rich resources of scriptural treatment of the human relationship to other creatures.

CRITICISMS OF STEWARDSHIP: (2) STEWARDSHIP EXCLUDES GOD'S OWN ACTIVITY IN THE WORLD

This second criticism is a more theological parallel to the first. It alleges that the notion of human stewardship neglects God's own continuing involvement with his creation. Extreme advocates of stewardship have even suggested that God has entirely delegated his governance of the world to humans. This is supposed to be the meaning of the fact that, in Genesis 1, God created humans on the sixth day of creation, at the end of all his acts of creation, and then rested on the seventh day. With the creation of humans God had nothing more to do himself, having put the world into the hands of humans, and so could now rest. Such a view is even more subject to the charge of hubris than those discussed in the previous section. It states outright that humans assume the role of God in relation to the world.

Such a conclusion can be reached most easily in a secular context in which God is for all intents and purposes dead. In the absence of God, whether resting or dead, humans must play God and exercise a divinely powerful and extensive dominion over creation. But of course this is not the biblical view. God is constantly active in his creation in ways that have nothing to do with humans as well as in ways that do. Humans should care for creation within the context of God's own caring for it, not in place of God's caring for creation.

CRITICISMS OF STEWARDSHIP: (3) STEWARDSHIP LACKS SPECIFIC CONTENT

A different kind of problem is that stewardship has proven to be a very flexible term. Once we get beyond the rather general ideas we have already noticed, there are a whole range of different understandings of what our stewardship of the Earth actually requires of us. For example, is it a hands-on or a hands-off job? When the idea of human stewardship of the Earth was first used in the seventeenth century, especially by the lawyer Matthew Hale, it went with a very high view of the need for human intervention in the rest of creation for creation's good.[18] Nature would run horribly wild if humans were not there to keep it in order.[19] For many environmentally minded Christians today, on the other hand, stewardship is mainly a matter of preserving creation from human damage to it – letting nature be itself, intervening only to protect, not to improve.[20] Stewardship is about preserving, not changing.

There are very different evaluations of wilderness in play here. For seventeenth-century people, wilderness was a waste and a mess that needed clearing up and putting in order. In the modern period too, nature has often been viewed as something sadly unfinished until humans set about improving it.[21] On the other hand, for environmentally sensitive contemporary people, it would seem that wild nature can do perfectly well without us. Intervention is likely to spoil it, not improve it. But then again, there are enthusiasts for biotechnology who see the Genesis dominion as a mandate for scientists to take control of the evolutionary process, to bring nature to new stages of development it has not yet reached, and cannot without us to transform it technologically.[22] So the notion of stewardship as such offers little guidance as to how we should relate to nature beyond exhorting us to seek the good of other creatures as well as of ourselves. But what is that good?

Stewardship certainly implies that the rest of creation somehow needs us. But why, and how? In a contemporary context one could easily imagine that the rest of creation would be much better off without us humans. It is we who have made such a mess of the world. It is our unstoppable interference, our arrogant assumption that we can improve nature, that has destroyed so much of it. One illustration Christopher Southgate gives of how humans might contribute to the healing of nature, instead of its destruction, is 'a reduction of extinction', i.e. of the extinction of species, though he admits that this 'would take a great deal more wisdom as well as a great deal more knowledge than we currently possess'.[23] But how significant is this in the context of contemporary ecological disaster? Doubtless we humans could preserve a few species that might, apart from us, die out (species have been going extinct continuously since life began on Earth). But, in practice today, it is hardly possible to distinguish those rather few naturally occurring extinctions from the much larger number of species that have died out or are in danger of dying out because of human activity. (Global warming will bring about the extinction of vast numbers of species.) We humans are surely in practice the only competitors that count.

So it is hardly surprising that many Christian advocates of stewardship today see stewardship as a matter of protecting nature from harm by humans, and repairing the damage humans have done to it. This view of stewardship implies that it is a task that is only needed because we humans are in the world. Without us, creation would get along perfectly well (and did so, of course, for millions of years before we came on the scene),[24] but, since God wanted to put us here, nature now needs us to protect it from us.

An analogy might be: suppose you tell a child to tidy their room; the room does need tidying, but only because there is a child there who makes it untidy.[25] Is human stewardship of the Earth like that? Such a modest account is attractive but I find it difficult to believe that the dominion in Genesis 1 means no more than that. On the other hand, the more positive interpretations on offer tend to sound highly unrealistic to anyone who is properly aware of how destructive our relationship with creation really has been in the modern period. In this context, ideas of humans as co-creators with God or co-redeemers with God[26] are nothing but red rags to bulls. Whatever might be said of them in the abstract, in the context of the modern technological project of total domination of nature they pander to the hubristic modern aspiration to the role of gods over the world. Whatever the rest of creation may need from us, it is certainly not the tyranny of pretended divine power. I have long found the question 'why should the rest of creation *need* us?' the hardest question about the meaning of the Genesis dominion and the human relationship to the non-human creation.[27]

CRITICISMS OF STEWARDSHIP: (4) STEWARDSHIP SETS HUMANS OVER CREATION, NOT WITHIN IT

The fourth criticism of the notion of stewardship – one that is central to my aims in this book – is that it depicts the relationship of humans to other creatures in a purely vertical way, without a corresponding horizontal dimension. By that I mean that it places us above creation, in a sort of hierarchy:

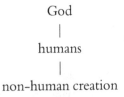

The notion of stewardship does not encourage emphasis or reflection on the fact that humans are also creatures, rooted like other creatures in this earthly home that we share with them. Stewardship puts us in authority over, but not in community alongside and with other creatures.

Another aspect of this limitation is that the stewardship model is a one-way relationship, in which humans rule and care for creation, but creation is merely the passive recipient of our work. A broader picture of a community of creatures in which we participate will open up reciprocal relationships, recognising our fundamental dependence on other creatures and the benefits they give us.

In my view, it is the exclusive focus on a vertical relationship to the rest of creation – whether it be called rule or dominion or stewardship or even priesthood – that has been one of the ideological driving forces of the modern technological project of dominating nature. Modern western people, beginning with the Renaissance, forgot their own creatureliness, their embeddedness within creation, their interdependence with other creatures. They sought to liberate themselves from nature, to transcend their own dependence on nature, and conceived themselves as functionally gods in relation to nature.[28] While stewardship avoids the themes of domination, exploitation and re-creation that fuelled the modern project, it retains the purely vertical relationship. This by no means simply invalidates it, but it is a limitation that suggests that the stewardship model by itself could be a perilously one-sided model for a relationship so complex as the human relationship to other creatures.[29]

CRITICISMS OF STEWARDSHIP:
(5) STEWARDSHIP TENDS TO ISOLATE ONE SCRIPTURAL TEXT

Finally, a criticism that leads directly into what I shall do in the rest of this book. It is that the idea of stewardship depends for its biblical support on the same single scriptural locus as the talk of rule or dominion: Genesis 1:26 and 28. Admittedly, the location of this text in the Bible highlights its special significance: it is connected with the very creation of humans. For a canonical reading of Scripture, Genesis 1:26 and 28 can certainly not be left aside. But nor should it be lifted out of the rest of Scripture. Too

---

often this text has been isolated from its context in the canon of Scripture. A major aim of this book is to place the Genesis concept of dominion within its wider biblical context, indicating both the ways in which it is interpreted by other texts and also that it is one theme among several that the Bible uses to speak of the place of humanity within creation. It will open up some of the rich and diverse resources the Bible as a whole offers us for thinking about our human relationship with the rest of creation and for responding to the ecological destruction of our time and the ecological threats of the future.

However, it will be useful to begin by reconsidering the passage in Genesis 1 on which the whole discussion of stewardship ultimately rests. We need to place the commands to 'subdue the Earth' and to 'have dominion' over other creatures in their context in the Bible's opening account of creation in seven days (Gen. 1:1—2:4), and to reconsider their meaning within that context.

UNDERSTANDING GENESIS 1: (1) THE SIX DAYS OF CREATION

Genesis 1:1—2:4 uses the biblical notion of a week, in which there are six days for working and the seventh day for rest, as the framework for an account of creation in which God creates on six days and rests on the seventh. The passage is carefully and intricately structured, and much of the meaning is embodied in the structure. The following diagram explicates the most important elements in the structure of the six days narrative:

Environments and Names	Inhabitants and Tasks
[pre-creation: Earth, waters, darkness: formless and unproductive]	
(**Day 1**) Light – separated from darkness *God saw that it was good* God names: Day and Night	(**Day 4**) Heavenly lights Task: to separate day from night, to give light, to rule *God saw that it was good*
(**Day 2**) Firmament – separates waters God names: Sky	(**Day 5**) Water produces water creatures Birds in sky *God saw that it was good* God blesses Task: to be fruitful and fill
(**Day 3**) Dry land – by gathering waters God names: Land and Sea *God saw that it was good* Land produces vegetation *God saw that it was good*	(**Day 6**) Land produces land creatures *God saw that it was good* Humans in God's image God blesses Task: to be fruitful and fill and subdue Dominion over creatures of (5) and (6) All creatures of (5) and (6) to live from vegetation of (3) *God saw all that he had made and it was very good*

Despite the use of a scheme of days, the allocation of material to the days follows primarily a spatial rather than a chronological arrangement. On the first three days God creates the three environments that constitute the ordered space of creation, and then, on the fourth, fifth and sixth days, he creates the inhabitants of each of these cosmic habitats in turn. Each of the habitats is named by God, and two of them (the waters and the land) participate in the creation of their inhabitants. Vegetation is treated as an aspect of the third environment, rather than as inhabitants of it, because it is viewed as part of the land's provision for the living creatures that inhabit it. The inhabitants are all animate creatures, including the heavenly bodies (seen as animate at least because of their regular and autonomous movement). Whereas God names the environments, he gives to each category of inhabitants (with the exception of the non-human land creatures[30]) a task that relates both to their specific environment and to the continuance of the created order in the future. In the cases of the creatures of sea and air and of humans, the task is given along with God's blessing because it is this that enables them to procreate and multiply, sharing to that extent in God's creative work.

The scheme is primarily spatial. There is also a degree of logical sequence: the work of the third day has to follow that of the second, and the environments have to be created before their respective inhabitants. What is lacking, however, is any sense of building towards a culmination. Humans, the last creatures to be created, have a unique role within creation, but they do not come last because they are the climax of an ascending scale. The 'creeping things' (reptiles and insects), created on the sixth day, are not higher, in some order of being, than the birds, created on the fifth day. So this scheme of creation has nothing in common with that progressivist reading of evolution that envisages a process of increasing complexity and increasing intelligence that culminates in human beings.

If the scheme is primarily spatial rather than chronological, we may wonder why it is set in a framework of seven days. One function of the temporal framework is to convey that, along with creating a spatially ordered creation, God created a temporal structure for that creation (the perpetuation of which is entrusted to the heavenly lights). But the fact that the number seven symbolises completeness (not unconnected with the fact that a week has seven days) is also important. As well as the sequence of seven days, the micro-structure of the account is replete with series of sevens, of which the most important is the sevenfold occurrence of the word *bara'* (to create).[31] That God completed his whole work of creation in the six days is emphasised in the account of the seventh day, on which he rested, presumably with the implication that he rested in appreciation of all that he had brought into being. The seventh day (rather than the creation of humans) is the true culmination of the work of creation, but not in the sense of ending a series that moves progressively towards it. Rather, the seventh day, radically different in kind from the others, relates directly to each of the six, and forms the vantage point from which the work of all six days may be seen, not as a sequence, but as a whole.

God's approbation and appreciation of every part of his creation is conveyed by the refrain, repeated at each stage of creation: 'God saw that it was good.' This indicates that each part of creation has its own value that does not depend on its value for other parts. The environments, for example, are not valued only because they serve as environments for their inhabitants. While the account stresses the importance of vegetation as food for the land animals, it does not require us to think that this is its only value. God appreciates the trees and plants also for their own sake. Nevertheless, the creation was designed to be an interconnecting and interdependent whole, and so the refrain is varied at the end of the work of the sixth day: 'God saw everything that he had made, and, behold, it was very good' (1:31).[32] The value of the whole is more than the value of the sum of its parts.

In its own way, the Genesis 1 account of creation is 'ecological'. It stresses the profusion and diversity of living things, and it portrays the creation, animate and inanimate, as an interdependent whole. Humans belong integrally to that interdependent whole. They are essential to the design of the whole, but so are the other parts of creation. The view, which was common in much of the Christian tradition, that the rest of creation was created for the sake of humans, finds no support in the text. It is within that context of creation as an interdependent whole that we need to understand the special role that they are undoubtedly also given.

UNDERSTANDING GENESIS 1: (2) THE HUMAN PLACE IN CREATION

Humans are one of two categories of creatures to whom God gives the special task of 'ruling': the sun and the moon 'rule' (*mashal*) the day and the night (1:16–18), while humans 'rule' (*radah*) all the creatures that inhabit sea, air and land (1:26 and 28). The latter are created in 'the image of God' presumably, whatever more precisely the phrase may mean, because this is what makes it possible or appropriate for them to rule over other living creatures. But we need to look quite closely at the way the human dominion is introduced and described in the two divine speeches:

> Let us make humankind in our image, according to our likeness, and **let them have dominion** (*radah*) **over the fish of the sea, and over the birds of the air, and over the cattle, and over all the wild animals**[33] **of the land, and over every creeping thing that creeps upon the land**. (1:26)

> Be fruitful and multiply, and fill the land and subdue (*kabash*) it, and **have dominion** (*radah*) **over the fish of the sea and over the birds of the air and over every living thing that moves upon the land**. (1:28)

The dominion is described in the portions of the text printed in bold type. Despite much confusion by exegetes,[34] the words that begin the second quotation are not part of the mandate of dominion. They correspond rather to what God has said to the sea creatures and the birds:

> Be fruitful and multiply and fill the waters in the seas, and let birds multiply on the land. (1:22)

The only difference is that humans are told to 'subdue (*kabash*)' the land. When this verb is used with humans as its object, as it mostly is in the Hebrew Bible, the meaning seems to be something like 'to take by force' or 'to make subject' (e.g. 2 Sam. 8:11; Esth. 7:8; Jer. 34:11), but when 'land' (*'eretz*) is the object, the meaning seems more like 'to occupy' or 'to take possession' (Num. 32:22, 29; Josh.

18:1; 1 Chr. 22:18). The action, in these cases, requires defeating the enemies who previously occupied the land, but the land itself has only to be possessed. It is not itself an enemy to be forcibly subjugated.

In Genesis 1:28 the 'land' that is to be 'subdued' is the same 'land' that is to be 'filled' by humans (i.e. all the land in the world), and the two actions are closely connected. It seems likely that 'subduing' the land here refers to agriculture, since the only way humans are able to fill the land is to cultivate it and so to make it yield more food than it would of its own accord. As we have noted, the element of force may not be intrinsic to the verb *kabash*, but if it is, then the reference is to the fact that farmers must work the land to make it yield crops.[35]

Agriculture makes the difference between fish and birds, on the one hand, and people, on the other. Without agriculture the land does not produce enough food for humans to fill it. Since God's command to humans is not only that they should multiply, but that they should do so to the extent of filling the land, they must also 'subdue' the land, i.e. farm it. Other land animals, confined to habitats that supply their food without needing to be farmed, cannot fill the land. (As well as farming, it is possible that 'subduing' the land alludes also to mining metals and quarrying stone; cf. Deut. 8:7–10.)

Of course, the command to 'fill the land' should not be taken over-literally. The biblical writers were aware that there were some areas of wilderness in which humans could not live. But a more serious issue is that the creation account clearly assigns the land also to all the land animals. So God can hardly intend humans to 'fill the land' at the expense of other animals. This is why, rather oddly, God's grant of 'every green plant' to the land animals for food (1:30) is not spoken to the animals themselves, but appended, as information for humans, to his grant to them of seed-bearing plants for food (1:29). The point must be that humans should not grow food for themselves (and so fill the land) to an extent that competes with the livelihood of other living creatures. Humans and other creatures are to share the land, and humans are responsible for seeing that their own use of the land does not negate this sharing.

For the mandate to fill the land and subdue it, we may appropriately use the term stewardship, since it is a right to responsible use of the land that belongs ultimately to God. But (contra most exegetes) in Genesis this is to be distinguished from the dominion over other living creatures. There is, implicitly, a connection between the two. The uniquely human practice of agriculture enables humans to multiply and spread so that they become the dominant species on Earth (even in the Old Testament period this must have seemed to be the case). But the dominion granted by God presupposes more than this fact of power. It also presupposes that humans bear the divine image, so that God can authorise them to use their superior power in a way that reflects God's own rule over his creation. Whereas they are to 'subdue' the Earth, they are to 'rule' (*radah*) the other living creatures.[36]

Unlike *kabash*, which is elsewhere used of land as well as people, *radah* is used, outside Genesis 1, almost exclusively with human individuals or groups as its object.[37] It is not surprising that, since it refers to rule or supremacy, it is often associated with violence or force, but this does not mean that violence or force is integral to the meaning of the word. In Ezekiel 34:4, it is used of the shepherds of the flock (representing rulers of the people) who are accused of not caring for the sheep but instead ruling (*radah*) them 'with force and harshness'. The implication is probably that they should have ruled (*radah*) with care and compassion, as God, the true shepherd of his people, does.

It is not clear whether the dominion over other living creatures includes the right to use them in any way. In the context of Genesis 1, there is no question of killing them for food: both humans and animals are vegetarian. Other uses of animals – as beasts of burden, for wool or milk – can apply only to the domestic animals, and so could constitute only a minor part of what dominion over all living creatures – in the sea, in the air and on the land – could mean. It seems better to exclude use of animals from the meaning of dominion. The human dominion, like God's, is a matter not of use but of care.

It is therefore significant and intelligible that the image of God is connected not with the subduing of the Earth but with the dominion over other living creatures. When humans obey the command to be fruitful and to multiply, to fill the Earth and to subdue it, they are not imitating God in a unique way but behaving like other species. All species use their environment and, though agriculture is unique to humans, it can be seen as a peculiarly human extension of the right of all animals to use their environment in order to live and to flourish. If the human dominion over other creatures were merely a matter of power, it too would be only the superlative version of what other creatures have. What links it to the image of God is that it is a delegated participation in God's caring rule over his creatures.

The fact that humans are commanded to do what other species do as well as, uniquely, to exercise dominion over other species, is important to our understanding of the latter. Creation in the image of God does not make them demi-gods. They are unequivocally creatures. They are land animals who must live from the land as all land animals must. They participate in the ordered interdependence of the creatures as Genesis 1 portrays them. The dominion God gives them is over fellow-creatures and it reflects God's rule in a necessarily creaturely way. It is to be exercised within the created order that God has established and must serve that order.

The dominion is over living creatures, not inanimate nature. This makes the verb *radah*, which elsewhere has only humans as its object, appropriate. Unlike the sun and the moon, who rule only the day and the night, humans rule other sentient beings, who are to some degree subjects of their own lives just as humans are. Genesis does distinguish quite sharply between living creatures and the rest of creation. The covenant of Genesis 9 is made by God with Noah and his descendants and 'with every living creature that is with you, the birds, the domestic animals, and every animal of the Earth with you, as many as came out of the ark' (9:9–10). It is assumed that, unlike trees and mountains, animate creatures are suitable partners in a covenant (cf. also Hos. 2:18). (Our modern use of the term 'the environment' – as a single term embracing landscape, flora and fauna – thus fits the perspective of Genesis very badly.)

We have contextualised Genesis 1:26 and 28 in their context in the creation account of Genesis 1:1—2:4. In the rest of this chapter we shall consider aspects of their context in the rest of the Torah (Pentateuch), picking up those passages that can function as further exposition of the human role in creation initially set out in Genesis 1. In this treatment I am not concerned to distinguish the various sources that scholars recognise in the early chapters of Genesis and in the Torah as a whole. Other studies of our subject have taken the approach of distinguishing the theologies of the two creation narratives (Gen. 1:1–23 and Gen. 2:4–25) and of the several sources that can be traced through the rest of the Torah.[38] Doubtless such sources existed, but in the Torah as we have it they have been combined by editors who surely did not simply cut and paste them, but brought them together intelligently into what they perceived as a coherent whole. It is this final form of the text that constitutes Scripture for Jewish and Christian readers, and so it is this final form that exegetes have primarily the responsibility of interpreting. This matters especially in our reading of Genesis 2, the second creation account. It is, of course, a distinct narrative, and its interests and emphases are significantly different from those of the first account. Therein lies its value. But the editors of Genesis evidently did not see the two accounts as incompatible. It makes good sense to read the second as complementing what we have learned from the first.

UNDERSTANDING GENESIS 2: (1) HUMAN SOLIDARITY WITH THE REST OF CREATION

Whereas the seven-days creation account ensures the creatureliness of humans by placing them within the order of creation, the Eden account does so, perhaps more emphatically, by stressing Adam's kinship with the Earth and the other creatures of Earth.

God, we are told, 'formed the human being (*'adam*) from the dust of the soil (*'adamah*)' (2:7)[39] – the pun draws attention to the relationship and indicates its appropriateness. (Loren Wilkinson offers an English equivalent to the Hebrew pun: 'God made humans out of humus',[40] while Carol Newsom puts it: 'we share common ground with the Earth because we are *common ground*'.[41]) This earthiness of humans signifies a kinship with the Earth itself and with other earthly creatures, plants and animals.[42] Human life is embedded in the physical world with all that that implies of dependence on the natural systems of life.

It is for neglecting this earthiness of humans that John Haught has criticised the idea of stewardship: 'a theology of dominion or stewardship fails to accentuate that we belong to the Earth more than it belongs to us, that we are more dependent on it than it is on us, that we are *of* the Earth and not living *on* the Earth'.[43]

The animals are created from the soil, all of them individually moulded, like Adam, by God (2:19). God animates the clay figure of Adam by breathing into him 'the breath of life' (2:7), which is the same breath that animates all living creatures (7:22). Though not specifically mentioned in the account of the creation of the animals (2:19), it must be assumed, because otherwise the animals would not be alive. The summary account probably assumes that, just as God himself formed both Adam and the animals from the soil, so God himself breathed the breath of life into both Adam and the animals (where else would it have come from?). The phrase 'living being' (*nefesh hayyah*), used of Adam in 2:7, elsewhere always refers to animals. Nothing in their created constitution differentiates humans from other animals, according to this account.

UNDERSTANDING GENESIS 2: (2) CARING FOR THE LAND

Moreover, Adam's life remains bound up with the soil. Before we hear of him, we hear of the soil's need of him: 'there was no one to till (*'avad*) the ground (*'adamah*)' (2:5). Once created, Adam is placed by God in the garden he has planted 'to till (*'avad*) it and to keep (*shamar*) it' (2:15). Following the description of the rivers of Eden (2:10–14), which associate it with Mesopotamia,[44] where the rivers themselves were not sufficient to make most of the land fertile, Adam's task is probably to irrigate the land in order to sustain the trees God has planted there.[45] Later he is sent to perform the same task outside Eden: 'to till the ground from which he was taken' (3:23).[46] The man from the soil must work the soil in order to live from the soil's produce.[47] We should also note that Noah, a sort of new Adam with whom creation is given a fresh start after the Flood, was also 'a man of the soil (*'adamah*)' (Gen. 9:20).

Adam's task of tilling the soil is probably much the same as that intended by the command to 'subdue the land' in Genesis 1:28, but here there is a stronger sense of humanity's close relationship with the soil. It seems to be a reciprocal relationship: the soil needs Adam's work and he needs the soil's produce. There is also, in the word 'keep' or 'preserve', the implication that Adam takes care of the soil. He avoids exhausting it. (Several recent studies of the passage have proposed translating *'avad* as 'to serve', either as the sole meaning or as an additional overtone.[48] But, whereas this verb with a personal object means 'to serve', there is a consistent usage of the verb to mean 'to work' or 'to cultivate' when the object is inanimate (Gen. 3:23; 4:12; Deut. 28:39; Isa. 19:9; cf. Prov. 12:11; 28:19; Zech. 13:5). This is the obvious meaning in Genesis 2.)

Adam has the right to make a living from the soil, but also the duty to care for it. The aspect of stewardship, entailing responsibility as well as right to usufruct, emerges here more clearly than in Genesis 1:28.

UNDERSTANDING GENESIS 2: (3) HUMANS AND OTHER ANIMALS

It is tempting to see in Genesis 2:19–20, in which God brings the newly created animals to Adam for him to name them, another expression of the human dominion over other living creatures that is granted to humans in Genesis 1:26 and 28. But, although the passage has often been read that way, in fact there is no good reason to see in Adam's naming of the animals an assertion of authority over them.[49] Rather, he is recognising them as fellow-creatures with whom he shares the world. He cannot, he finds, enjoy with them the very special relationship that is only possible with his fellow-human, 'flesh of his flesh', Eve. But in their own way, in Eden, they are companions of humans.[50]

THE FLOOD AND THE COVENANT

While the Christian tradition has focused on Genesis 3 as recounting the 'fall' of humans from original innocence into sin and its consequences, the Genesis narrative itself appears to envisage something more like a gradual descent into sin, which begins in Genesis 3 and the expulsion from Eden, continues through the story of Cain and his descendants (Gen. 4), and reaches its nadir in the corruption of the Earth in the period preceding the Flood (Gen. 6:1–7 and 11–13). Whereas Genesis 3 roots the fall in the temptation to be like God, the subsequent narratives portray this original sin taking the form of violence (Gen. 4:8 and 23–24; 6:11–13). In fact, it seems that the violence includes the animals too, not only as victims of human violence but as perpetrators of violence against humans and other animals. This appears to be the best way to understand the statement that 'all flesh had corrupted its ways upon the Earth' (6:12), since 'all flesh' in subsequent verses (6:13 and 17; 9:11, 16 and 17) certainly refers to all living things.[51] The account has to be read against the background of the way Genesis 1 portrays humans and animals as originally vegetarian. God gave them only plants for food (Gen. 1:29–30). In view of the change that is recognised after the Flood (Gen. 9:2–3, 5–6), we are probably to understand that the violence that led to the Flood included killing for food.

The harmonious relationships of Eden have broken down. Humans fail to exercise their role of responsible care for living creatures, beginning to kill them for food, and animals take to attacking humans and to predation of other animals. This is evidently envisaged as the consequence of humans filling the Earth (cf. 6:1: 'when people began to multiply …'). The statement that 'the Earth is filled with violence' (Gen. 6:11) echoes, with a kind of irony, God's command to humans to 'fill the Earth and subdue it' (1:28). Their taking possession of the Earth has actually filled the Earth with violence. Instead of an appropriately limited use of the Earth's resources, humans have over-exploited the Earth, with the result that they engage in violent competition among themselves, they deprive the wild animals of their food, and both humans and animals resort to meat-eating.

The Flood is a kind of de-creation, a reversion to chaos,[52] though not a complete one. So extreme is the desecration of the Earth by violence that God makes virtually a fresh start. However, there is one man, Noah, who alone (with his family, we should probably presume) 'walked with God', like his great-grandfather Enoch, almost as though he were still in the Garden of Eden (Gen. 6:8–9; cf. 5:24). Because of Noah, God does not have to replace the original creation, but can make a fresh start that is still continuous with the original creation. Noah and his family will survive to populate a purified Earth, and with them they will ensure the survival of the other kinds of living creatures, so that they too may repopulate the Earth (8:17). What has rarely been observed is the relationship of this narrative to the human dominion over the animals. Noah is the epitome of the kind of responsible care for other creatures with which humans had been entrusted by God at creation. This is all the more striking when we realise that the state of violence that led to the Flood was the consequence of the abuse of the dominion by the rest of Noah's generation. While violence had come to dominate the relationships of other humans and animals, Noah, in his conservation of species (as we might call it), modelled the peaceable and caring relationship with animals that had been God's creative ideal.[53]

The story of the Flood is somewhat disappointing because we expect a fresh start to creation that begins again from Genesis 1—2. Instead, we find a reformulation of God's original charge to humans (Gen. 9:1–7). Violence, it seems, is endemic and can only be limited, not eliminated. Humans will not live peaceably with animals, but will be safe from attack by animals only through instilling fear into them.[54] They are permitted to eat meat, though with the proviso that they do not drink the blood of living creatures. Abstaining from the lifeblood is acknowledgement that all life is given and belongs to the Creator. Humans have no dominion over the life of living creatures.[55] They may not take life at will. Killing for food is a concession granted them by God, which may be exercised only with the recognition that they have no natural right to it. While it is true that the new concession falls below God's original ideal of a vegetarian – and so wholly non-violent – creation, when we see its function as a kind of remedy for the unrestrained violence of the time before the Flood, its function is not to promote but to restrain violence.[56]

In canonical retrospect we can see that God's reformulation of the role of humans in Genesis 9 is a kind of holding operation, restraining violence until the time when something more radical would be done about it. God will not resort to another flood (Gen. 8:21; 9:11–15) because he has in view a better way of rescuing his creation from evil, one that, unlike the Flood, will really enable a realisation of God's original ideal for his creation. For the time being, the covenant he makes is with all living creatures (9:9–10 and 16–17), not just with humans, for it was only within this community of creatures that God had ever envisaged his human creatures living. God continues to care for all his creatures, having the salvation of all in ultimate view.

Robert Murray is right when he explains that, in Genesis 9,

> mutual relations between creatures here on Earth are now envisaged *as they are*, not as they were idealized in Gen. 1 and 2, or in any other vision of universal peace. The Bible contains, in fact, two models for thinking about humans and animals: one paradisal, the other this-worldly and realistic.[57]

Not only Genesis 2, but also Genesis 1, portrays an ecotopia,[58] and it is a serious mistake to relate the world within which we live to Genesis 1, without taking account of Genesis 9. That the Garden of Eden is a paradise lost (for the time being) is generally recognised, but that Genesis 1 also portrays the world not as it is, but as it ideally should be, is less usually admitted. The fully harmonious whole that God pronounced 'very good' still awaits its realisation. Here and now we must reckon with a world that is much better than it could be (as the world after the Flood was much better than the unrestrictedly violent one before the Flood), but in which some concessions to violence have to be made. They are, as we have seen, strictly limited concessions. How much of our actual production and consumption of meat is really compatible with the carefully conditional concession of Genesis 9:3–4?

On the other hand, the original ideals of creation are not irrelevant, partly because, in the light of the whole biblical narrative, we know that God has not by any means abandoned them. In chapters 4 and 5 we shall discuss the ecotopias the Bible envisages for the future, when the promise of Genesis 1 and 2 will be fulfilled and even surpassed. Especially in the light of the salvation that is already ours in Jesus Christ, we should not opt simply for the realism of Genesis 9 rather than the idealism of Genesis 1—2. Here and now, both are relevant.

STEWARDSHIP AND DOMINION IN ISRAEL'S LAND LAW

In the Mosaic law we can see that the Torah as a whole does not endorse a simple option for the realism of Genesis 9 rather than the idealism of Genesis 1. Both are reflected. The way that Israel is to live in and from the holy land, by means of agriculture, models the way humans are to fill and to subdue the Earth according to Genesis 1. Very explicitly, Israel is a tenant and steward of the land that belongs to God, with the right to live from the land but also the responsibility to care for it.[59]

This is a large topic, and we must be content with some particularly interesting examples. The laws authorise Israel's use and enhancement of the land, but they also impose strict limits, especially in the form of the sabbatical institutions: the weekly sabbath, the sabbatical year, every seven years, and the jubilee year (the sabbath of sabbaths), every fifty years. These laws are not just about good farming practice,[60] but about keeping the economic drive in human life within its place and not letting it dominate the whole of life. They also give Israel occasion to remember that the land is God's, given to them in trust; not a commodity but a gift, and a gift given to the whole community, not to the acquisitive alone.

In Israel's land legislation, both the human right to subdue the Earth and the human dominion over other living creatures are exercised as much in restraint as in active use. Particularly striking is the concern for wild animals. In the sabbatical year, fields, vineyards and orchards are to be left to rest and lie fallow, 'so that the poor of your people may eat; and what they leave the wild animals may eat' (Exod. 23:11 NRSV; similarly Lev. 25:7). Thus, even within the cultivated part of the land, wild animals are expected to be able to live. This is an application of the principle we have seen implied in Genesis 1:29–30: that both humans and other land animals have a right to the produce of the Earth and humans, in their production and consumption of food, must recognise that they share the Earth with other species and have no exclusive right to its resources.

This provision for the wild animals to live even where Israelites farmed the land could be seen as a kind of symbol of respect for wilderness, reminding both ancient Israel and later readers of Scripture that dominion includes letting wild nature be itself. There is value that should be respected and preserved in the wild as well as in the humanly cultivated.

The time has come to attempt a synthesis of what we have learned about the human place in creation, according to Genesis 1 and its interpretation elsewhere in the Pentateuch, with a view to its contemporary significance for God's people today.

SYNTHESIS: (1) HUMAN SOLIDARITY WITH THE REST OF CREATION

While the Genesis creation narratives do distinguish humans from other creatures, giving them a unique place within creation, they also place humans unambiguously within creation. Humans are not demi-gods with creative power, set like God above creation, but creatures among other creatures, dependent, like other creatures, on the material world of which they are part, and immersed in a web of reciprocal relationships with other creatures. The unique tasks and roles of humans, given them in Genesis 1:26 and 28, are bound to be misunderstood and abused unless the fundamental solidarity of humans with the rest of creation is recognised as their context.

SYNTHESIS: (2) RESPONSIBLE USE OF THE EARTH'S RESOURCES

All living creatures need to make use of other creatures, animate or inanimate, in order to live and to flourish. Humanity is different only in the extent, diversity and ingenuity of its use of other creatures. Since, properly speaking, all creation belongs to God its Creator and to God alone, creatures can make use of other creatures only by divine permission. The creation narrative in Genesis 1 makes this explicit when God declares that he has *given* every green plant for food to all the animals that live on land (1:30). The task of subduing the Earth that God grants humans is, primarily, the human equivalent. However, for humans, this task can be understood as stewardship in the sense of responsible care for the Earth that God himself still owns and has entrusted to humans for their sustenance and delight. Adam's farming of the Earth in Eden included preserving it, and Israel's use of the land was limited so that it would not be exhausted.

Contemporary, environmentally sensitive interpreters of Genesis tend to gloss over the human right to use the resources of creation. But this is a serious mistake. Human use of the Earth and its creatures is part of the fundamental interdependence of the whole creation. It is a necessary feature of human life and accounts for much human activity. Contemporary interpreters are rightly wary of justifying the unrestricted exploitation of the Earth and its creatures which has had such disastrous results in the twentieth century, and which was justified in the past by use of these texts in Genesis 1. But it is better to stress how the Bible limits human use of other creatures than to eliminate this theme from the text altogether. God's original purpose for humanity does entitle us to make limited use of other creatures for human life and flourishing. As Stephen Clark puts it: 'we are allowed our modest use of parts of nature explicitly upon condition that we leave it at peace, that we not take all of it.'[61]

I have distinguished, in Genesis 1:26 and 28, the subduing of the Earth from the dominion over other living creatures. The latter would seem to be a matter of caring responsibility, rather than use. Are humans therefore not given by God the right to use other living creatures in any way? With regard to eating meat, there is clearly a change between the original mandate and its reformulation after the Flood (Gen. 9:3), although, as we have seen, the right to kill for food is a concession and one that has restrictive conditions attached to it. But animals were useful to humans in the Old Testament period in ways that do not entail killing: donkeys, camels and horses for transport, oxen for ploughing and grinding, sheep for wool, dogs as watch dogs, sea shells for ornament, the skins, horns and feathers of animals that die naturally for clothing, tools, and so forth. Genesis does portray at least some of such uses before the Flood (Gen. 4:2–4 and 20–21; cf. 3:21), and it is notable that in Genesis 1:24–25 domestic animals are already distinguished from wild animals at the time of their creation, as though the role of domestic animals in human society was God's intention from the beginning.[62] Whether we see the human right to use other living creatures for their own life and flourishing as part of the task of subduing the Earth (does the agriculture envisaged in Genesis 1:28 include roles for domestic animals, such as oxen?) or as an aspect of the dominion over other living creatures, may not be very important. In some respects, the two categories converge. But we should bear in mind that Genesis does often distinguish animate from inanimate nature, and that distinction should surely be observed in the ways we make use of other creatures. We should recall also that the use of other living creatures is not itself something unique to humans; many other living creatures do it. The distinctively human task is to keep that use within a larger role of caring responsibility for other creatures.

SYNTHESIS: (3) IN THE IMAGE OF GOD

In Genesis 1, God marks out humanity from other living creatures by creating them in his own image and by granting them dominion over others. What it means to be made in the image of God has been much debated by exegetes and theologians.[63] Attempts to draw a hard distinction between human nature and animals have often been hung on this text, but scientific research makes it increasingly difficult to identify any absolute difference.[64] In the text itself the image of God is closely related to the dominion over other creatures, and this is the best clue to its meaning. The image must be whatever it is that gives us power unlike that of any other creatures. But the image must also be whatever it is about humans that makes it possible for us to exercise that power in a responsible and caring way. We do not need to say that we are the only creatures with moral values[65] or that we are the only creatures conscious of God.[66] The point is that we have that *kind* of awareness of God and that *kind* of moral sense that enable us to feel and to exercise responsibility in creation on such a large scale. It cannot be that other creatures in no way reflect their Creator, but that we have a particularly broad participation in God's governance of creation and need therefore also to reflect God's care for his whole creation on this Earth.

The close relationship between the image of God and the dominion means that the latter is an exercise of rule *on behalf of* God, not *instead of* God. Only humanity in relationship with God, knowing its own dependence on God, can exercise dominion as God's image.[67] Conversely, humanity's inveterate aspiration to replace God, to be gods, has been expressed, especially in the modern period, through domination of nature. By the project of total control of the natural world, modern humans have sought the means of making themselves gods, subject to none, supreme over all. Christians have been surprisingly slow to appreciate the connection between the modern world's rejection of God and the ecologically disastrous modern project of technological conquest of nature. That humans are made in the image of God, to exercise dominion on God's behalf, not in God's stead, is one important theological antidote to this modern mistake.

SYNTHESIS: (4) RULING LIKE GOD

Many interpreters have rightly seen in Genesis 1:26 the implication that the human dominion is some sort of reflection of God's rule, and therefore that in some sense the Bible's portrayal of God's rule should be the model for humanity's.[68] Reflecting it must surely begin with learning to value it in the ways God does. Then we can appreciate that God rules for the good of all his creatures. It is his compassionate and salvific care for all creatures. For example, Psalm 145 recalls the classic biblical statement of the character of God (from Exod. 34:6) and uses it to characterise God's rule, not only over humanity, but over all creatures:

> The LORD is gracious and merciful,
> slow to anger and abounding in steadfast love.
> The LORD is good to all,
> and his compassion is over all that he has made. (Ps. 145:8–9 NRSV)

This kind of rule is surely what the human dominion is intended by God to be: a form of caring responsibility for God's creatures.

However, because modern humanity has been so prone to forget this, we should add that human dominion is *unlike* God's rule in very significant other respects: it is restricted, it is exercised within rather than over creation, it may not aspire to divine omnipotence, and, perhaps above all, it is exercised in relation to fellow-creatures.

SYNTHESIS: (5) RULING FELLOW-CREATURES – HIERARCHY QUALIFIED BY COMMUNITY

As we have seen, our creatureliness is more fundamental than our distinctiveness among creatures. Our creation in the image of God and the unique dominion given to us do not abolish our fundamental community with other creatures. The vertical does not cancel the horizontal.

Indeed, the horizontal relationship with fellow-creatures is vital to the proper understanding of the vertical relationship of authority over others. Since Genesis 1 presents this authority as a kind of kingly rule, it is relevant to recall the only kind of human rule over other humans that the Old Testament approves. The book of Deuteronomy permits Israel to have a king, but interprets this kingship in a way designed to subvert all ordinary notions of rule (17:14–20). If Israel must have a king, then the king must be a brother. He is a brother set over his brothers and sisters, but still a brother, and forbidden any of the ways in which rulers exalt themselves over and entrench their power over their subjects. His rule becomes tyranny the moment he forgets that the horizontal relationship of brother/sisterhood is primary, kingship secondary.[69] Similarly, the human rule over other creatures will be tyrannous unless it is placed in the context of our more fundamental community with other creatures.

SYNTHESIS: (6) RULING WITHIN THE ORDER OF CREATION – SHARING THE EARTH

Genesis 1 presents a picture of a carefully ordered creation. The order is already established before the creation of humans. It does not need humans to put it in order. The human dominion is not granted so that humans may violate the already given order of creation and remake creation to their own design. It is taken for granted that the God-given order of the world must be respected by the human exercise of limited dominion within it.

We have observed how Genesis 1:29–30 implies that human use of the Earth is not to compete with its use by other living creatures. They also have a right of use. This is a massive restriction of human rights to the Earth's resources and chimes well with contemporary concerns. A similar point is made in Genesis 9:8–17, where God's covenant is made not only with Noah and his descendants but also with 'every living creature of all flesh' (v 15). It is for the sake of them all that God promises never again to destroy the Earth in a universal deluge. The Earth is home for them all and they all have a stake in that covenant. Even within the sphere of human agriculture Israel's land laws recognise that some provision for wild creatures must be left.

SYNTHESIS: (7) PRESERVING CREATION

Ruling – understood as caring responsibility for – other creatures can include saving them from destruction. If biblical warrant for saving species from extinction is required, surely it is in the story of Noah and the Flood. But we should also note, with Rowan Williams, that 'the story is clearly about how the saving of the human future is inseparable from securing a future for *all* living things'.[70] That it was so important to save other living creatures along with humanity testifies to the interconnectedness and interdependence of the creation of which humans are a part.

SUMMARY

Does God's mandate to humans at creation encourage us to become controllers and managers of the whole of creation on this planet? No. It ascribes to God's gift the unique degree of power within creation that realistically our species has, and we should neither underestimate nor exaggerate that if we are to exercise it responsibly, as the mandate requires.

Granted our limited place within the God-given order of creation, the power we do have is to be exercised with loving care for the rest of creation. Our right to use the Earth's resources for human life and flourishing is strictly limited by the responsibility to conserve and by the rights of the other living creatures who share the Earth with us.

A role of caring responsibility for other living creatures, our 'dominion', is not a role that sets us above creation but a specific role that humans have within creation. It is rightly practised only when we recognise it to be dominion over fellow-creatures.

There are indications in the Torah that we should not consider the special human role within creation only in terms of intervention and change, but also in terms of restraint and letting be.

The human relationship to the rest of creation, as intended by God according to the biblical material we have studied in this chapter, cannot be easily summed up by a single term such as stewardship. It includes, most fundamentally and profoundly, being one creature among others. It requires at every point respect for the God-given order of creation. It is differentiated – entailing a major difference in how humans relate to living creatures and to inanimate nature. It includes a limited right to use of the Earth's resources for human life and flourishing. It calls for a caring responsibility for other creatures that reflects but does not usurp God's own care for his creation.

HUMAN ENHANCEMENT OF CREATION

I have left this topic until the last section of this chapter because the necessary discussion arises less directly out of exegesis than other issues we have discussed in this chapter. Interpretations of the Genesis dominion have traditionally given much prominence to human culture – in the broad sense of what humans make out of nature by transforming it into something humanly made. The most obvious example within Genesis, which we have discussed, is agriculture. It is clear that when Adam tills the soil he is collaborating with nature to make out of it what it would not make of itself without him. Without Adam's irrigation the fruit trees in the Garden of Eden would not grow. This is a kind of human enhancement of creation, and it is evidently a role that God intended within the order of creation. Often it has been regarded as 'improvement' of wild nature,[71] but, as we shall see, 'enhancement' is a better term.

Genesis 4:17–22 narrates the origins of other human cultural practices: building cities, making musical instruments, and forging metal tools, including weapons.[72] These are celebrated, but at the same time ambiguous:[73] they occur among the descendants of Cain, not in the line of Seth, while the invention of metal weapons enables Lamech's excess of violent revenge (4:23–24). In view of the importance of the escalation of violence in the Genesis account of early humanity, we must take very seriously the fact that the story of the origins of culture ends on this note, but it does not mean that culture itself is denigrated. Rather its potential for evil as well as good is highlighted. It is all too easily abused.

By 'enhancement' of creation I mean what humans do when they modify nature in ways that are not destructive but productive. This can be done in largely non-intrusive ways, as, for example, in art. In all kinds of art, humans make something different of nature from what it is purely in itself. We do not in the process replace nature in itself but add something else to it. A landscape painting does not replace the landscape itself, nor does it devalue the landscape itself, as though the landscape had no value until Constable painted it, but the painting does add something of fresh and different value. It is not a matter of benefiting other creatures, but it adds something to the created world. In that sense, it is an enhancement of creation. 'Improvement' would not be the right word, because it is not implied that the value of the landscape is increased by the painting. The painting is something, indebted to the landscape, that humans have added to the sum of value in creation.

A more, but still only gently intrusive example, with which most environmentalists have no problem, is gardening. A garden is a humanly modified version of nature. Few of us now feel, as the seventeenth-century pioneers of stewardship ideas did, that gardens are much preferable to wild nature. We value wild nature for itself, while also enjoying gardens as having different value. This is an example of a principle we can apply also to much more radically transforming things that humans do with nature: building homes and cities, crafting and manufacturing goods. Of course, the greater the extent to which the natural creation is transformed by these human creations the greater the danger that they will prove destructive of nature. Such remaking of nature without proper regard for the integrity and order of creation is not enhancement but loss.

The key is to add but not to replace. Humanly modified nature is not better, but different. We are not improving nature, but we are fashioning something with fresh value. Can wild nature not look after itself perfectly well without our intervention? Yes, of course, it can. Is not our intervention destructive? Yes, very often, and especially in the modern period it has been. But can we not add value to wild nature? Yes, if we enhance while also letting be.

Chapter 2

oooooooooooooooooooo

PUTTING US IN OUR PLACE

A major concern of this book is for us to recognise that there is much more to the Bible's understanding of the relation between humans and the rest of creation than the mandate of human dominion given us in Genesis 1. One reason it is important to seek out the other biblical perspectives on the matter is that, in the modern history of the West, the idea of human dominion has been the ideological justification of human domination and exploitation of nature. It has been associated with the dangerous modern human aspiration to godlike and creative power over the world. Under the banner of human dominion we have thought ourselves liberated from any given place within the order of God's creation. The modern culture of materialistic excess has developed in the context of a notion of dominion as an unrestricted right of masters and owners to exploit all the resources of creation.

To counter such hubris and excess, strong medicine is needed. Careful exposition of dominion as responsible stewardship may not be enough. We need to rediscover those biblical accounts of the human place in creation that are completely unconcerned with dominion and that do not set humans above other creatures. The point is not to replace an exclusive focus on Genesis 1 with an exclusive focus on these other passages, but to learn from the full range of biblical perspectives on the matter. To break the habit of gross misuse of the idea of dominion, we need the perspectives that counter-balance this idea with others. Before we can adequately reconceive the dominion as a distinctive role within the created order, we need to be put back within the created order. No part of Scripture does this more firmly and effectively than the book of Job. Here, if anywhere, we will find ourselves turned from hubris to humility. The strong antidote provided by God's answer to Job may taste, as it did to Job, like a somewhat bitter pill to swallow. But with the pain of relinquishing hubris goes also the exhilarating experience of the overwhelming wonder of God's universe. For addicts of domination and excess the book of Job offers a healing and transforming vision of both the Creator and his creation. Here we shall find that it is good to be put in our place.

THE CREATION IN GOD'S ANSWER TO JOB

Chapters 38—39 of the book of Job are the longest passage in the Bible about the non-human creation. This in itself ought to have guaranteed them a larger place than they have had in discussions of biblical views of creation. But they are also potent poetry. Bill McKibben calls them 'the first great piece of modern nature writing', and claims that nothing quite comparable with their appreciation of wild nature is to be found subsequently until the writings of John Muir.[1] He may be right.

A further reason for taking these chapters very seriously is that the author of the book puts them into the mouth of God. For thirty-five chapters, readers of Job have listened to Job and his friends debating God's ordering of the world. We have heard Job's anguished accusations against God and his seemingly hopeless desire at least to be allowed to put his case to God and to receive an answer. For a first-time reader, it must be a shock to reach the beginning of chapter 38: 'Then the LORD answered Job out of the whirlwind.' Chapters 38—39 purport to be God's answer to Job. After a brief response from Job, God continues through two more chapters (40—41). How exactly these two divine speeches are an answer to Job's question is the most debated issue in studies of the book.[2]

For our present purposes we can set the scene for these chapters quite briefly. Job is a righteous man, even a blameless man, whose suffering drives him to pose the biggest problem for believers in the biblical God: how can God, the all-powerful ruler of the world, be just if he leaves righteous people to suffer while wicked people prosper? Why do bad things happen to good people? Job's friends take the traditional line: bad things do not happen to good people. Since Job is suffering greatly, he must be a great sinner. But Job maintains his innocence. Neither he, nor anyone else in the book, questions that God is the all-powerful and all-wise ruler of nature and history. So Job is left with the conclusion that God cannot be just. He accuses God of wielding power with flagrant injustice (e.g. 9:21–24). It is this accusation that God is answering when he speaks out of the whirlwind.

The debate in the earlier chapters of Job has been about the moral order of the world. Surely the all-powerful, all-wise, perfectly righteous God will order the world so that people get what they deserve? This theme of God's ordering of the world is the obvious point of connection with what God says in answer to Job. But God's speeches approach it from a completely different angle. What God does is to invite Job into a vast panorama of the cosmos, taking Job on a sort of imaginative tour of his creation, all the time buffeting Job with questions. Virtually every sentence is a question. A strange way of answering Job, we might think. Job's questions seem to be answered only with questions. But the effect is to deconstruct and reorder Job's whole view of the world. God puts Job in his place.

God starts as he evidently means to go on: with a question that puts Job definitively in his cosmic place vis-à-vis God the Creator and his creation:

> Where were you when I laid the foundation of the Earth? (38:4)

The divine speech in fact starts as a kind of creation narrative, imaged differently from Genesis 1, that moves from creation in the beginning to God's ordering of creation's activity in the present.

THE PHYSICAL UNIVERSE IN GOD'S FIRST ADDRESS TO JOB (38:4–38)

We shall consider first the ten poetic strophes that lay out a panorama of the physical universe:

1 Creation of the Earth (38:4–7)

> 'Where were you when I laid the foundation of the Earth?
>> Tell me, if you have understanding.
> ⁵Who determined its measurements – surely you know!
>> Or who stretched the line upon it?
> ⁶On what were its bases sunk,
>> or who laid its cornerstone
> ⁷when the morning stars sang together
>> and all the heavenly beings shouted for joy?'³

God is pictured here as the cosmic architect and builder of the huge edifice of the world. It has a carefully planned design that stems from the wisdom of God. But Job, of course, was not privy to that design. This would not really be news to Job. He would never have claimed to understand the design of the universe. But God's tactic is to require Job really to take in what he already knows in theory.

2 Formation of the oceans (38:8–11)

> 'Or who shut in the sea with doors
>> when it burst out from the womb? –
> ⁹when I made the clouds its garment,
>> and thick darkness its swaddling band,
> ¹⁰and prescribed bounds for it,
>> and set bars and doors,
> ¹¹and said, "Thus far shall you come, and no farther,
>> and here shall your proud waves be stopped?"

God's creation also entailed containing the forces of disorder and destruction in the world. The sea is here both the symbol of these and also the literal sea. There is a sense both that the sea has its place in creation, but also that it is a well-nigh uncontrollable force that, given its head, would destroy creation. Against that possibility God sets firm bounds. If the emphasis in the first strophe was on the wisdom of God creating an ordered cosmos, here it is on the power of God to contain the forces opposed to that order.

3 Regulation of the dawn (38:12–15)

> 'Have you ever in your lifetime commanded the morning,
>> and caused the dawn to know its place,
> ¹³so that it might take hold of the skirts of the earth,
>> and the wicked be shaken out of it?
> ¹⁴It is changed like clay under the seal,
>> and it is dyed like a garment.
> ¹⁵Light is withheld from the wicked,
>> and their uplifted arm is broken.'

One of the broadest features of the workings of the world which began at creation and continues daily ever since is the dawn. The first dawn of creation is new again every morning. We should notice the key phrase: 'caused the dawn to know its place'. Creation is a matter of ordering things, keeping them in their place, and in the case of the dawn that means its regularity and its scope. One function of this regulation of the dawn is to keep in check the wicked who love darkness. Just as God's command of the sea keeps cosmic disorder in check, so his command of the dawn keeps moral disorder in the human world within limits. This is the only explicit reference to human beings (other than Job) in this whole panorama of the physical cosmos.[4]

4 The underworld (38:16–18)

> 'Have you entered into the springs of the sea,
>> or walked in the recesses of the deep?
> ¹⁷Have the gates of death been revealed to you,
>> or have you seen the gates of deep darkness?
> ¹⁸Have you comprehended the expanse of the earth?
>> Declare, if you know all this.'

Below the great expanse of the Earth lie the shadowy realm of the dead and the watery abyss that is the source of the oceans. Job knows nothing of these realms. For all his suffering he has not penetrated the mystery of death or the sources of disorder in the cosmos. These are the dark mysteries of the cosmos that no mortal can know. It should be noted that stanzas 2, 3 and 4 all deal with aspects of evil in the world.

5 Light and darkness (38:19–21)

> 'Where is the way to the dwelling of light,
>> and where is the place of darkness,
> 20that you may take it to its territory
>> and that you may discern the paths to its home?
> 21Surely you know, for you were born then,
>> and the number of your days is great!'

There is heavy sarcasm here: surely Job knows all about this? After all, he was there (wasn't he?) at the creation when God separated light from darkness! The sarcasm is designed to puncture Job's hubris. Also notable is the combination of knowledge and power, ignorance and impotence. If Job knew … then he could control … as God does. But he does not know.

6 Adverse weather (38:22–24)

> 'Have you entered the storehouses of the snow,
>> or have you seen the storehouses of the hail,
> 23which I have reserved for the time of trouble,
>> for the day of battle and war?
> 24What is the way to the place from which the lightning
>> forks, and the east wind is scattered upon the earth?'

With this strophe we move to a series concerned with various phenomena of the heavens, beginning with weather. This strophe refers to destructive weather: snow storms, hail storms, and the sirocco wind that dries up everything in its path.[5]

7 Lifegiving weather (38:25–27)

'Who has cut a channel for the torrents of rain,
    and a way for the thunderbolt,
[26]to bring rain on a land where no one lives,
    on the desert, which is empty of human life,
[27]to satisfy the waste and desolate land,
    and to make the ground put forth grass?'

The literally vital need of rain in the Middle East is evoked by this strophe, but at the same time God is said to direct the life-giving rain to places where no human lives. This may be a preliminary indication of God's care and provision for animals, which will be the main subject of 38:39—39:30.

8 The mysteries of the weather (38:28–30)

'Has the rain a father,
    or who has begotten the drops of dew?
[29]From whose womb did the ice come forth,
    and who has given birth to the hoarfrost of heaven?
[30]The waters become hard like stone,
    and the face of the deep is frozen.'

Once again Job is confronted with phenomena he cannot explain.

9 Controlling the stars (38:31–33)

'Can you bind the chains of the Pleiades,
    or loose the cords of Orion?
[32]Can you lead forth the Mazzaroth in their season,
    or can you guide the Great Bear with her children?[6]
[33]Do you know the ordinances of the heavens?
    Can you establish their rule on the earth?'

Ancient people, without strong artificial light in the hours of darkness, knew the stars much better than most modern people do. Even so, it is quite obviously beyond Job's knowledge or power to guide the constellations on their courses across the sky.

10 Controlling the weather (38:34–38)

'Can you lift up your voice to the clouds,
    so that a flood of waters may cover you?
³⁵Can you send forth lightnings, so that they may go
    and say to you, "Here we are"?
³⁶Who has put wisdom in the inward parts (?),
    or given understanding to the mind (?)?
³⁷Who has the wisdom to number the clouds?
    Or who can tilt the waterskins of the heavens,
³⁸when the dust runs into a mass
    and the clods cling together?'

This strophe returns to the meteorological phenomena of earlier strophes, but now the emphasis is on Job's inability to command them as God does, rather than on Job's incomprehension of them.

REFLECTIONS ON JOB 38:1–38

Before we continue with the rest of the speech as it turns to the animals, we will pause for some reflections on the depiction of the physical cosmos that we have read:

(1) The characteristic of the cosmos that is at the forefront of the descriptions is cosmic order. God has designed and maintains an ordered creation in which the various creatures – inanimate creatures so far, for the most part – have their allotted places. The order is not simply set up by God at the beginning. He is continuously active maintaining it.

(2) What Job lacks is both knowledge and power, the latter in consequence of the former. In Francis Bacon's words (at the origins of modern science): knowledge is power. Because Job does not understand he cannot control, whereas God in his infinite wisdom designed and also controls nature.

(3) The effect of this barrage of cosmic questions on Job (and readers of the book) must surely be cosmic humility. Before the immensity and mystery of the creation we know ourselves to be creatures whose own place in the world is limited. Viewing the

cosmos to a very small degree from God's perspective, we realise we are not God. Humility is not a popular virtue in our culture of self-assertion. But in this context it is something essential to being properly human. To be human is to have a limited place in the cosmic scheme of things, a less limited place than many other creatures, but limited nonetheless.

(4) This is a far from anthropocentric vision of the cosmos. Most of the features of creation described do have some relevance to human life, but hardly any reference is made to this human relevance. This is a universe that is what it is quite independently of us. The effect on Job must be to decentre him away from his preoccupation with his own case.[7] He is taken out of himself and given a broader vision of the universe and God's ways with it. What brings home to him the incalculable wisdom and power of God is the *otherness* of the cosmos, precisely that it is not a human world.

(5) God's barrage of questions designed to put Job in his place might seem brutal. In seeking to induce humility in Job, is God simply humiliating the man? In a sense the rhetoric of the passage *is* brutal, even in places sarcastic, but at the same time there is no indication of anger on God's part. What most distinguishes God's speech from mere brutality is the imaginative effect of the poetry. Job is confronted imaginatively with all these aspects of the cosmos, almost as though he were actually taken to see them. This is what takes Job out of himself and overwhelms him with the vastness, the grandeur, the wildness and the order of things. The effect is stunning and humbling, but also healing. Job is being confronted with the reality of how things are. For Job to realise his true position in the scheme of things is painful, but the pain is the sort of pain that can be necessary for effective healing. Job's whole stance towards the world and towards God is reorientated in a way that no mere reasoning, but only encounter with otherness, can effect.

Two further reflections on the passage arise from reading Job in our own context:

(1) What can we make of the fact that science can now explain a lot of what mystifies Job? We know pretty well, for example, how the meteorological phenomena of this passage work. Our knowledge of the universe has expanded vastly since Job's time, but nevertheless the difference is comparatively superficial. For the story of science is that each advance in knowledge merely opens up new areas of mystery. As Arthur Peacocke puts it, 'Our awareness of our ignorance grows in parallel with, indeed faster than, the growth in our knowledge.'[8] John Maddox comments:

> The big surprises will be the answers to questions that we are not yet smart enough to ask. The scientific enterprise is an unfinished project and will remain so for the rest of time.[9]

Only recently has it become apparent that much of the universe is full of so-called dark matter, but still no one really has the slightest idea what it is. The quest for a unified theory that will explain the whole universe ('a theory of Everything') shows no sign of reaching its goal, and, even should it do so, would not in fact explain everything, only the laws of sub-atomic physics.[10] As John Barrow argues, 'Theories of Everything are far from sufficient to unravel the subtleties of a universe like ours ... [T]here is more to Everything than meets the eye.'[11] Moreover, there is no basis at all for supposing that human minds will some day be able to understand everything. It is quite possible that they will come up against limits to knowledge that human minds are inherently incapable of crossing.[12]

(2) Cosmic humility is a much needed ecological virtue.[13] We need the humility to recognise that our place in the world is a limited one. We need the humility 'to walk more lightly on this Earth, with more regard for the other life around us'.[14] We need the humility to recognise the unforeseeable risks of technology before we ruin the world in pursuit of technological fixes to all our problems. We need the humility to know ourselves as creatures within creation, not gods over creation, the humility of knowing that only God is God.

THE WILD ANIMALS IN GOD'S FIRST ADDRESS TO JOB (38:39—39:30)

After the ten strophes on the physical universe, God's answer to Job turns to animals, and asks Job to consider ten selected animals and birds. The questions are much the same: does Job know, can he comprehend, can he control, as God does? But in the case of these living beings, there is also another question: can Job provide for these creatures, as God does?

1–2 The lion and the raven (38:39–41)

'Can you hunt the prey for the lion,
  or satisfy the appetite of the young lions,
⁴⁰when they crouch in their dens,
  or lie in wait in their lair?
⁴¹Who provides prey for the raven
  when his fledglings cry to God,
and wander about for lack of food?'

3–4 The mountain goat (ibex) and the deer (39:1–4)

'Do you know when the mountain goats give birth?
  Do you observe the calving of the deer?
²Can you number the months that they fulfill,
  and do you know the time when they give birth,
³when they crouch to give birth to their offspring,
  and are delivered of their young?
⁴Their young are strong, they grow up in the open;
  they leave them and do not return.'

5 The wild ass (onager) (39:5–8)

'Who set the wild ass free?
  Who loosed the bonds of the swift ass,
⁶to whom I have given the steppe for his home,
  the salt flats for his habitat?

> [7]He scorns the tumult of the city;
> > he hears no shouts from a driver.
> [8]He ranges the mountains for pasture,
> > and searches for any green thing.'

6 The wild ox (buffalo) (39:9–12)

> 'Is the wild ox willing to serve you?
> > Will he spend the night by your crib?
> [10]Can you tie him in the furrow with ropes,
> > or will he harrow the valleys behind you?
> [11]Can you rely on his massive strength,
> > and leave your heavy labour to him?
> [12]Can you depend on him to come home,
> > and carry your grain to your threshing floor?'

7 The sand grouse[15] (39:13–18)

> 'The wings of the sand grouse rejoice,
> > her pinions and plumage are gracious.
> [14]She lays her eggs on the earth,
> > and lets them be warmed in the dust,
> [15]forgetting that a foot may crush them,
> > that a wild animal may trample them.
> [16]She makes her young grow hardy without her
> > and does not worry that her labour may be in vain.
> [17]For God has denied her wisdom,
> > and given her no share in understanding.[16]
> [18]When she soars on high,
> > she laughs at the horse and its rider.'

8 The war horse (39:19–25)

> 'Do you give the horse his might?
> > Do you clothe his neck with mane?
> [20]Do you make him leap like the locust?
> > His majestic snorting is terrifying.

^{21}He paws violently, exults in his strength,

 he goes out to meet the weapons.

^{22}He laughs at fear, and is not dismayed;

 he does not recoil from the sword.

^{23}On his back rattles the quiver,

 the flashing spear, and the javelin.

^{24}With fierceness and rage he swallows the ground;

 at the sound of the trumpet he cannot stand still.

^{25}When the trumpet sounds, he shouts "Hurrah!"

 He smells the battle from afar,

 the thunder of the captains, and the shouting.'

9–10 The hawk and the vulture[17] (39:26–30)

'Is it by your wisdom that the hawk soars,

 and spreads his wings toward the south?

^{27}Is it at your command that the vulture mounts up

 and makes her nest on high?

^{28}She lives on the rock and makes her home

 in the fastness of the rocky crag.

^{29}From there she spies the prey;

 her eyes see it from far away.

^{30}Her young ones suck up blood;

 and where the slain are, there she is.'

REFLECTIONS ON JOB 38:39—39:30

We can now reflect on some aspects of this second half of God's first address to Job:

(1) We should notice how each of the animals is described in ways quite specific to its species. We are not given visual descriptions – readers are expected to know what the animals look like – but we are given details, in many cases, of habitat, characteristic behaviour, feeding, and treatment of the young. These features no doubt continue the emphasis on the order of creation that was prominent in the account of the physical universe. God has created

each animal with its own proper habitat and way of life, means of sustenance and generational continuance.

(2) In the Old Testament there is usually a sharp distinction between domestic animals, which belong to the human world, and wild animals which do not. All the animals in this passage are wild, with the only apparent exception of the war horse. But the wonderful description of the war horse (39:19–25) is devoted to showing that in reality there is nothing tame or domestic about him. His ferocity and courage are natural to him. He needs no compulsion to play his part in battle. On the contrary, he evidently enjoys it. This horse is very much his own horse. That he actually has a rider is only obliquely indicated. Also especially notable in this connection is the wild ox (39:9–12). Remarkably and uniquely among these descriptions, we are told nothing about the wild ox except that he does not behave like his domestic cousin. He will not be Job's servant. Job cannot use him for agricultural work as he does the domestic ox. This ox is wild by nature. Similarly, it is the freedom of the wild ass that dominates the description of him (39:5–8). He keeps well away from the human world, where his domesticated cousin suffers often very burdensome servitude. He runs free as God has made him. In general, the point about the wildness of these ten animals is not that they are threats to humans (few of them were) but that they are entirely independent of humans. They have lives of their own. They neither serve humans nor, like domestic animals, need to be provided for by humans. God provides for them.

(3) As part of God's answer to Job, these imaginative portraits of animals continue to decentre and reorient Job in his world. They do so perhaps more forcibly because they come closer to home. In a sense, the panorama of the physical world stated the obvious. No one in Job's world would have supposed they understood or could control those aspects of the cosmos. Job himself had come close to admitting this in an earlier speech (26:7–14). The point was obvious but still needed to be assimilated by Job if his hubris was to be countered. In the case of the wild animals, on the other hand, might not Job have reasonably expected that he could become

dominant over them? The human dominion assigned by God in Genesis 1:26 was over all living things. Norman Habel argues that God's answer to Job subverts and undermines the Genesis mandate of dominion.[18] At the very least we must say that it puts another side to the picture. It limits or qualifies dominion, which seems here to be limited to the animals that belong to the human world.[19] It strikes a blow at the anthropocentrism and hubris that are encouraged by treatment of the dominion as the only thing that needs to be said about the human relationship to other creatures. It is also important that other creatures have their own lives, given them by God, that can be fulfilled only in independence of humans. Job is not the centre or the apex of the animal world. He is a creature among others.

(4) The passage begins and ends with the predatory behaviour of carnivorous animals and in particular the feeding of their young (38:39–41 and 39:26–30). At the beginning, the young lions wait in their dens for their parents to bring them meat, while the raven also seeks meat for its youngsters. At the end, the baby vultures suck up the blood from the pieces of carrion their parent has brought them.[20] Perhaps this close thematic link between the beginning and the end of the passage, such that the end puts one in mind of the beginning, is meant to suggest the cycle of nature, in which death nourishes new life and new life could not continue without death. In any case, from the point of view of this passage, the carnivorous nature of some animals is simply part of the God-given order.[21] Indeed, the opening verses suggest that it is God himself who provides the prey for the lion and the raven.

(5) Besides the function of this passage in putting Job in his place, there is surely another dimension of the descriptions.[22] They express God's sheer joy in his creatures, their variety and idiosyncracies, the freedom of the wild ass and the massive strength of the wild ox and the horse, the soaring flight of the hawk and even the apparent stupidity of the sand grouse. Their divine designer and provider is also proud of their independence, delights in their wildness and rejoices in the unique value of each. Job is invited to join God in this delight. This wild world of the animals,

so different from Job's own world of sheep and camels, draws him out of himself into admiration of the other.

Four further reflections on the passage arise from reading Job in our own context:

(1) It is no longer true that wild animals and birds such as these are so wholly free of any impact humans could have on them. We have encroached on their habitats, which are no longer so out-of-bounds for humans as they were for Job. Species go extinct every day as a result of human activity, while climate change will affect most of life on this Earth and is likely to lead to the extinction of vast numbers of species. Like Job, we cannot tame the wild animals, but unlike Job we can either ensure or prevent their survival, and so we have responsibilities for them that Job never had. We must preserve their habitat and respect their various ways.

(2) As in the case of the physical universe, our knowledge of these and other animals has, of course, increased vastly since Job's time. Ancient people did observe animals carefully, as these descriptions show, but that observation was limited. Job cannot answer the question about the period of a mountain goat's pregnancy because these shy animals in inaccessible habitats were not easily observed (39:1–3). Now we can see far less accessible natural events on television wildlife documentaries. But we still cannot understand fully how the hawk migrates. Mysteries remain. New species are still being discovered all the time.

Moreover, beyond factual scientific knowledge about animals, there remains a greater mystery: the mystery of other beings. What is it like to be a wild ox or a sand grouse? God knows; we can only very partially imagine. Among the descriptions in Job those of the wild ass, and especially the marvellous poem about the horse, are examples of imaginative portrayal of what it might be like to be one of these creatures so different from ourselves. The mystery remains.

(3) The descriptions presuppose that the animals are 'subjects of their own lives'.[23] The descriptions are in fact very restrained in their anthropomorphisms, that is, in their attribution of human feelings and intentions to the animals (see 39:7, 13–18 and 21–25).

But only by means of anthropomorphism have we any means at all of empathy with other conscious creatures. Against a standard modern critique of applying anthropomorphic language to animals, cognitive ethologist Marc Bekoff defends such language, even in scientific study, on the grounds that we have no other way of accessing the experience of animals. Renouncing anthropomorphism altogether is bound to be reductionist, explaining animal behaviour in wholly mechanistic terms. To use anthropomorphic language need not imply that we recognise no difference between our own feelings and those of animals; only that we postulate something similar on the basis of the behaviour we observe. For a horse to feel excitement and pleasure cannot be the same as for us to do so; but it is reasonable to suppose the horse experiences something of the sort: horse-excitement and horse-pleasure. Bekoff argues for the scientific use of anthropomorphism provided it is used carefully and 'biocentrically', meaning that we make every attempt to understand who animals are in their own world.[24]

Of course, there is no reason to expect such scientifically cautious limits on the use of anthropomorphism in ancient poetry like the book of Job, but as a matter of fact these biblical descriptions of animals seem to come remarkably close to it. They do not indulge in undisciplined projection of human thoughts and emotions onto animals, but stay close to the animal's observed behaviour, attributing only emotions quite plausibly expressed by this behaviour. They respect the mystery of other beings, while treating them as subjects with awareness and feelings akin to some of our own.[25] (For this reason, it is unfortunate that most modern translations use the pronoun 'it' with reference to these animals; the translation above, following Habel,[26] uses the personal pronouns, 'he' and 'she', because they are more appropriate to the way the descriptions treat the animals as subjects with awareness and feeling.) This cautious degree of anthropomorphism is very important for human relationships with other animals. It enables us to recognise them as subjects of their own lives and not mere objects for human use.

(4) Bill McKibben, noting that Job in this passage is called both to cosmic humility and to share God's delight in his creation, makes a significant point about the need for both these ecological virtues in our current context of ecological crisis:

> The challenge before us is to figure out how to link these two callings, these two imperatives from the voice in the whirlwind – the call to humility and the call to joy. Each one, on its own, is insufficient. Humility by itself is an arid negativism; a gleeful communion with the Earth around us can quickly turn into some New Age irresponsibility … But together they are reinforcing, powerful – powerful enough, perhaps, to start changing some of the deep-seated behaviors that are driving our environmental destruction, our galloping poverty, our cultural despair. And fortunately the two can go hand in hand.[27]

GOD'S SECOND ADDRESS TO JOB (CHAPTERS 40—41)

It is God's second address to Job that finally brings Job to his senses. Chapters 40 and 41 describe two fearsome animals called Behemoth and Leviathan. Who are these animals and what do they add to God's argument with Job? They have often been identified as the hippopotamus and the crocodile, and there is a good deal in the text to support that identification (especially 40:15; 40:21–23; 41:13–17).[28] If they are no more than the hippopotamus and the crocodile, the chapters 40—41 simply continue the same argument already made in chapter 39. Behemoth and Leviathan are evoked to reinforce the point made in chapter 39: that Job is not able to control wild nature. These are particularly ferocious wild animals that Job must find it inconceivable that he could capture, control or rule over. One problem with this view is that, unless these very long and elaborate descriptions of Behemoth and especially Leviathan make some point that chapter 39 has not already made, their function does not seem equal to the stress that is laid upon them by their length and their position as the climax of God's whole argument with Job.

Most contemporary scholars take the view that these are not ordinary animals like those in chapter 39, but mythical monsters. This does not mean ignoring the features of the descriptions that do recall the hippopotamus and the crocodile. Rather, the author has certainly modelled his monsters partly on those real animals,[29] but also added features which would be quite unrealistic features if they were supposed to characterise the hippo and the crocodile. One of the most obvious is that Leviathan breathes fire, a point which the author hammers home through three whole verses (41:19–21).[30] Some would say that such features are poetic embellishments,[31] but we should remember that there were no such unrealistic embellishments in the descriptions of the animals in chapter 39. Introducing such embellishments now, in the accounts of Behemoth and Leviathan, would surely undermine the case being made. Job would be being intimidated, convinced that he could not capture or control these animals, by means of fictional additions to their real character. In fact, we know that hippos and crocodiles were successfully hunted in the ancient world. What God challenges Job to do would not be completely impossible if only these two fearsome animals were in view.

Moreover, whereas the animals in chapter 39 are called by their ordinary names, Behemoth and Leviathan are not the names of ordinary animals. Behemoth is actually the plural form of the ordinary word for a four-legged mammal (*behema*), but the plural is here used as a singular. It must mean something like 'The Animal' or 'the beast *par excellence*'.[32] Leviathan is undoubtedly the name of the primordial chaos monster (Ps. 74:13–14; Isa. 27:1), and it is actually used in this sense earlier in Job (3:8). The names – the first thing we are told about each of these creatures – immediately cause readers to think of monsters, not regular animals.

If Behemoth and Leviathan are mythical monsters, what are they doing here in God's address to Job? Before turning to the texts, we must attend to the fact that God's second address to Job includes another passage of argument before he gets to Behemoth, an argument important for understanding the two monsters (40:10–14). In this argument, God challenges Job to rule the human world. This continues, in a way, the great panorama of creation in chapters 38—39. God has reminded Job of how he cannot control the cosmos, the sun, the stars, the weather or the wild animals. But what about the human world? This would seem rather more plausible. Earlier in the book, Job has recounted his role as a village elder, dispensing justice (chapter 28). Could he do this on a world scale? In other words, could Job himself do what he has complained that God is not doing – rule the human world with justice, making sure that every sinner gets due punishment?:

Can Job rule the human world? (40:10–14)

'Adorn yourself with majesty and dignity;
    clothe yourself with glory and splendour.
[11]Unleash the fury of your wrath,
    and look on all who are proud, and abase them.
[12]Look on all who are proud, and bring them low;
    tread down the wicked where they stand.
[13]Bury them all in the dust together;
    shroud their faces in the grave.
[14]Then I will also acknowledge to you
    that your own right hand can give you victory.'

Of course, Job cannot do it. He lacks the power. The description of the wicked here as proud, a typical biblical way of referring to tyrants and oppressors, people who arrogantly behave as though they were gods, is an important point for its relevance at a later stage of our discussion.

After that discussion of the human world, God turns to Behemoth and Leviathan. He can hardly be just returning to more animals. Their placing in the narrative must mean that these are another facet of creation altogether, one that Job can have no hope of ruling.

Can Job control Behemoth? (40:15–24)

'Look at Behemoth,
   whom I made just as I made you;
   he eats grass like an ox.
^{16}His strength is in his loins,
   his potency in the muscles of his belly.
^{17}He stiffens his tail like a cedar;
   the sinews of his thighs are knotted together.
^{18}His bones are tubes of bronze,
   his limbs like bars of iron.

'^{19}He is the first of the great acts of God–
   even his Maker can only approach him with a sword.
^{20}The mountains bring him their tribute
   where all the wild animals play.
^{21}Under the lotus plants he lies,
   hidden among the reeds in the marsh.
^{22}The lotus trees conceal him in their shade
   the willows of the brook surround him.
^{23}If the river rages, he is not alarmed;
   he is confident even though Jordan surges against its
      mouth.
^{24}Can anyone capture him by the eyes
   or pierce his nose with hooks?'

Can Job control Leviathan? (40:1–34)

'Can you draw out Leviathan with a fishhook,
   or tie down his tongue with a cord?
^{2}Can you put a rope through his nose,
   or pierce his jaw with a hook?
^{3}Will he make many supplications to you?
   Will he speak soft words to you?
^{4}Will he make a covenant with you
   to be taken as your servant forever?

[5]Will you play with him as with a bird,
>   or will you put him on a leash for your girls?[33]
[6]Will traders bargain over him?
>   Will they divide him up among the merchants?
[7]Can you fill his skin with harpoons,
>   or his head with fishing spears?
[8]If you lay a hand on him,
>   you will remember the battle; and you will not do it again!

[9]There is no hope of subduing him;
>   the very sight of him is overwhelming.
[10]No one is so fierce as to dare to stir him up.
>   But who can stand before my face?
[11]Whoever confronts me I will requite,
>   for everything under the heavens is mine.
[12]Will I not silence his boasting,
>   his mighty words and his fine argument?

[13]Who can strip off his outer garment?
>   Who can penetrate his double coat of mail?
[14]Who can pry open the doors of his mouth?
>   Terror is all around his teeth.
[15]His back is a row of shields,
>   tightly sealed together.
[16]Each is so near to the next
>   no air can come between them.
[17]They are joined tightly to one another;
>   they are interlocked and cannot be separated.
[18]His sneezes flash forth lightning,
>   and his eyes are like the eyelids of dawn.
[19]Firebrands pour from his mouth;
>   sparks of fire leap out.
[20]Smoke billows from his nostrils
>   as if from a boiling pot over a fire of reeds.
[21]His breath sets coals ablaze,
>   and flames dart from his mouth.

²²Strength resides in his neck,
>	and terror dances before him.
²³The folds of his flesh cling together,
>	so that they are firm and immovable.
²⁴His breast is hard as rock,
>	as hard as a lower millstone.
²⁵When he rises up the gods are afraid;
>	they retreat before his crashings.
²⁶The sword that reaches him has no effect,
>	nor does the spear, the dart, or the javelin.
²⁷He treats iron as straw,
>	and bronze like rotten wood.
²⁸No arrow can make him flee;
>	slingstones are turned to chaff for him.
²⁹A club seems to him just a piece of straw;
>	he laughs at the rattle of javelins.
³⁰His underparts are like sharp potsherds;
>	he spreads himself like a threshing sledge on the mire.
³¹He makes the deep boil like a cauldron;
>	he makes the sea like a pot of ointment.
³²Behind him he leaves a luminous path;
>	one would think the deep had white hair.

³³On earth he has no equal,
>	created as he was without fear.
³⁴He looks down on all the arrogant;
>	he is king over all who are proud.'

What can we say about these two monsters? Behemoth is the monster of the land, supreme over all the land animals, while Leviathan is the sea monster, 'king over all who are proud' (41:34). The description of Behemoth is much the shorter, suggesting that Leviathan is the more important. Much of what is said of both monsters dwells on their stupendous strength, their complete fearlessness, the impossibility of capturing or controlling them, the impossibility even of wounding or killing them. But the implication is also that there is just one who is indeed, unlike Job, able to capture and control these monsters: God.

Leviathan was a chaos monster, a personification of the destructive forces in nature that threaten the order of God's creation. These forces are most often in the Old Testament portrayed under another image: the Sea. To ancient Israel the terrifying, destructive power of the raging ocean was the most dangerous thing they knew in nature. So they thought of the primeval chaos as the waters of chaos. God's act of creation involved restricting the waters of chaos within strict limits and so making room for the order of the created world. But God did not abolish these forces of chaos: he confined them and continues to control them, to keep them within definite boundaries. Otherwise they would engulf and destroy creation. The Old Testament tends to see them as always awaiting their opportunity to do that. Only at the end of history will God finally abolish chaos – dry up the Sea or slay Leviathan (Isa. 27:1).[34]

In fact, the story of creation at the beginning of God's first speech to Job includes, as we have noted, this theme of God's containing the chaos waters and fixing impassable limits for them (38:8–11; cf. also 2:12 and 26:12). There God addresses the Sea: 'Thus far shall you come, and no farther, and here shall your proud waves be stopped' (38:11). Significantly, the Sea's waves are proud. The Sea is arrogant because it aspires to burst out of its limits, to rebel against God's order. This is one point that connects the Sea in chapter 38 with Leviathan in chapter 41. Leviathan is closely associated with the primordial deep. He stirs it up to boiling point (41:31). When he rears up, his crashing waves terrify even the heavenly beings (41:25). The very last thing God says about Leviathan – which is also the end of all God has to say to Job – is that 'He looks down on all the arrogant; he is king over all who are proud' (cf. also the reference to Leviathan's boasting before God in 41:12). Both the Sea and Leviathan represent the forces of destruction in the world, both characterised as proud or arrogant in their rebellion against the order God has given to creation. Leviathan indeed is the very prince of rebellion, looking down from the height of his own arrogance on all other proud creatures.

As for Behemoth, he is probably best seen as another symbol of the forces of destruction in creation. The two figures – one supreme on land, the other in the sea – make up a comprehensive symbol of the anti-God powers in creation, active both on land and in the waters.[35] (It may be relevant to note that in Egyptian mythology both the hippopotamus and the crocodile appear as forms taken by the evil god Seth in his battle against the god Horus.[36] They correspond, therefore, to the place of Leviathan in the Canaanite mythology to which Israel's myth of God's victory over the forces of chaos was indebted.) Thus, whereas the first of God's speeches to Job focused on the order of creation, established and maintained by God, with only passing reference to the forces of destruction that God keeps within bounds (38:8–11 and 38:15), the second divine speech focuses all of Job's attention on the forces of chaos that continually threaten the created order. The message seems to be that not only has God restrained these powers but also he must win a final victory over them (41:10–12).[37] Whether God's victory over Leviathan described in these verses is understood to be past or future is not of decisive significance. That God has vanquished the forces of evil in the past, at creation, shows that he is capable of doing so again whenever it may prove necessary to secure his creation against destruction.[38]

Who are the proud over whom Leviathan rules? Some of them at least must be the wicked described in 40:11–12, the proud people whom God challenged Job to rule. In moving from that passage to the descriptions of Behemoth and Leviathan, God moves from the arrogant human sinners to the monstrous creatures that personify arrogant rebellion against God. If Job wants to order the universe more justly than God, then these are what he is up against. Job has to realise that only God can cope with them. There are forces of chaos and destruction in creation that God contains and controls, but has not yet abolished. Job, in his ignorance of all that God is doing in the wider world beyond his own preoccupations, has no way of understanding how God's dealings are, ultimately, just. He can know only that God has evil under control and will in the end abolish it.

Thus, in this last part of God's address, Job has to come to terms with the darkest aspect of creation. Theological discussions of the non-human creation often raise the question whether there is anything like evil in the natural world, independently of human evil. These passages in Job may go as far as the Old Testament ever goes in answering that question. But there is a less speculative aspect to the matter. Norman Habel has argued that the full significance of the second speech of God is that Job himself is being compared with Behemoth and Leviathan. Job, in his arrogant rebellion against God, questioning the order of creation God has established, is like Behemoth and Leviathan, and God will silence Job as he did Leviathan:[39]

> As in a mirror, Job is shown Leviathan stirring up chaos.
> Yahweh is hinting that Job has taken on heroic proportions
> and that like a chaos figure he has roused Yahweh to appear
> in a whirlwind and challenge him … If Yahweh's Lordship
> involves controlling the forces of chaos and evil in the
> world, both of which he admits are present, Job needs to
> recognize he is part of that world. He can either be like
> Leviathan and stir chaos or be like God and seek to control
> it.[40]

I do not find this reading convincing, because it runs contrary to the clear implication of the description of Leviathan: that Job has no chance of controlling it. Job's arrogance is challenged, not by inviting him to compare himself with Leviathan, but by showing him that he cannot vanquish or control Leviathan.

However, there is something to be learned from Habel's idea that Job is confronted with the option of being like Leviathan or like God. While we contemporary humans, like Job, cannot in the last resort defeat the destructive forces in creation, we can help to unleash them. Human action that threatens the order of God's creation and leads to destruction of creation aids and abets Behemoth and Leviathan. Human aspiration to godlike creative power

Putting Us in Our Place

over the world, challenging the divinely given order, shares the arrogance of Leviathan. Humans in this case join the proud over whom Leviathan is king (41:34).

THE COMMUNITY OF CREATION

A major proposal of this book is that the image of a community of creation, in which we humans are fellow-members with God's other creatures, is a helpful way of synthesising important aspects of the relevant biblical material. It also provides a broader context within which to situate the special and distinctive roles of humans in creation, recognising these without lifting humans out of creation as though we were demi-gods set over it. All God's creatures are first and foremost creatures, ourselves included. All earthly creatures share the same Earth; and all participate in an interrelated and interdependent community, orientated above all to God our common Creator. It is a community of hugely diverse members whose mutual relationships are therefore enormously rich and diverse. Modern ecological science is constantly revealing more and more of the complex balance and flux of interrelationships within the biosphere of the Earth and its component ecosystems,[1] but a great deal remains to be known, probably much more than we already know. Biblical writers were not able to plot such interconnections scientifically, but they articulate a vision of creation that is coherent with the science, while focusing, as science properly cannot, on matters of value, ethics, responsibility and, especially, the creation's relation with God.

PSALM 104 – SHARING THE EARTH

There are some striking resemblances between Job 38—39 and Psalm 104 (which is the second longest biblical account of the non-human creation).[2] Both begin with poetic evocations of God's initial creation of the world, more like each other than either is to

Genesis 1, and both move smoothly from there into a panoramic view of the parts and members of creation. Both deny humans a place of supremacy. But Psalm 104 puts us in our place in the world in a much gentler way than God's answer to Job. Here, there is no indication that human hubris needs shattering. Rather there is a sense that within the praise of God for his creation we fall naturally into the place he has given us alongside his other creatures.

> Bless the LORD, O my soul.
>> O LORD my God, you are very great.
> You are clothed with honour and majesty,
>> 2wrapped in light as with a garment.
> You stretch out the heavens like a tent,
>> 3you set the beams of your chambers on the waters,
> you make the clouds your chariot,
>> you ride on the wings of the wind,
> 4you make the winds your messengers,
>> fire and flame your ministers.
>
> 5You set the earth on its foundations,
>> so that it shall never be shaken.
> 6You cover it with the deep as with a garment;
>> the waters stood above the mountains.
> 7At your rebuke they flee;
>> at the sound of your thunder they take to flight.
> 8They rose up to the mountains, ran down to the valleys
>> to the place that you appointed for them.
> 9You set a boundary that they may not pass,
>> so that they might not again cover the earth.
>
> 10You make springs gush forth in the valleys;
>> they flow between the hills,
> 11giving drink to every wild animal;
>> the wild asses quench their thirst.
> 12By the streams the birds of the air have their habitation;
>> they sing among the branches.
> 13From your lofty abode you water the mountains;
>> the earth is satisfied with the fruit of your work.

^{14}You cause the grass to grow for the cattle,
and plants for people to cultivate,
so as to bring forth bread from the earth,^{3}
^{15}and wine to gladden the human heart,
oil to make the face shine,
and bread to strengthen the human heart.
^{16}The trees of the LORD are watered abundantly,
the cedars of Lebanon that he planted.^{4}
^{17}In them the birds build their nests;
the stork has its home in the fir trees.^{5}
^{18}The high mountains are for the wild goats;
the rocks are a refuge for the coneys.^{6}

^{19}You have made the moon to mark the seasons;
the sun knows its time for setting.
^{20}You make darkness, and it is night,
when all the animals of the forest come creeping out.
^{21}The young lions roar for their prey,
seeking their food from God.
^{22}When the sun rises, they withdraw
and lie down in their dens.
^{23}People go out to their work
and to their labour until the evening.

^{24}O LORD, how manifold are your works!
In wisdom you have made them all;
the earth is full of your creatures.
^{25}Yonder is the sea, great and wide,
creeping things innumerable are there,
living things both small and great.
^{26}There go the ships,
and Leviathan that you formed to sport in it.

^{27}These all look to you
to give them their food in due season;
^{28}when you give to them, they gather it up;
when you open your hand, they are filled with good
things.

The Community of Creation

^{29}When you hide your face, they are dismayed;
when you take away their breath, they die
and return to their dust.
^{30}When you send forth your spirit, they are created;
and you renew the face of the ground.

^{31}May the glory of the LORD endure forever;
may the LORD rejoice in his works –
^{32}who looks on the earth and it trembles,
who touches the mountains and they smoke.
^{33}I will sing to the LORD as long as I live;
I will sing praise to my God while I have being.
^{34}May my meditation be pleasing to him,
for I rejoice in the LORD.
^{35}Let sinners be consumed from the earth,
and let the wicked be no more.
Bless the LORD, O my soul.
Praise the LORD!

REFLECTIONS ON PSALM 104

(1) This is a psalm of praise to God for his 'generous extravagance'[7] in creation and in provision for his creatures, for a world of huge diversity and complexity, a world of fecundity and abundance of life. There is a pervasive sense of the world as God's gift to all living creatures. The God of this psalm is God the generous giver from whom all good things come (cf. Jas. 1:17).

(2) God's 'extravagance' in creating so many diverse creatures appears in what William Brown calls the psalm's 'veritable taxonomy of zoological species',[8] as well as in the particular mention of the fecundity of the sea (v 25: 'creeping things innumerable ... living things both small and great'). Indeed, the psalmist interrupts his 'taxonomy' in order to comment: 'LORD, how manifold are your works!' (v 24).

(3) God's generous provision for all these living creatures (humanity, animals (domestic and wild), birds and sea creatures) can be put into the following six categories:

the breath of life – This is life itself, the fundamental gift that underlies all others and determines the limit of all others. The life, the breath of living things, is God's breath ('spirit') that he gives and takes as he pleases, continually renewing life on Earth (vv 29–30). As Odil Steck puts it, humans 'and all living creatures are "elementally dependent" on God'.[9]

water – This is essential for all life – and its need is especially obvious in the Middle East. It is very prominent here (vv 10–13 and 16).

food – According to verse 28, God opens his generous hands and provides good things for all of his creatures. Even the lions, hunting in the forest at night, seek their prey *from God* (v 21) – an image we have already encountered in Job.

habitat – The availability of water and the appropriate food depends on the specific habitat God has provided for each kind of creature: trees by water for birds, mountains for mountain goats, rocky crags for coneys, arable land for humans, forests for lions and many others, sea for the innumerable creatures of the ocean. Our contemporary awareness that we are destroying creatures by destroying their habitats follows very directly from the kind of ecological understanding of nature that is to be found already in Psalm 104.

times and seasons – The alternation of day and night, the regularity of the seasons of the year are an essential aspect of the Earth's habitability for living creatures, which accommodates different creatures differently (vv 19–23 and 27).

joy – The life God gives and resources is no mere utilitarian survival, but has its goal in God's creatures' joy in life: the birds sing for joy (v 12),[10] God's provision for humans includes wine to gladden the heart and oil to make the face shine (v 15), while the great sea monster Leviathan was created by God to play in the ocean (v 26). There is a hint (v 31) that the creatures' joy is a participation in God's own joy, the pleasure he takes in all he has created.

(4) The psalm portrays creation as completely and directly dependent on God's generous giving. There is a strong sense of God's immediate and constant involvement with his creatures. But, at the same time as stressing dependence on God, the psalm sees this as empowerment. Birds build their nests, humans work the land and sail ships, Leviathan plays.

(5) As well as the general categories of birds, wild animals, domestic animals, animals of the forest and sea creatures, seven living creatures are specifically named: wild asses, humans, storks, wild goats, coneys, lions, Leviathan. The number seven may be deliberate, since, as the number of completeness, it can be used to indicate that seven specific items are representative of the whole. More significantly, it is worth noticing that, of the six non-human creatures listed here, three are also among the ten animals in God's challenge to Job: wild asses, mountain goats and lions. This highlights the fact that the animals named are especially those that were beyond the control of humans. Of course, this is also true of Leviathan, who appears here in a much more innocent role than he has in Job.

(6) What place do humans have in this panorama of creation? They do receive a little more attention than other living things (vv 14–15, 23 and 26).[11] There are hints at a certain exceptionality: references to domesticated animals (v 14: God makes the grass grow for cattle), to agriculture (v 14), viticulture and arboriculture (v 15), and to ships on the ocean (v 26). But there is no trace of human supremacy over the creatures in general. The impression is rather of fellow-creatureliness. Like other living creatures, humans have their own place in a creation where there are also innumerable fellow-creatures for whom God also provides life, place and sustenance. Humans are part of God's wonderfully diverse creation. Brown comments that, compared with the anthropocen-

tricity of Psalm 8, Psalm 104 'moves toward an ecocentric profile'.[12] I would prefer to say that this psalm is primarily theocentric, and that its picture of an ecological creation belongs within its theocentric praise of God for his creation. 'With no stain of human dominion, this Psalm plays out joy in God and nature both.'[13]

(7) The whole picture is almost without exception positive. There is reference to death, but it seems to be simply accepted as a part of the natural cycle of life and death (v 29). God apparently causes earthquakes and volcanic eruptions (v 32: he 'looks on the earth and it trembles', he 'touches the mountains and they smoke'). But these are probably understood as aspects of theophany, as they were at Mount Sinai, manifestations of God's glory (v 31), rather than as causing innocent suffering. This entirely positive view of creation resembles that of Genesis 1.[14] For whatever reason, the psalmist resolutely withholds any indication that there might be anything wrong in God's created world – *except* (and the exception is therefore all the more remarkable) that, almost at the end of the psalm, interrupting his praise, the psalmist prays: 'Let sinners be consumed from the earth, and let the wicked be no more' (v 35a). Humans are the creatures who spoil the otherwise rosy picture of the world. Walter Brueggemann suggests that the sinners

> are those who refuse to receive life in creation on terms of generous extravagance, no doubt in order to practice a hoarding autonomy in denial that creation is indeed governed and held by its Creator. Creation has within it the sovereign seriousness of God, who will not tolerate the violation of the terms of creation, which are terms of gift, dependence and extravagance.[15]

This human despoiling of creation is in fact the psalm's strongest indication of human exceptionality.

(8) In the account of the sea there is specific mention of 'ships' and 'Leviathan' (v 26), as though both were species of sea creature, illustrations of the 'small' and 'great' creatures mentioned in the

preceding verse. Humans sailing the sea can certainly feel very small, while Leviathan is perhaps the only creature sufficiently large to seem at home in the vast ocean. The reference to ships might suggest that humanity is not so limited to a particular habitat as other animals are, but it also portrays humans at their most vulnerable. Knowing Leviathan from other passages of the Hebrew Bible, including Job, we may see him as personifying the chaos that God overcame at creation and must thereafter keep at bay lest it reduce creation back to chaos. As such he is closely associated with the sea, itself a manifestation of the primeval waters of chaos. The vulnerability of humans foolhardy enough to travel by sea (ancient Israelites rarely did so) appears in the juxtaposition of their ships with Leviathan. And yet Leviathan is not here the agent of destruction, as he is in Job, but merely a monster (a whale?) playing in the ocean.[16] Similarly, he appears in Genesis 1, if at all, only in the reference to sea monsters, created with other sea creatures, on the fifth day (Gen. 1:21). Thus both Genesis 1 and Psalm 104, by contrast with Job, have tamed the chaos monster[17] and so have already eliminated the conflict of chaos with order and the threat of cosmic destruction that Leviathan represents. In this respect, as in others, they both portray creation in an ideal or utopian or eschatological way.

(9) After instancing many species individually, stressing their diversity, the psalm goes on to bring them all together, humans and other animals alike, in their common dependence on the Creator (vv 27–30). What gives wholeness to this psalm's reading of the world is not human mastery over it or the value humans set on it, not (in contemporary terms) globalisation, but the value of all created things for God. This is a theocentric, not an anthropocentric world. God's own rejoicing in his works (v 31) funds the psalmist's rejoicing (v 34), as he praises God, not merely for human life and creation's benefits for humans, but for God's glory seen in the whole creation. In a different way from Job, the psalmist is taken out of himself, lifted out of the limited human preoccupations that dominate most of our lives, by his contemplation of the rest of God's creation. This is the kind of appreciation of God's

creation, sharing in God's appreciation of it,[18] that can enable us to live rightly within it, to join with other creatures in living for the praise of his glory.

MATTHEW 6:25–33 – SHARING GOD'S PROVISION FOR HIS CREATURES

From the great creation psalm of the Old Testament, we turn to a New Testament passage, part of the Sermon on the Mount,[19] in which Jesus draws on the creation theology of the Hebrew Bible, probably on Psalm 104 itself,[20] in order to teach his disciples the kind of lifestyle that is appropriate to living in such a world, the world of God's generous extravagance, in which God provides abundantly for all his creatures.

Matthew 6:25–33

'Therefore I tell you, do not worry about your life, what you will eat or what you will drink, or about your body, what you will wear. Is not life more than food, and the body more than clothing? [26]Look at the birds of the air; they neither sow nor reap nor gather into barns, and yet your heavenly Father feeds them. Are you not of more value than they? [27]And can any of you by worrying add a single hour to your span of life? [28]And why do you worry about clothing? Consider the lilies of the field, how they grow; they neither toil nor spin, [29]yet I tell you, even Solomon in all his glory was not clothed like one of these.[30] But if God so clothes the grass of the field, which is alive today and tomorrow is thrown into the oven,[21] will he not much more clothe you – you of little faith?[31] Therefore do not worry, saying, "What will we eat?" or "What will we drink?" or "What will we wear?" [32]For it is the Gentiles who strive for all these things; and indeed your heavenly Father knows that you need all these things. [33]But strive first for the kingdom of God and his righteousness, and all these things will be given to you as well.'

Jesus' teaching was, of course, deeply rooted in the Hebrew Bible and the Jewish tradition, but it is probably not sufficiently recognised how far Jesus draws on the creation theology of the Old Testament. There seems to be no reference in the Gospels to the human dominion over the animals of Genesis 1:26, but here in the Sermon on the Mount we find that Jesus has very much made his own the psalmist's understanding of the creation as a common home for living creatures, in which God provides for all their needs. The consequence Jesus draws, in turning the teaching of the psalm into advice on how his disciples should live, is that we need have no anxiety about our day-to-day material needs, but should live by radical faith in the Father's provision for us. Because the generous and wise Creator takes care of all these things for us, we are free to give our attention instead to seeking God's Kingdom and God's righteousness in the world.

Jesus holds up for us the example of the birds, for whom God provides, as he does for all his creatures. But he adds a reflection not in the psalm: 'Look at the birds of the air; they neither sow nor reap nor gather into barns, and yet your heavenly Father feeds them.' Interpretations of this verse have varied. Some interpreters suppose that Jesus contrasts the birds who do not work with people who do. The point would be that, if God feeds even the idle birds, how much more will he provide for people who work hard for their living? Other interpreters suppose that Jesus compares the birds who do not work with his disciples who do not work either. But note that the saying does not actually say that the birds do not work. It does not deny the rather obvious fact that many birds spend a lot of energy and effort in finding their food. It merely says that they do not then have to process their food ('they neither sow nor reap nor gather into barns') the way humans do.

Probably neither of these explanations is correct. Rather the point is that, since the birds do not have to labour to process their food from nature, but eat it as they find it, their dependence on the Creator's provision is the more immediate and obvious. Humans, on the other hand, preoccupied with the daily toil of supplying their basic needs, may easily suppose that it is up to them to provide themselves with food. This is the root of the anxiety about basic needs that Jesus is showing to be unnecessary. The way in which humans get their food by farming allows them to focus on their own efforts and to neglect the fact that much more fundamentally they are dependent, like the birds, on the resources of creation without which no one could sow, reap or gather into barns. The illusion is even easier in modern urban life. But the birds, in their more obvious dependence on the Creator, remind us that ultimately we are no less dependent on the Creator than they. It follows that Jesus is not here talking about special providential provision by God for followers of Jesus. He is speaking of our dependence on the resources of creation that God provides for all, humans and other living creatures, to live from.

He is, of course, speaking of basic needs. The presuppositions of Jesus' creation theology are very far from the wasteful excess and the constant manufacture of new needs and wants in our contemporary consumer society. Jesus intends to liberate his disciples from that anxious insecurity about basic needs that drives people to feel that they never have enough. But in our society that instinctive human anxiety about having enough to survive has for most people long been superseded by the drive to ever-increasing affluence and an obsessive anxiety to maintain an ever-rising standard of living. It is this obsessive consumption that is depleting and destroying the resources of nature and depriving both other species and many humans of the means even of mere subsistence.

It would be easy to regard Jesus' teaching here as cruelly unrealistic in the light of the famine and scarcity of food and water that afflict many parts of the world (and that climate change is likely to exacerbate). Is not Jesus, like the author of Psalm 104, seeing the world through rose-tinted glasses? An important consideration is that, just as Jesus here presupposes the ordinary agricultural means by which food reaches people, so he can presuppose the provisions of the Torah that are intended to supply the basic needs of the poor who do not have economic resources of their own. Such institutions as the triennial tithe (Deut. 14:28–29 and 26:12–15) and the requirement that farmers should leave some of the harvest for the poor to glean (Lev. 19:9–10) can be taken into account along with the ordinary generous almsgiving of which Jesus himself speaks in the Sermon (Matt. 6:2–4). Both hard work and community sharing are channels by which the Creator's provision supplies the needs of all.

Both Psalm 104 and Jesus challenge us with the conviction that the God-given resources of creation are sufficient for all God's creatures – that is, for the reasonable needs of all God's creatures, not for the kind of excess in which, of all God's creatures, only humans indulge. God's provision is sufficient if equitably shared. Living from God's provision means also living within limits, those ecological limits of creation that we in the affluent parts of the world are finally having to recognise. For Jesus and the psalmist the world around them spoke of God's extravagant generosity in providing for all. It is because we are so addicted to excess that we feel instead the painful necessity of reducing our consumption to reasonable limits.

Living within ecologically necessary limits may seem more possible if we can enter the way of seeing the world that Jesus offers us when he directs our attention to the birds of the air and the lilies of the field. These are not mere picturesque illustrations of his argument, as modern urban people have been apt to suppose. The birds and the flowers are essential to the argument. We cannot appreciate Jesus' message in this passage unless we place ourselves as creatures within God's creation, along with our fellow-creatures the birds and the wild flowers. We cannot appreciate Jesus' message unless we see ourselves not as masters of creation entitled to exploit its resources to our heart's desire, but as participants in the community of God's creatures. No doubt we are eminent participants. Jesus does say we are of more value than the birds,[22] though he says this not in order to disparage the birds, who do have value of their own, but to reassure the anxious. No doubt we are eminent participants in the community of creation, but participants nonetheless. Considering these other creatures we see a natural world of abundance and beauty that exists by the Creator's gift, independent of all our efforts to create our own world of plenty and beauty for ourselves. If we can recover our own real relationship to that world of God's creatures, then we can begin to seek God's Kingdom and further his purposes for his creation.

Jesus' teaching may seem extreme, and it is true that hyperbole is characteristic of his pedagogic technique.[23] However, our addiction to excess is also extreme. Most of us in the affluent parts of the world have a long way to go in learning to live within reasonable limits before we get anywhere near even the level at which most ordinary people lived in Jesus' time. In the contemporary West, with our frenetic pursuit of more and more, we have lost the very concept of 'enough'.[24] But the changes that ecological limits require of us concern not only our personal consumption but also the broad economic assumptions and goals that drive our consumer society and its globalisation.

PRAISING OUR MAKER TOGETHER

Psalm 104 can help us recover a sense of co-creatureliness through recognising that we share the Earth with God's other living creatures and that we depend, with other creatures, on God's generous provision of the resources from which we live. But the most profound and life-changing way in which we can recover our place in the world as creatures alongside our fellow-creatures is through the biblical theme of the worship all creation offers to God. The theme of the worship of God by all creatures, animate and inanimate, is widely present in the Psalms (65:12–13; 69:34; 89:12; 96:11–12; 97:7–8; 103:22; 145:10 and 150:6) as well as in some other parts of the Bible (1 Chr. 16:31–33; Isa. 35:1–2; 40:10; 43:19 and 55:12; Phil. 2:10; Rev. 5:13).[25] But the most extensive example in the Hebrew Bible is the magnificent Psalm 148.[26]

Psalm 148

> Praise the LORD!
>
> Praise the LORD from the heavens;
>   praise him in the heights!
> [2]Praise him, all his angels;
>   praise him, all his host!

³Praise him, sun and moon;
   praise him, all you shining stars!
⁴Praise him, you highest heavens,
   and you waters above the heavens!

⁵Let them praise the name of the LORD,
   for he commanded and they were created.
⁶He established them forever and ever;
   he fixed their bounds, which cannot be passed.

⁷Praise the LORD from the earth,
   you sea monsters and all deeps,
⁸fire and hail, snow and frost,
   stormy wind fulfilling his command!

⁹Mountains and all hills,
   fruit trees and all cedars!
¹⁰Wild animals and all cattle,
   creeping things and flying birds!

¹¹Kings of the earth and all peoples,
   princes and all rulers of the earth!
¹²Young men and women alike,
   old and young together!

¹³Let them praise the name of the LORD,
   for his name alone is exalted;
   his glory is above earth and heaven.
¹⁴He has raised up a horn for his people,
   praise for all his faithful,
   for the people of Israel who are close to him.

Praise the LORD!

The catalogue of creatures who make up this cosmic choir of praise is comprehensive: more than thirty categories of creatures are addressed. Some of these are representative of a whole class of creatures: for example, 'fruit trees and all cedars' (v 9) doubtless stand for the whole vegetable creation. In the injunctions to praise, the word 'all' occurs eight times, scattered through the text. The catalogue of creatures is in two parts, representing the heavens (vv 1–4) and the Earth (vv 7–12). Both spheres praise their Maker, who himself is categorically beyond all creation: 'his glory is above the earth and the heavens' (v 13). Two passages explaining why it is appropriate that God's creatures should praise him (vv 5–6 and 13–14) follow, respectively, the two parts of the catalogue of creatures. He is to be praised because he is the Creator of all (vv 5–6) and the only One exalted above all creation (v 15). Finally, at the only point where Israel comes into the picture, God is to be praised for exalting his own people to a place of honour within the created world (v 14).

I spoke of the depiction of creation in this psalm as a 'cosmic choir'. Perhaps an even more appropriate analogy would be a symphony orchestra. The various creatures contribute to a symphony by being both individually different and mutually complementary. As Terence Fretheim notes, 'Each entity has its own distinctiveness, with varying degrees of complexity. But each is also part of the one world of God contributing to the whole.' (This raises the possibility that, 'if one member of the orchestra is incapacitated or missing altogether', the praise of the whole will be adversely affected.[27] We shall return to this possibility towards the end of this chapter.)

Humans are placed at the end of the catalogue of worshippers, just as they come at the end of the works of creation in Genesis 1 and at the end of the survey of creatures in Psalm 104. In this case, no more than in those, can they be the climax of an ascending scale of value. There is no reason to suppose that angels are the least valuable of creatures or that reptiles are more valuable than fire. In any case, the notion of such a scale of value makes no sense: how could one weigh the value of a mountain against that of a sea monster, snow against a fruit tree? But it may be that humans are the creatures who are most reluctant to praise their creator, and are placed last so that they may be encouraged to worship by the vision of the whole of the rest of the cosmos praising its Creator. After all, it was not actually true, in the psalmist's world, that all the kings of the Earth and the peoples of the Earth were actually worshipping YHWH. The psalm is an invitation to them to do so, and presumably relates to the hope of the prophets that all the nations of the Earth would come to worship YHWH in the future. Within such a context, the worship of the creatures who do praise God has a witnessing role, declaring God's praiseworthy reality to the human world (cf. Ps. 19:1–4).[28]

When modern Christians encounter the theme of all creation's worship of God in Psalm 148 or in other passages of Scripture, they are apt not to take it very seriously. They may take it to reflect some kind of pre-scientific animism or pan-psychism that attributes rational consciousness to all things, even mountains, rain and trees. Or they may take it to be mere poetic fancy.[29] Both reactions miss the significance of this biblical theme. These passages about creation's praise are, of course, metaphorical: they attribute to non-human creatures the human practice of praising God in language (or, in the case of the trees in Isa. 55:12, clapping their hands!).[30] But the metaphor points to a reality: all creatures bring glory to God simply by being themselves and fulfilling their God-given roles in God's creation. A tree does not need to do anything specific in order to praise God; still less need it be conscious of anything. Simply by being and growing it praises God:

> Creation's praise is not an extra, an addition to what it is, but the shining of its being, the overflowing significance it has in pointing to its Creator simply by being itself.[31]

It is distinctively human to bring praise to conscious expression in voice, but the creatures remind us that this distinctively human form of praise is worthless unless, like them, we live our whole lives to the glory of God.

Before the modern period, the praise of all the creatures seems to have been more widely appreciated in the Church. The reasons why it has fallen out of most modern Christians' consciousness must be urban people's isolation from nature, which deprives them of a living sense of participation in nature, and the modern instrumentalising of nature, which turns it into mere material for human use. But these reasons also suggest how valuable it might be to recover a living sense of participation in creation's praise of God. It is the strongest antidote to anthropocentrism in the biblical and Christian tradition. When we join our fellow-creatures in attributing glory to God, there is no hierarchy and no anthropocentricity. In this respect all creatures, including ourselves, are simply fellow-creatures expressing the *theocentricity* of the created world, each in our own created way, differently but in complementarity. As Psalm 148:13 says, in this worship God's name alone is exalted: there is no place in worship for the exaltation of any creature over others. Moreover, to recognise creation's praise is to abandon a purely instrumental view of nature. All creatures exist for God's glory, and we most effectively learn to see other creatures in that way, to glimpse, as it were, their value for God that has nothing to do with their usefulness to us, when we join them in their own glorification of God.

There is another aspect of this call to universal worship that Christians in earlier periods felt more at home with than most modern Christians do: the participation of the angels in heaven. Many traditional liturgies and hymns express the notion that in human worship we join the choirs of heaven. The cosmology of Psalm 148 is not, of course, ours. It envisages the created universe as composed of 'the heavens' and 'the earth', and the heavens as comprising the highest heavens where the hosts of angels worship and the lower heavens where the sun, moon and stars move across the sky in the courses ordained for them at creation (vv 1–6). We should note that no part of 'the heavens' or the creatures that inhabit them is included in the human dominion of Genesis 1:26 and 28. The dominion is over the sea creatures, the birds and the land animals only, while the heavenly bodies, according to Genesis 1:14–18, have a dominion of their own. So we should not be tempted to see the psalmist's role in calling on all creatures to praise God as some kind of exercise of the human dominion.[32] The psalmist invites both the creatures of the heavens and the creatures of the Earth to worship. Were we to read the psalm hierarchically, we should have to recognise that the whole of the first half of its catalogue of worshippers are superior to humans, not subject to human dominion. In fact, however, the praise of God by all creation levels all creatures before their common Creator, angels and heavenly bodies included.

We can take the cosmology figuratively. It functions as a way of classifying the creatures. But we need not abandon the idea that there are intelligent creatures of God who worship him in his manifest presence. It is not easy to recover the sense of connection with them that pre-modern Christians had, but the psalm should remind us that the visible world we know is not the sum of created reality and we are certainly not the only creatures who worship with conscious awareness of God and of the wholeness of his creation.[33] Too many modern Christian comments on human uniqueness ignore the angels.

What then, finally, are we to make of the fact that the *psalmist invites* all the creatures of the heavens and the Earth to praise God? Does it indicate a special role for humanity in the cosmic choir? It cannot be that other creatures do not praise God until called on to do so by humans. The angels undoubtedly do not await a human invitation before praising their Creator. Nor do the other creatures form a choir of harmonious praise only when humans 'conduct' them. The cosmic order has been given them by God in creation. An attractive suggestion is that what is unique about humans enables 'us to see the created world whole, and offer it up in praise'.[34] This probably is unique to humans among the creatures of Earth, but it is also one of those statements about human uniqueness that ignores the angels. In this context of cosmic praise the angels clearly matter, and they presumably are able to see the created world whole, perhaps even more adequately than we can.

The psalmist does not assemble the universal choir in fact, nor are humans the only creatures able to do so in thought. But the psalmist does assemble the cosmic choir *for us*, in our human awareness, so that we can worship in conscious participation in the worship of all creation. The psalmist invites us into a world that is wholly orientated to the glory of God. He enables us to see it as it is, which is at the same time to be directed by it to the glory of God. He 'profiles the non-human world as "models of praise" for the human world to emulate'.[35] There is a certain reciprocity in our praise.[36] The other creatures help us to worship, while we add to their worship by drawing it into our own. The more we appreciate the other creatures, the more they help us to worship, and the more we can take up their worship into the particular sort of thanksgiving for the whole creation that is possible for us humans. The interrelated and interdependent community of creation, embracing all creatures in heaven and on Earth, comes to fullest expression in the vast range of different but complementary ways of glorifying God that come together in the cosmic choir.

The choir is not yet complete. As we have noted already, verses 11–12 are an invitation to which all human societies and individuals have not yet responded. But the psalm does not mention this lack. By dealing in imperatives rather than indicatives, it can give a wholly positive impression of creation's universal praise of its Creator. This unqualified positivity matches that of Genesis 1, which, as we have noted, is an ideal or utopian account of creation that already anticipates the eschatological fulfilment of creation. Psalm 148 invites all its hearers, singers and readers into just such an eschatological fulfilment. This universe of praise is what creation was made to be, and every human voice that joins this worshipping community enables the whole to be more fully what it was made to be.

COSMIC CELEBRATION

Brian Swimme and Thomas Berry speak of 'celebration' as characterising the whole universe:

> If we were to choose a single expression for the universe it might be 'celebration', celebration of existence and life and consciousness, also of color and sound but especially in movement, in flight through the air and swimming through the sea, in mating rituals and care of the young ... [T]he universe as a community of diverse components rings with a

certain exultation and joy in being ... Everything about us seems to be absorbed into a vast celebratory experience. Whatever be the more practical purposes of existence it appears that celebration is omnipresent, not simply in the individual modes of its expression but in the grandeur of the entire cosmic process.[37]

This is a powerful vision, but essentially a pantheistic one. The universe celebrates itself, revels exuberantly in its own life. From a biblical perspective we may warm to the image of cosmic celebration, but may also wish to give it another dimension: the relationship of creation to Creator that turns celebration into celebratory worship. Worship is more than exultation and joy in being. It is that ecstasy of being that takes one out of oneself into thanksgiving and praise to the Source and Goal of one's being. Because all creatures, by virtue of being creatures, are intrinsically related to their Creator, they can fully celebrate their own life only by also praising their Creator.

ARE HUMANS PRIESTS OF CREATION?

The praise of God by all creation levels all creatures before their common Creator. To say this is not to eradicate the vast diversity of the creatures, who worship in a vast variety of ways that corresponds to their own diversity. But, in my view, it would be a mistake to try to assimilate this aspect of our human place within creation to any of the hierarchical models that seek to interpret the Genesis dominion. Such models highlight our God-given power over and responsibility for the other creatures. They work well only when combined with a lively sense of our own creatureliness, our co-creatureliness with the other creatures, and it is that sense that our participation in all creation's worship of God can foster. Hierarchy seems inappropriate in this context. When we are taken up into the praise that the other creatures are constantly offering to God we probably do best to forget the dominion. It certainly has no place in the biblical depictions of creation's praise.

For this reason I do not warm to the idea that humans are the priests of creation, mediating the praise of creation to God.[38] This notion was given classic expression in the Anglican tradition by the poet George Herbert, who pictures the creatures as unable to put their praise into words and so requiring humans to 'present the sacrifice for all'.[39] It has also become popular in the Orthodox tradition[40] (to which Jürgen Moltmann's account of it is indebted[41]), where it is associated especially with the idea of an offering of all creation to God in the Eucharist. The idea has recently been taken up also by Christopher Southgate, who integrates it into his evolutionary theodicy and interprets it to mean that humans are not only 'contemplatives of creation' but also co-redeemers, engaged with God in the redemption of creation from evil.[42]

Priesthood in this connection implies some form of representation and mediation: humans represent the rest of creation in offering creation's praise up to God. In some accounts, humans form the necessary and only link between God and the rest of creation. John Zizioulas, for example, writes that the Christian

> regards the human being as the only possible link between God and creation, a link that can either bring nature in communion with God and thus sanctify it; or condemn it to the state of a 'thing', the meaning and purpose of which are exhausted with the satisfaction of man.[43]

But the view that other creatures are related to God only through human mediation is surely a relic of some of the more grossly anthropocentric views of the creation in Christian history, and has no support from the Bible, where other creatures have their own direct relationships with God (Gen. 9:10 and 16; Job 38–39; Pss. 50:4; 104:21 and 104:27–28; Isa. 45:8; Joel 1:20; Matt 6:26; Rev. 5:13).

In response to such criticism of Orthodox theologians, however, Elizabeth Theokritoff points out that in most Orthodox writing about humans as priests of creation it is not denied that other creatures do relate directly to God.[44] She herself places the emphasis on the 'eucharistic offering' of creation to God as thankfulness for creation:

> The connection between creation's own offering of praise and our offering on behalf of all might be set out in these terms: in the other creatures around us, we encounter a 'wordless word' expressing God's will for that creature and its own natural response, which is its 'praise' in a real though metaphorical sense. This is the praise it offers on its own behalf. But it is our specific gift to have a conscious awareness both of the creature and of the Creator whose Word it echoes, and *to articulate the connection by offering up the creature's praise as our thankfulness to the Creator.*[45]

This comes close to the implications of Psalm 148 as I suggested them above, so long as we recognise that the angels are as capable as humans of this kind of holistic appreciation and offering of creation's praise, and so long as we see it as one side of a reciprocal relationship, in which the other creatures help us to worship and we develop theirs by taking it up into our own thanksgiving for all creation. But to call this human role priesthood seems to me to obscure the reciprocity and to accentuate hierarchy inappropriately. I am certainly not suggesting, as Theokritoff fears, an individualistic world in which each creature praises God independently of all others, but I do not think the wholeness of creation's worship is *created* by human mediation. Human acknowledgement of it and rejoicing in it are the channel by which the other creatures help us to worship.[46]

The psalmists and we ourselves can put creation's wordless praise into human words, but we cannot suppose that God needs us to do this before he can hear and appreciate other creatures' praise. When Psalm 19:1–4 declares that the heavens are telling the glory of God, doing so without words, the point is that they manage very well without words. Their voice does go out through all the Earth, even though they speak no audible language. Perhaps, in order to hear creation's praise, to echo it in our own praise and thus to join the universal choir, we need to set words aside for a while. We need to attend to the wordless praise of the other creatures. Then we may be inspired to 'translate' it into human language, or, alternatively, into music or visual art. These distinctively human gifts can make it our praise too and add our own praise to it. All good translation is both less and more than what it translates. We may enhance but at the same time we do not exhaust creation's praise. The more we attend to the creatures, the more they will lift our hearts to God, borne on their praises.

NATURE – DIVINE, SACRED OR SECULAR?

The biblical and Christian tradition has been both praised and blamed for de-divinising and de-sacralising nature.[47] For supporters of the modern project of scientific-technological domination of nature, it was of great value that the Bible and the Christian tradition had allegedly de-divinised nature, opposing all forms of nature religion, clearing away all superstitious reverence for nature, clearing the way for objective scientific investigation of nature and technological use of nature for human benefit. Modern green criticism of the Christian tradition has often accepted this account but held it against the Bible and Christianity.[48] By de-divinising nature, Christianity exposed it to the ruthless exploitation that has brought us to the brink of ecological disaster. We need to recover religious reverence for nature.

From the biblical material we have considered in this chapter, we should be able to see that such judgements pose a false alternative between, on the one hand, a pantheistic or animistic vision of nature as divine (and so to be worshipped) and, on the other hand, a modern scientific and secular view of nature as a mere object of human use. The biblical vision of the worship of God by the whole of creation illuminates another possibility.

We can usefully distinguish the words 'divine' and 'sacred'. These are not synonyms. 'Sacred' means, not 'divine', but 'dedicated to or associated with the divine'. In the Bible (and the Christian tradition before modern times), nature is certainly de-divinised but it is not de-sacralised.[49] The creatures are not divine, but they belong to God, are valued by God, and point us to

The Community of Creation

God. Adequately perceived, they do not let our attention rest purely on themselves, but take us up into the movement of glorification of God that is their own existence. To deny them divinity is not to depreciate them but to let them be truly themselves in all the variety of their endlessly specific ways of being and doing. Pantheism absorbs them into a vague divine synthesis. Seeing them as creatures of God allows them their quiddity, their being each precisely that specific and different creature God has made them. It is attention to that quiddity that continually assists our praise of the God who gives them themselves and always surpasses them and us. They belong to a theocentric community of creation whose purpose is to give back to God in praise the being he has given them.

THE COMMUNITY OF CREATION[50]

The use of the term 'community' to describe the ecosystems in which humans and the rest of nature interrelate probably originates in the work of Aldo Leopold, the pioneering American conservationist. He used the terms 'land community' and 'biotic community' interchangeably, but his stress on the former particularly indicates the fundamental importance of the intricate, organic interdependence of soil, water, flora and fauna, in which humans also belong.[51] One of his concerns was to develop an ethic in which humans have obligations not only to each other and to human society but also to the whole land community:

> We abuse land because we regard it as a commodity belonging to us. When we see land as a community to which we belong, we may begin to use it with love and respect.[52]

> [A] land ethic changes the role of *Homo Sapiens* from conqueror of the land community to plain member and citizen of it. It implies respect for his [*sic*] fellow-members, and also respect for the community as such.[53]

Whether interdependence as such can impose moral obligations that would not otherwise exist is debatable,[54] but it need not concern us here.[55] What is important for us about Leopold's image of a biotic community is that it models the kind of commonality and interdependence of humans and all other creatures that the Hebrew Bible recognises and which, at the same time, is so clear from our contemporary ecological plight, especially the effects of climate change. Differently from Leopold, who brings no religious perspective to his thought, the community the Bible envisages is a *theocentric* community of *creatures*.

Hence Wendell Berry speaks of humans as 'creatures of God, members of the holy community of Creation'.[56] Elsewhere, speaking of the 'Great Economy' (a term for the whole creation in its interconnectedness), he says that

> It is not the 'sum of its parts' but a *membership* of parts inextricably joined to each other, indebted to each other, receiving significance and worth from each other and from the whole. One is obliged to 'consider the lilies of the field', not because they are lilies or because they are exemplary, but because they are fellow members and because, as fellow members, we and the lilies are in certain critical ways to be alike.[57]

What we have in common with the lilies of the field is not just that we are creatures of God, but that we are fellow-members of the community of God's creation, sharing the same Earth, affected by the processes of the Earth, affecting the processes that affect each other, with common interests at least in life and flourishing, with the common end of glorifying the Creator and interdependent in the ways we do exactly that.

A community may consist of a great diversity of members. This is obviously true of many human communities. In the community of creation the diversity is much greater but this by no means reduces the interdependence that constitutes community membership. In some respects the interdependence is greater: a human may at least survive without other humans, but not without earth, air, water and plants, and not outside a natural context that has been shaped by many other creatures into a form that can accommodate human life. Membership of a common community does not, of course, preclude different roles for different members within the community. The community of creation again requires a very much greater diversity of roles within it than the human community. Species of life and inanimate forms of nature are all highly specialised in the diverse contributions they make to the whole. A realistic understanding of the natural world must recognise that these roles often entail fierce competition, but even more co-operation (something that the Darwinian emphasis on 'survival of the fittest' tended to obscure but which ecology has made us much more aware of).[58] The diverse roles operate within the community, and the distinctive roles of humans (of which there are surely many) are no exception. Exceptional though we may be in various ways, our exceptionality is embedded in the community of creation to which we belong and would be impossible without it. We are not aliens imposing ourselves on, or intruding ourselves within, the community of creation, but natural members of it.

Among other distinctives, humans have exceptional power over the rest of creation on this planet. We are very far from omnipotent, and we do well to remember that the rest of the biotic community would thrive in its own ways without us,[59] just as it did long before we appeared on the scene. Our huge destructive potential consists, of course, in our ability to trigger vast forces and operations of nature other and much greater than ourselves, especially without our intending to. All of our positive and creative achievements are ways of working with the potential of other creatures. We would be nothing without them. It is highly misleading to contemplate our power over the rest of creation without remembering our even greater dependence on the rest of creation. Because urban people now live in such a humanly constructed world this is less immediately obvious than it has been to most people in history, and that is part of our current problem, but it does not take much thought, let alone ecological catastrophe, to remind ourselves of it. We understand both ourselves and the biblical understanding of us much better the more we attend to the prominence of the non-human creation in the Bible, instead of passing over it as not part of the Bible's relevance to people in a technology-encased culture such as ours. Wendell Berry makes the point:

> I don't think it is enough appreciated how much an outdoor book the Bible is. It is a 'hypaethral book', such as Thoreau talked about – a book open to the sky. It is best read and understood outdoors, and the farther out of doors the better.[60]

To realise our membership of the community of creation does not mean abdicating the distinctive sort of powers we undoubtedly have. It does mean being alert to their limitations. Much of the ecological problem of the modern age has been the result of an illusory aspiration to omnipotence which duped us into all sorts of well-meaning technological projects that turned out to have unforeseen results we could not control. Climate change is the climactic sum of many such miscalculations, as well as reckless irresponsibility. Realising our membership of the community of creation dispels the illusion of omnipotence and enables us to think more realistically about the power we do have. It is the way to begin to exercise that power with the caring responsibility that is our 'dominion' over other living creatures.

The distinctively human role of 'dominion' is not something that sets us apart from the rest of creation, as though we were independent of it and external to it. It is a role that we should exercise within the community and precisely as members of the community relating to fellow members. When we see it in the context of all the other aspects of what it means for humans to be part of the interdependent network of relationships in the community of creation, when we realise that our distinctive power is rooted in a more fundamental dependence on the rest of creation, then we can see that the dominion has its place within a wider pattern of *reciprocity*. It has nothing to do with the modern project of liberating ourselves from the rest of nature, as though we could stand over and above it and make of it what we wish.

The Community of Creation

Leopold saw *Homo sapiens* as a 'plain member and citizen' of the land community. We can certainly endorse 'member and citizen', but perhaps not 'plain'. Leopold himself speaks of an 'ecological conscience' which clearly only humans can have, and proposes a land ethic that only humans can consciously practise. We might say that humans are eminent members and citizens, but members and citizens nonetheless.

Who are the members of the community of creation according to biblical depictions? In Genesis 1 and Psalm 104 it looks as though the members are the animate creatures (humans and animals), while the rest of creation, including vegetation of all sorts, is environment and provision for them. But in those psalms where the creatures are called on to praise God, all parts of the natural world are included. Besides the comprehensive coverage of the whole creation in Psalm 148, we might note Psalm 96:11–13a:

> Let the heavens be glad, and let the earth rejoice;
> let the sea roar, and all that fills it;
> let the field exult, and everything in it.
> Then shall all the trees of the forest sing for joy
>   before the LORD ... (cf. also Ps. 98:7–9; Rev. 5:13)

All creatures worship God, and God values them all for their own sakes as well as for the roles they play within the complex interrelationships of creation. However, the distinction between the environments and the living creatures in passages such as Genesis 1 and Psalm 104 is also significant. In the modern period the words 'nature' and 'the environment' have often been used in ways that obscure differentiations within the natural world, especially that between sentient creatures and inanimate nature. Such usage perpetuates the impression that all the other creatures are more like each other than any of them are like human beings, and therefore the tendency to set humans apart from the rest of creation. In various contexts it is no doubt necessary or useful to refer to, on the one hand, humans and, on the other, the non-human creation, just as British people may sometimes distinguish Britain and 'the rest of the world' without implying that all other countries are more like each other than any are like Britain. This kind of distinction can be useful so long as it is recognised as a matter of perspective, not ontology.

If creation is a community of creatures living in complex interrelationships, then the activities of some must have consequences for others. Human life is not a self-contained affair, but takes place in relationship both to the Creator and to the rest of the creation. Our modern ecological awareness of the disorder and destruction wrought in the natural world by human activities is already foreshadowed in the Hebrew prophets, as we shall see in our next section.

THE WHOLE CREATION MOURNS

As well as passages which depict all the creatures praising their Creator, there is another series of passages in the Hebrew Bible that also metaphorically attribute voice to the non-human creatures but depict them not rejoicing but *mourning*. (The parallel and contrast between praising and mourning is the more striking in that the mourning, like the praising, is directed to God (Jer. 12:11).) Creation's mourning is for what we might call ecological death, the kind of devastation of land, through severe drought or desertification, that leaves its vegetation withering and its animal life failing. Usually it is 'the land' or 'the earth' (sometimes it is hard to decide whether 'eretz refers to the land of a locality or to the whole Earth) that mourns (Isa. 24:4 and 33:9; Jer. 4:28; 12:4 and 23:10; Hos. 4:3; cf. Joel 1:10, where the soil ('adamah) mourns; Jer. 12:11; Amos 1:2).[61] What the land mourns is the effect human wrongdoing has had on all its non-human inhabitants, both flora and fauna. For example, Jeremiah asks:

> How long will the land mourn,
> and the grass of every field wither?
> For the wickedness of those who live in it
> the animals and the birds are swept away,
> and because people said, 'He is blind to our ways'. (Jer. 12:4)

While in some cases the effect is on the domestic sphere of nature – agriculture and domestic animals – and so functions as judgement on humans for their wickedness (as in Deut. 28:15–44), in other cases the non-human creation is blighted on a much larger scale. Especially instructive is this passage from Hosea:

> Hear the word of the LORD, O people of Israel;
>> for the LORD has an indictment against the inhabitants
>>> of the land.
> There is no faithfulness or loyalty,
>> and no knowledge of God in the land.
> ²Swearing, lying, and murder,
>> and stealing and adultery break out;
>> bloodshed follows bloodshed.
> ³Therefore the land mourns,
>> and all who live in it languish;
> together with the wild animals
>> and the birds of the air,
>> even the fish of the sea are perishing. (Hos. 4:1–3)

The destructive effect even on the creatures of the sea seems extraordinarily hyperbolic, but this is an example of a phenomenon we find in some other cases in biblical prophecy. What can only seem grossly hyperbolic in its original context looks only too realistic in the context of our own situation of worldwide ecological catastrophe.

It may be that verse 3 depicts a kind of 'un-creation', because it lists the creatures (humans, wild animals, birds, fish) in the reverse order to the sequence in which they appear in Genesis 1. Another passage about the mourning of the Earth undoubtedly portrays a kind of reversion to the chaos or nothingness before creation:

> I looked on the earth, and lo, it was waste and void;
>> and to the heavens, and they had no light.
> ²⁴I looked on the mountains, and lo, they were quaking,
>> and all the hills moved to and fro.
> ²⁵I looked, and lo, there was no one at all,
>> and all the birds of the air had fled.

> ²⁶I looked, and lo, the fruitful land was a desert,
>> and all its cities were laid in ruins
>> before the LORD, before his fierce anger.
> ²⁷For thus says the LORD:
>> The whole land shall be a desolation; yet I will not
>> make a full end.
> ²⁸Because of this the earth shall mourn,
>> and the heavens above grow black;
> for I have spoken, I have purposed;
>> I have not relented nor will I turn back. (Jer. 4:23–28)

The curious phrase 'waste and void' (*tohu vabohu*) in the first line of this passage occurs in the Hebrew Bible only here and in Genesis 1:2, where it describes the state of nothingness before anything was created.[62] Again we have a hyperbolic image, suggesting the un-creation of all creation,[63] but a more limited image of the desolation of the land of Israel apparently occurs in the midst of the universal one (v 26).

Human evil has ecological consequences.[64] As Walter Brueggemann puts it, 'Covenantal Israel held the staggering notion that human conduct matters for the well-being of creation.'[65] This idea coheres with the Hebrew Bible's strong sense of a created order by which relationships in the community of creation should be ordered.[66] Most of the time other creatures observe this order, but humans all too often flout it:

> Even the stork in the heavens knows its times;
> and the turtledove, swallow, and crane observe the time of
>> their coming;
> but my people do not know the ordinance of the LORD.
> (Jer. 8:7; cf. also 18:14–16)

Their 'not knowing' is wilful ignorance; they do not wish to know the moral order of things that God has ordained. Humans are the disorderly factor in the world, disrupting its harmony and its natural rhythms, with destructive consequences both for humans themselves and for other creatures. Sometimes the prophets can

The Community of Creation

speak of these consequences of human evil as the direct interventions of God in judgement (e.g. Isa. 24:1–4; Zeph. 1:2–3), sometimes as though they are processes built into the order of creation as God has created it (e.g. Hos. 4:1–3). The two are not necessarily in contradiction. The prophets understood that the behaviour of humans and the well-being of the rest of creation are intimately interconnected, but they did not, of course, have the scientific understanding of the connections that modern ecology is giving us. On the whole, we have become aware of such connections only as our ignoring of them has led to consequences too considerable to be ignored. But in many such cases the human activities that have led and are leading to such destructive consequences have not been pursued through pardonable ignorance or simple foolishness. They have been driven by greed or the will to power, arrogance or aggression, and not infrequently injustice and oppression in human society have gone hand in hand with ecological destruction.[67] The natural order and the moral order are by no means unconnected.[68]

The prophets' image of the mourning of the Earth is taken up by Paul in Romans 8:18–23.[69]

Romans 8:18–23

I consider that the sufferings of this present time are not worth comparing with the glory about to be revealed to us. [19]For the creation waits with eager longing for the revealing of the children of God; [20]for the creation was subjected to futility, not of its own will but by the will of the one who subjected it, in hope [21]that the creation itself will be set free from its bondage to decay and will obtain the freedom of the glory of the children of God. [22]We know that the whole creation has been groaning and in travail together[70] until now; [23]and not only the creation, but we ourselves, who have the first fruits of the Spirit, groan inwardly while we wait for adoption, the redemption of our bodies.

What exactly is the plight of creation, from which it longs for deliverance? Understanding of this has been obscured by the habit of interpreters and translators of assuming that the 'groaning' of verse 22 is the groaning of a woman in birth pains. Modern translations therefore tend to run the two Greek verbs (*sustenazein*, meaning 'to groan together', and *sunodinein*, meaning 'to be in travail together') into one English verb with an adverbial expression, e.g. the NRSV's translation: 'the whole creation has been groaning in labour pains until now.' But the two verbs can equally well be understood as making two different points. The first echoes the passages in the prophets that say that the Earth mourns, while the second takes up an Old Testament metaphor for experiencing God's judgement (e.g. Jer. 4:31; and cf. 1 Thess. 5:3).[71] The verb translated 'to groan' (*sustenazein*) is actually the verb *stenazein* with the prefix *sun* ('with'), and so should be translated 'to groan with' or 'to groan together'. Without the prefix, the verb recurs in verse 23 ('we ourselves ... groan inwardly') and is echoed by the corresponding noun (*stenagmos*, 'groan' or 'sigh') in verse 26. The verb could be translated 'to mourn', which would make the connection with the passages in the prophets more obvious, but I have kept the familiar translation 'to groan'.

According to verse 20, the creation was 'subjected to futility' by God. Most exegetes have seen here a reference to the fall of Genesis 3, where God curses the ground because of Adam's sin, with the result that farming will be harder work (Gen. 3:17).[72] But this does not seem an adequate basis for Paul's claim that the whole creation is in 'bondage to decay', 'groaning and in travail' as it longs for future liberation. In the prophets, on the other hand, we find the notion that the non-human creation as a whole suffers the effects of human sin and God's judgement on it. Though the effect, in particular contexts in the prophets, may be localised, it is often, as we have seen, portrayed in universal language, extending even to the ocean (Isa. 24:1–7; Jer. 4:23–25; Hos. 4:3; cf. Zeph. 1:2–3). What the Earth mourns is the withering and destruction of its inhabitants, flora and fauna, and so Paul's phrase 'bondage to decay' or 'bondage to a process of destruction' (v 21) is an appropriate description of the state to which God has assigned the creation because of human sin.[73] When Paul says that 'the creation was subjected to futility' (v 20), using the noun *mataiotes*, he may mean, as the translation 'futility' suggests, that creation was emptied of meaning or purpose by its condemnation to decay and destruction, much as human death, if it is conceived as the end of existence, makes life seem pointless.[74] This seems the most likely meaning. But the root meaning of *mataios* is 'empty', and the related verb *mataioun* means 'to bring to nothing', and so it is possible that Paul has in mind Jeremiah's vision of the whole Earth as 'waste and void' (*tohu vabohu*), returned to the nothingness that preceded creation. In that case, Paul would mean that, because of human sin, God set creation on course for un-creation.

If this line of interpretation is correct, then Paul is not referring to some drastic change in the natural world that followed from the fall of Adam and Eve, such as the introduction of death for the animal creation. This traditional view is impossible to reconcile with modern knowledge (animals were dying many millions of years before the first humans appeared on Earth)[75] and, in any case, is not really supported by Genesis 3. On the interpretation that I have suggested, Paul is thinking of ecological degradation and desertification of the kind the prophets indicated when they portrayed the Earth mourning, the soil losing its fertility, plants withering, animals dying. Joel's account is the most vivid and may serve to fill out Paul's rather abstract language:

> The fields are devastated,
>> the ground mourns;
> for the grain is destroyed,
>> the wine dries up,
>> the oil fails.
>
> [11]Be dismayed, you farmers,
>> wail, you vinedressers,
> over the wheat and the barley;
>> for the crops of the field are ruined.

¹²The vine withers,

> the fig tree droops.

Pomegranate, palm, and apple –

> all the trees of the field are dried up;

surely, joy withers away

> among the people …

¹⁷The seed shrivels under the clods,

> the storehouses are desolate;

the granaries are ruined

> because the grain has failed.

¹⁸How the animals[76] groan!

> The herds of cattle wander about

because there is no pasture for them;

> even the flocks of sheep are dazed.

¹⁹To you, O LORD, I cry.

For fire has devoured

> the pastures of the wilderness,

and flames have burned

> all the trees of the field.

²⁰Even the wild animals cry[77] to you

> because the watercourses are dried up,

and fire has devoured

> the pastures of the wilderness. (Joel 1:10–12 and 17–20)

It is notable that in this passage, whereas the other prophets speak of the mourning of the Earth, Joel depicts all kinds of creatures mourning, lamenting and groaning to God: the ground (v 10), the domestic animals (v 18), the wild animals (v 20), as well as the farmers (v 11), the people (v 12) and the prophet himself (v 19). It is easy to see here how Paul could generalise the mourning as that of the whole creation. The desiccation and devastation of nature, also extensively depicted by Joel, are the object of the mourning, and represent, in Paul's terms, creation's subjection to futility. Joel's panorama of creation is not unlike Psalm 104, but here their environments no longer support the living creatures that depend on them. In effect, the Creator's provision for his creatures, so lavish in Psalm 104, has been withdrawn, and the joy depicted in that psalm has given way to lament and desperate supplication to the Creator.

According to Romans 8:20–21, 'the creation was subjected to futility … in hope that the creation itself will be set free'. If I am right to find the background to this idea of subjection to futility in the prophets, then perhaps Paul also found in the prophets the warrant for representing it as a subjection 'in hope'. For the prophets expect the degradation of creation to be reversed in the future through a divine regeneration of the natural world. For example:

> The wilderness and the dry land shall be glad,
> the desert shall rejoice and blossom;
> like the crocus ²it shall blossom abundantly,
> and rejoice with joy and singing.
> The glory of Lebanon shall be given to it,
> the majesty of Carmel and Sharon.
> They shall see the glory of the LORD,
> the majesty of our God.
> (Isa. 35:1–2; cf. 32:15–20; and 51:3; Amos 9:13–14; Joel 3:18)

In such passages, these revivifying effects on the natural world accompany the redemption of the people of God who have suffered judgement for the wrongdoing that brought degradation on the natural world. If there is hope for the people, then there must also be hope for the non-human creation. To the extent that it is humans who have brought devastation on the rest of creation their hopes and destinies are bound up together. This is precisely what we see also in Romans 8:19–21.

The liberation of creation is to happen at the end of history, when Christian believers will attain their full salvation in the glory of the resurrection (vv 21 and 23).[78] Since creation's bondage is due to human sin, its liberation must await the cessation of human evil at the end. It might seem, therefore, that this passage cannot mandate human activity for the relief of creation from the burden of human mistreatment now. It is true that that is not Paul's concern in the passage. But, if we accept the diagnosis that human wrongdoing is responsible for ecological degradation, it follows that those who are concerned to live according to God's will for his world must be concerned to avoid and to repair damage to God's creation as far as possible. Like the coming of the Kingdom of God, we cannot achieve the liberation of creation but we can anticipate it.[79]

Romans 8:19–23 has been described as 'an environmental mantra',[80] meaning that appeal is often made to it as a kind of ecological proof-text, mandating environmental activity by Christians, without engaging in exegetical detail with the problems of interpreting the passage. I hope that reading the text against the background of the theme of the mourning of the Earth in the Old Testament prophets has helped to elucidate it. Crucially, what becomes clear is that Paul assumes the same kind of close relationship between human wrongdoing and the well-being of the non-human creation that the prophets do. Paul and the prophets share what Ellen Davis calls 'the biblical understanding of the world, in which the physical, moral and spiritual orders fully interpenetrate one another – in contrast to the modern superstition that these are separable categories'.[81] This is not to say that Paul or the prophets understood the connection between human behaviour and ecological degradation in the way that we are now able to do, but what modern scientific knowledge makes possible is mainly a fuller understanding of how human physical behaviour (burning fossil fuels, over-fishing the oceans and so forth) has extensive and destructive consequences for the ecosystems of the planet. For the ethical and spiritual dimensions that pervade such human behaviour it is we who can learn from the biblical writers.

For many contemporary Christians, the most difficult matter in the biblical material we have discussed in this section will be the understanding of ecological destruction as divine judgement. It can be helpful to recognise that frequently in the Bible language of divine judgement describes the way acts have consequences in this world.[82] Disruptions of the created order of things cause further disruption that rebounds on the perpetrators. This can be conceptualised either as a process inherent in the created order or as the intervention of God, but the two are treated by the biblical writers as perfectly compatible. God's just purpose for creation works out through the processes he has ordained, though it would be a mistake to think of these operating in a fully automatic way that would allow no scope, for example, for God's merciful delay of judgement or revocation of judgement in response to repentance, both of which are prominent in biblical accounts of God's ways with the world. God's justice and mercy are both at work, but it is recognised that this kind of judgement on a large scale is bound to be, the world being as it is, relatively indiscriminate.[83] Those most responsible are by no means always those who suffer most. In the case we are considering here, there is clear recognition in both the prophets and Paul that, while there is some justice in human wrongdoers suffering from the lack of the essential resources of the Earth, the non-human creatures themselves are the undeserving victims of the consequences of human behaviour. What is being said is that God leaves humans and the rest of creation to the consequences of human actions, and this occurs within God's overall providential ordering of the world. However, it is also essential to say that the biblical writers look for the coming liberation of the whole created order from the entail of human sin. The biblical response (not solution) to the problematic of evil in the world is to a large extent eschatological, and this is Paul's approach in Romans 8:19–23. The eager longing of the whole groaning creation will be satisfied by God's unimaginable transformation of that whole creation to reflect his own glory and to participate in his own eternal life.

PRAISE AND LAMENT

I began the last section by pointing out that the Bible depicts the whole created world both as joining in praise of its Creator and as directing laments to its Creator on account of the devastation of the Earth and its creatures. This is parallel to the way in which the

Psalms depict and direct human address to God as both praise and lament, in probably equal quantities and in a variety of relationships. Lament does not stifle praise, nor does praise suppress lament. A clue to the way they relate in the relationship of the non-human creatures to God may lie in the passage quoted above from Isaiah 35:1–2:

> The wilderness and the dry land shall be glad,
>   the desert shall rejoice and blossom;
> like the crocus ²it shall blossom abundantly,
>   and rejoice with joy and singing.

Here it is at the fulfilment of creation's eager longing for liberation that the Earth breaks out into joyful praise (as also in Isa. 44:23 and 55:12–13).

The non-human creation glorifies God for making it what it is and by being what he has made it. The non-human creation mourns before God for the ways in which God's human creatures have polluted, degraded and destroyed it, in so many ways preventing it from being what God made it to be. Its very ruin is a lament to its Creator. It reflects God's glory but it also reflects humanity's desecration of God's glory in it. Psalm 148 then is not just a paean of undiluted praise. For those who read or sing it with the desecration of God's world in mind, it is praise in defiance against evil and in hope of new creation. Its invitation to all to praise the Creator will continue to ring out until the day when mourning is subsumed into the eschatological joy of all creation.[84]

Chapter 4

WHERE THE WILD THINGS ARE

Among the ecological failings of which the Bible has been accused is that it promotes a negative view of wilderness. Roderick Nash, in his classic work, *Wilderness and the American Mind*, claims that the Old Testament portrays wilderness as 'a cursed land', 'the environment of evil, a kind of hell'.[1] Although wilderness also features in the Bible as a place of spiritual testing and encounter with God, there 'was no fondness in the Hebraic tradition for wilderness itself'.[2] Speaking of the American Puritans, he comments: 'their Bibles contained all they needed to know in order to hate wilderness.'[3] More recently, Robert Leal, while allowing that there are also positive evaluations of wilderness in the Bible, focuses on what he sees as a widespread biblical attitude to wilderness as the realm of chaos, lawlessness and evil.[4]

THE GARDEN OF EDEN – ORCHARD OR FOREST?

A good place to start a response to such claims is in the Garden of Eden, which may or may not be wilderness.

Genesis 2:8–15

> And the LORD God planted a garden in Eden, in the east; and there he put the man whom he had formed. [9]Out of the ground the LORD God made to grow every tree that is pleasant to the sight and good for food, the tree of life also in the midst of the garden, and the tree of the knowledge of good and evil. [10]A river flows out of Eden to water the garden, and from there it divides and becomes four

branches. [11]The name of the first is Pishon; it is the one that flows around the whole land of Havilah, where there is gold; [12]and the gold of that land is good; bdellium and onyx stone are there. [13]The name of the second river is Gihon; it is the one that flows around the whole land of Cush. [14]The name of the third river is Tigris, which flows east of Assyria. And the fourth river is the Euphrates. [15]The LORD God took the man and put him in the Garden of Eden to till it and keep it.

What sort of place is the Garden of Eden? Certainly a place of ideal happiness, since the name Eden probably means 'bliss' or 'delight'. It is a garden in the sense that it had been deliberately planted, though, unlike all other gardens, the hands that planted it were God's own hands. It is apparently not the kind of formal garden the ancient Persians enjoyed, even though the word 'paradise' (used of the Garden of Eden first in the Greek translations of the Hebrew Bible) is borrowed from their usage. Gardens in the Bible are usually either vegetable gardens or orchards. From verse 9, it would seem clear enough that this garden is an orchard: 'the LORD God made to grow every tree that is pleasant to the sight and good for food'. These are fruit trees. 'Pleasant to the sight' might mean that they look as though they will taste good, but we should expect this to be said of the fruit, not the trees, and so the meaning is probably that they are aesthetically beautiful. The fact that the trees of the garden produce edible fruit (later God tells Adam he may eat the fruit of all of them except the tree of knowledge) does not mean they are purely utilitarian. A well-watered, fragrant, luxuriant orchard was a place of pleasure, as we can tell from the lover's description of his bride as one in the Song of Songs:

> A garden locked is my sister, my bride,
>> a garden locked, a fountain sealed.
> Your channel is an orchard of pomegranates
>> with all choicest fruits,
>> henna with nard,

nard and saffron, calamus and cinnamon,
    with all trees of frankincense,
myrrh and aloes,
    with all chief spices –
a garden fountain, a well of living water,
    and flowing streams from Lebanon. (S. of S. 4:12–15)

(Here the word translated 'orchard' is Hebrew *pardes*, 'paradise'.) In later Jewish tradition, the trees of the Garden of Eden were famous for their delightful fragrances.

However, in some references to it the Garden of Eden sounds more like a forest. The prophet Ezekiel tells a parable about the empire of Assyria, representing it as the highest tree in the world. It dwarfs even the trees in the Garden of Eden:

The cedars in the garden of God could not rival it,
    nor the fir trees equal its boughs;
the plane trees were as nothing
    compared with its branches;
no tree in the garden of God
    was like it in beauty.
I made it beautiful
    with its mass of branches,
the envy of all the trees of Eden
    that were in the garden of God. (Ezek. 31:8–9)

That sounds like a forest of magnificent trees, but not fruit trees. Why should a forest be called a garden? The answer is presumably that it is God's own garden, the garden he planted. Whereas gardens planted by humans are artificial, the garden God planted is wild nature. (Thus Psalm 104:16 says that God himself planted the cedars of Lebanon, the best known forest in the biblical world.) From this perspective, Eden looks as though it is the original, glorious heart of wild nature.[5]

So perhaps the Garden of Eden is both a forest and an orchard. Genesis 2 depicts the world before there was any difference, before wild nature and humanly cultivated nature became different, separated and often competitive spheres. In this forest Adam is at home as humans will never afterwards be in wild nature.

Adam's relationship to the garden is worth noticing carefully. When verse 8 tells us that 'the LORD God made to grow every tree that is pleasant to the sight and good for food', it would seem that he planted them for Adam. There are no animals yet in this story of creation. There is no one besides Adam to whose sight the trees would be attractive and no one besides Adam for whom their fruit would be good for food. But if this suggests that the garden was planted for Adam, we also read in verse 5 that, before Adam was created, 'there was no one to till the ground', while in verse 15 we find that 'the LORD God took the man and put him in the Garden of Eden to till it and keep it'.[6] Adam's role in the world, so far as this text goes, is to look after the garden. So, in a sense, the garden and Adam are made for each other. The garden is there to delight and to nourish Adam, and he is there to cultivate and to care for it. Fruit trees benefit from some attention and, it looks likely, in view of the preceding verses about the rivers that water the garden, that Adam also does some irrigation.[7] Eden does not depend on rainfall as the uplands of the land of Israel will have to do, with all the uncertainties of such dependence, since Eden is actually the source of the four rivers that water the whole Earth.[8] Adam has the job of channelling the river water where it is needed in the garden. But this is relatively easy work, not the back-breaking struggle with the soil that will be his task when he is expelled from Eden (3:17–18). His gardener's job, as Odil Steck puts it, 'is simply the carefree, satisfying activity of tilling and cultivating this garden'.[9] Israelites, though they depended on farming the land, often wished they could live just from vineyards and orchards.[10]

Adam is at home in the forest and his tending of its fruit trees does not make it less wild or natural. It does not resist him, as the soil with its thorns and thistles will outside Eden (3:18), and he does not disrupt the pristine condition in which it left its Maker's hands. This is nature and culture in harmony, and, when the animals enter the picture, and, as the climax of the narrative of Genesis 2, the woman also, the harmony embraces them too. Of course, central to the whole idyll is the harmony of God with all his creatures. Eden is God's garden, not only because he planted it, but because he enjoys it, he mingles with the trees, the animals and the people he has made. He takes his daily walk there in the cool of the evening (3:8). But the breach in God's harmony with the human couple destroys the whole idyll. Henceforth, wild nature and human culture cannot be the same. They may achieve relative harmony sometimes, but they remain different. The story of their tangled relationship is as formative of human history as is the story of human society itself. Because Adam and Eve ate the fruit of the tree of knowledge, nature has a history, humans have a history, and God has a history with both.

The purpose for which God put Adam in the garden was: 'to till it and to keep it'; or 'to cultivate and to care for it'; or 'to work it and to protect it' (2:15). In the garden, the combination was not a problem. But, after Eden, how do we both cultivate and protect nature? Evan Eisenberg suggests that this command to Adam can now be seen 'as a Hebrew koan ... a kind of riddle that we urgently need to solve. How do we protect nature from our work, and so keep from fouling the source of our own life? And how do we work with nature in a way that leaves both nature and human nature undiminished?'[11] The riddle has probably not puzzled too many people for most of human history, partly because wild nature did not seem to be endangered by humans. Beyond the humanly cultivated world in which most humans have lived, wild nature was always there, and was often perceived as waiting to reclaim human territory for itself at the slightest opportunity. It was civilisation that usually seemed fragile, not wild nature. Now it is the opposite. When Bill McKibben wrote his book *The End of Nature* (1990), he meant by the title that, especially by causing climate change, contemporary humanity has put an end to the idea of nature as independent of humans, beyond human influence or control.[12] This may be a somewhat exaggerated claim, but there is surely important truth in it, and it focuses the mind on that essential property of wild nature: that it is other than us. It is not the nature we have humanised, cultivated, absorbed, modified, reconstructed and reinvented. It is not, in our sense, a garden, but untouched wilderness, pristine, independent, just being itself – *other*.

It is the fragility of wilderness in the face of the massive human impact that modern civilisation not only does make, but at least until recently was designed to make on nature, that makes the preservation of wilderness, such as there still is, a matter of urgent concern for many. Of course, this is a disputed view. For some people, an end to wild nature, uncontrolled by us, is a goal to be desired and striven for. Total control and transformation of nature into what we want to make of it – what Teilhard de Chardin called the 'hominisation' of the world – has been the dream of the scientific-technological project from the seventeenth century onwards, and it is alive and well among the technological visionaries for whom bioengineering and artificial intelligence promise a future in which humans or their posthuman descendants will have wholly mastered the evolutionary process. There are also the economic pragmatists for whom the priority is the materialistic improvement of human life through transforming nature into the goods valued by consumerism. For such ways of thinking, there is at best a place for pockets of wild nature managed for the recreation or therapy of people who enjoy that sort of thing. Does wild nature really have any other sort of value?

Before leaving the Garden of Eden, there is an important final point to be made about it. Nash claims that the 'story of the Garden and its loss embedded into Western thought the idea that wilderness and paradise were both physical and spiritual opposites'.[13] There is some truth in this, but it is not quite how Nash represents it. He is able to quote two texts from the prophets that contrast the Garden of Eden with wilderness. Joel says of a plague of locusts: 'Before them the land is like the Garden of Eden, but after them a desolate wilderness' (Joel 2:3). Isaiah 51:3 speaks of the desolate wasteland to which Jerusalem had been reduced and of God's promise to redeem and bless: 'he will make her wilderness like Eden, her desert like the garden of the LORD'. Here (as also in Gen. 13:10) Eden represents a luxuriantly fertile place, while the

Where the Wild Things Are

wilderness is uninhabitable and unproductive wasteland. They are opposites, but they represent the two poles of the spectrum of land, from the perspective of humans needing to make a living from the soil. Neither designates ordinary arable land, such as most Israelite farmers farmed. It is not the case, as Nash supposes, that when Adam and Eve left the garden, they faced a 'wilderness' in the biblical sense of that term. They had to put hard work into cultivating land, but the land they cultivated was fit for cultivation. Wilderness, in the usual biblical sense, is not. This example shows how important it is to define our terms.[14]

WILD NATURE IN THE BIBLE

So far in this chapter I have used the terms 'wild nature' and 'wilderness' synonymously, but, because of a potential ambiguity of the term 'wilderness,' I have usually said 'wild nature'. In modern ecological discussion, 'wilderness' refers to all natural habitat that is not manipulated or managed by humans. Wilderness is the opposite of cultivated or managed land. It lies outside human culture and civilisation, and its living inhabitants are wild animals, as opposed to domesticated animals. In this sense, wilderness might be desert, jungle, forest, coastline, mountain, or almost any kind of land that has not come under human control and influence (sometimes even oceans can be designated wilderness). But English translations of the Bible use the term 'wilderness' (translating especially Hebrew *midbar* and Greek *eremos*) in a narrower sense: it refers to land that not merely is not farmed, but is unsuitable for farming: arid or semi-arid regions, barren, with little vegetation. We might call it wasteland – and that word captures something of biblical people's attitude to it. Wilderness in this biblical usage sometimes designates land that cannot be farmed but can be used for grazing livestock, such as goats and sheep (e.g. Joel 1:19 and 20, and 2:22: 'the pastures of the wilderness'). In that case it is the borderlands between arable land and desert. It can also refer to land devastated by war (e.g. Jer. 22:6–7). But mostly it is the desert, the land without water or vegetation, where humans can scarcely survive, let alone practise agriculture.[15]

However, 'wilderness' in this biblical sense is not the only part of the biblical world that is 'wilderness' in our modern sense. In particular, there is forest, a term that in the Bible covers both dense forest, made up of tall trees and undergrowth, and open woodland with low-growing trees and shrubs (maquis).[16] Considerable parts of Palestine were still forested in biblical times.[17] Forests were not as inhospitable and useless to humans as desert, especially since they provided timber, and the maquis could be grazed by domestic animals. But forests were nevertheless wild nature, largely untouched by human work, and full of dangerous wild animals that made them places for humans to avoid. Much of the cultivated land of biblical Palestine had, of course, once been wooded (cf. Josh. 17:15 and 18), and forest was what it would revert to if it ceased to be farmed (e.g. Hos. 2:12). The point is that, if we want to know how wild nature is perceived in the Bible, we must include forests as well as what the Bible calls wilderness.[18]

From one point of view, as we have seen, it was the expulsion from Eden that divided the world into the human and the non-human, the cultivated and the wild. From another point of view, it was Israel's adoption of settled agriculture that did this.[19] For biblical Israel, there is, on the one side, the land on which they live and in which their own life is embedded, though it belongs to God, not to them. This is a community of creation in which they not only participate but have the upper hand. Domestic animals are very much part of it: the Sabbath commandment, for example, prescribes rest from work not only by humans, but also by domestic animals (Exod. 20:10 and Deut. 5:14). When the king of Nineveh ordered a penitential fast, in response to the preaching of Jonah, not only human beings but also domestic animals had to abstain from food and drink and wear sackcloth (Jonah 3:7–8). This was a Persian, not an Israelite custom,[20] but its Israelite readers were presumably not to think it ridiculous.[21] These animals were part of the human world and shared, to some extent at least, its relationship to God.

Outside that world is forest and wilderness, where humans can scarcely survive. Fugitives might take refuge in forests (1 Sam. 22:5

and 2 Sam. 18:9), and nomads, usually with camels, survived in the desert (Gen. 21:20–21; Isa. 21:13–14 and Jer. 49:28–30).[22] But Israelites would do so only if left with no other choice. The wilderness wanderings were remembered as the period when only God's miraculous protection and provision for Israel enabled her to survive in 'the great and terrible wilderness, an arid wasteland with poisonous snakes and scorpions' (Deut. 8:15). Lions, bears and wild boar lived in the forests of Palestine. Not only did they make forests dangerous to humans (e.g. 2 Sam. 18:8), they would invade the cultivated land and the grazing land, threatening people and domestic animals.[23] These features certainly give wild nature strongly negative connotations. From the perspective of Israelite farmers, forest and especially wilderness were uninhabited, inhospitable and even threatening to humans, and this was a fairly realistic assessment. We can hardly expect any other from farmers living close to subsistence.[24]

In the prophets, there is a recurrent scene in which a city that comes under judgement by God, conquered and razed to the ground, becomes a desolate, uninhabitable place.[25] For example, this is Babylon:

> It will never be inhabited
>> or lived in for all generations;
> Arabs will not pitch their tents there,
>> shepherds will not make their flocks lie down there.
> [21]But wildcats will have their lairs there,
>> owls shall make their nests in the houses;
> there ostriches will live,
>> and satyrs will dance there.
> [22]Hyenas will howl in its towers,
>> and jackals in the pleasant palaces. (Isa. 13:20–22a)[26]

Note that this is not even wilderness good enough for grazing sheep or for nomads to settle temporarily. It belongs only to the wild creatures that frequent such places. Jerusalem is threatened with a perhaps somewhat less severe fate, reduced to grazing land for wild animals:

For the palace will be forsaken,
    the populous city deserted;
the hill and the watchtower
    will become dens forever,
the joy of wild asses,
    a pasture for flocks [of wild animals]. (Isa. 32:14)[27]

An interesting feature of such descriptions of the desolation to which the sites of destroyed cities are reduced is how knowledgeable the prophets are about the creatures that live in such places.[28] In fact, not all of the creatures can be identified with any confidence, because they are species that rarely occur elsewhere in the Hebrew Bible. The fullest list of desert creatures is in Isaiah's depiction of the desolated land of Edom, which I give here in Joseph Blenkinsopp's translation:

The hawk and the hedgehog will claim it as their own,
owl and raven will make it their home …
[13]Thorns will spring up in her palaces,
nettles and thistles in her forts;
it will become the haunt of jackals,
the abode of ostriches;
[14]wildcats will gather with hyenas,
the satyr will call to his mate,
there too will Lilith alight
and there find a spot for herself;
[15]there the owl will nest,
lay her eggs, hatch them, and give them shelter;
there too kites will gather,
no one without her mate. (Isa. 34:11a and 13–15)[29]

However, by contrast with Blenkinsopp's translations of the names of the creatures in this passage, Yehuda Feliks argues that ten of the twelve living creatures (all except the wildcats and the hyenas in v 14) in this passage are actually desert birds. Moreover, he identifies eight of the ten species of bird (all except the kite and the raven) as various species of owl.[30] He explains why owls of various kinds seem sinister and frightening:

> [N]o other group in the feathered world are more fitting than these birds to exemplify the horrors of destruction. They nest mainly in deserted buildings … In popular legend … they always appear as symbols of destruction and as portents of disaster. The reason for this is their strange and terrifying appearance: the large head surrounded by tufts of feathers in the form of ears, their wide-open and staring eyes underneath which there appear to be cheeks … In addition, they make a breathing noise like the stertorous breathing of a person in his death throes, or the moaning of a being in pain. Most of them are called after the sounds they make.[31]

They are, of course, creatures of the night, and their hooting sounds can sound distinctly spooky. Furthermore, the two remaining animals – those Blenkinsopp translates as 'wildcats' and 'hyenas' – have names that seem to mean yelper and howler. As with most of the birds, their identification is guesswork, but their names alone add to the general spookiness and desolation of the scene.[32]

At least five of the birds appear in the list of twenty-one unclean birds, those that may not be eaten, in the Torah (Lev. 11:13–19 and Deut. 14:12–18). This is because they are predators or scavengers. But the passage in Isaiah has not drawn on the legal list. What is remarkable is that all these species, including apparently many different species of owl, are known to the prophet, carefully distinguished by different names. He may not have been fond of these creatures, but he has observed them and learned their names. In some sense, surely, he appreciated them. What his writing about them conveys is their otherness, a quality that is easily perceived negatively but in fact has its own kind of positive value.

Isaiah's picture of the desert makes the point that it is certainly not a place where humans are supposed to live, but it has its own inhabitants who do belong in it. Ominous and scary though they are, they are the creatures of God to whom he has given this habitat. In other words, the perception of the wilderness is undoubtedly negative in the sense that, from a human point of view, it is uninhabitable, but this very judgement of it as the non-human sphere highlights the fact that it is the sphere of other creatures, whom God has made for it. The implication is precisely that not all habitats are for humans; some are for very different kinds of creatures.

This explains the fact that in Psalm 104 and Job 38—39, those two panoramas of creation in which humans have no privileged position, the areas of wild nature are not viewed negatively. They are simply part of the variety of habitats God has created. Just as humans live in fertile and cultivated areas, so forests are habitats for lions and storks, mountains for mountain goats and rock badgers, the wilderness for wild asses and sand grouse, the mountain crags for vultures. All that is 'wrong' with the wild places is that they are not for humans, but the Hebrew Bible does not suppose that all parts of the world are for human use or habitation. Despite first impressions, the Bible seems closer than we might have thought to contemporary appreciation of wild nature precisely as non-humanised nature, nature whose value lies not in its adaptation to human use or enjoyment, but in its unspoiled otherness.

While the Bible tends to view wilderness (in the biblical sense) negatively, from the point of view of human interests, this is much less the case with forests. Only very rarely is the desolation of a city portrayed as the land's reversion to forest (Hos. 2:12 and Mic. 3:12), and in fact there are more occasions on which the destruction of forests is seen as a lamentable part of the desolation of a land (Isa. 10:18–19 and 33–34; Jer. 21:14 and 46:23; Ezek. 20:45–48; and Zech. 11:1–3), though some of these may be figurative.[33] Since most arable land had originated from clearing forest, not cultivating wilderness, it is rather surprising that the Hebrew Bible's antipathy is directed very much more to wilderness than to forest. What this probably shows is that the antipathy had actually little to do with competition between arable land and wild nature. In fact, apart from Joshua 17:15–18, the texts show little indication of awareness that the land the Israelites farmed had been forest, and perhaps most of the deforestation had taken place too long ago to be remembered. Adam, after all, was warned that he must contend with thorns and thistles (Gen. 3:18; cf. Isa. 5:6), not that he would have to uproot trees. So, for Israel, what was 'wrong' with forest was not that it was not cultivated, but that it was inhabited by the dangerous wild animals who feature so prominently in the imagery of the Hebrew Bible. While this made it inhospitable to humans, it was the habitat God had provided for the wild animals that live in it (Ps. 104:30). Remarkably, Israelite land law even took account of the needs of wild animals (presumably those inhabiting pockets of forest between Israelite fields) by specifying that in the sabbatical year the produce of the land was to be left for the poor, the domestic animals and 'the wild animals in your land' (Lev. 25:7; cf. Exod. 23:11).

RETURN TO ECOTOPIA: (1) FORESTS

As well as visions of coming devastation, there are also in the prophets just as many visions of salvation, often on the far side of judgment.[34] These are utopias, in the sense that they project ideal conditions of human flourishing. We might better call them ecotopias,[35] since they regularly feature the non-human creation and imagine ideal relationships between humans and other creatures, both flora and fauna. In theological terms they are at least incipiently eschatological, to be taken up, from a New Testament perspective, into the Bible's overall vision of the future renewal of the whole creation, but they are also protological in the sense that, to a greater or lesser extent, they evoke the situation prior to the expulsion of Adam and Eve, and prior, therefore, to the historical disruption between humans and wild nature. We can see this both in the ecotopian visions that feature forests and in those that feature wild animals, and, when we remember that the only real problem of forests, from the perspective of biblical people, was that dangerous animals lived there, we can see that these two aspects are closely connected. But we shall take them one by one.

Following Isaiah's oracle of judgement on Jerusalem that we cited in the last section (Isa. 32:14), the prophet continues:

until a spirit from on high is poured out on us,
and the wilderness becomes a fruitful field,
and the fruitful field is deemed a forest. (Isa. 32:15)

Here the lifegiving divine Spirit rejuvenates the devastated land. There is an ascending scale of fruitfulness: wilderness, 'fruitful field' (*carmel*, apparently meaning 'orchard', or perhaps the best of the arable land), forest. The fruit garden will be so fruitful and flourishing it will be considered forest! We are surely back in the orchard-forest of Eden, where forest is not threatening but bounteous.

The prophecy continues:

Then justice will dwell in the wilderness,
and righteousness abide in the fruitful field.
[17]The effect of righteousness will be peace,
and the result of righteousness, quietness and trust forever.
[18]My people will abide in a peaceful habitation,
in secure dwellings, and in quiet resting places …
[20]Happy will you be who sow beside every stream,
who let the ox and the donkey range freely.
(Isa. 32:16–18 and 20)[36]

Verses 16–17 indicate not only that the flourishing of the natural world of soil, plants and trees will be accompanied by justice and well-being (*shalom*) in human society, but also that right relationships will unite human society and the natural world in perfect harmony. In other words, the created order will be respected. Animals, however, are not mentioned until verse 20, which means that people will be able to let their domestic animals roam freely because they will no longer be in danger from dangerous predators.[37] Wild animals will no longer be a threat, but we are not told here what has happened to them!

Another vision in which the wilderness becomes so fruitful it produces a forest is in Isaiah 35, which is the immediate sequel to the scene of desolation in Edom that we considered in the last section. As John Watts notes, chapter 35 is 'as extravagant in its language of renewal and new birth as 34:9–15 had been in its language of death and desolation'.[38] Here the prophet imagines the route the Israelites returning from exile will take across the desert, as it springs to life around them:

> The wilderness and the dry land shall be glad,
>> the desert shall rejoice and blossom;
> like the crocus[39] [2]it shall blossom abundantly,
>> and rejoice with joy and singing.
> The glory of Lebanon shall be given to it,
>> the majesty of Carmel and Sharon.
> They shall see the glory of the LORD,
>> the majesty of our God ...
> [6]... For waters shall break forth in the wilderness,
>> and streams in the desert;
> [7]the burning sand shall become a pool,
>> and the thirsty ground springs of water;
> the haunt of jackals shall become a swamp,
>> the grass shall become reeds and rushes ...
> [9]No lion shall be there,
>> nor shall any ravenous beast come up on it;
> they shall not be found there,
>> but the redeemed shall dwell there. (Isa. 35:1–2, 6–7 and 9)

Again, the problem of dangerous animals is averted simply by denying them access to this highway through the forest. The lifeless wilderness and arid land at once flower and break out into joyous singing. The culmination of the transformation is the gift of magnificent trees like those of the mountains of Lebanon, famously forested with cedars and other towering evergreens,[40] or the woods of Mount Carmel that sloped down into the valley of Sharon, the whole area well known for the abundance of its vegetation (the name Carmel is the same word as that translated 'fruitful field' or 'orchard' in Isa. 32:15, and, whether or not the mountain was named for this reason, the name and the term were surely associated).

What is especially remarkable about this passage is the parallelism in verse 2 between, on the one hand, 'the *glory* of Lebanon' and 'the *majesty* of Carmel', and on the other hand, 'the *glory* of the LORD' and 'the *majesty* of our God'. The implication must be that the splendour of the trees reflects God's own glory,[41] seen in the miraculous replenishment of creation with some of its most impressive members.

A similar prophecy, with more detail about the trees, is Isaiah 41:18–19:

> I will open rivers on the bare heights,
> > and fountains in the midst of the valleys;
> I will make the wilderness a pool of water,
> > and the dry land springs of water.
> [19]I will put in the wilderness the cedar,
> > the acacia, the myrtle, and the olive;
> I will set in the desert the cypress,
> > the plane and the pine together.

All these forest trees (and one large shrub: the myrtle) are useful: the tall trees were valued for their wood, the olive for its fruit, the myrtle for its aromatic branches, all for their shade. But their presence here is more than utilitarian. They make up a composite picture of the wild forests of the ancient Near East springing to glorious life at the touch of their Creator. A more positive view of forests would be hard to imagine (see also Isa. 55:13).

RETURN TO ECOTOPIA: (2) WILD ANIMALS

Biblical people feared dangerous wild animals (such as lions, bears and snakes) both as threats to their own lives and as threats to their domestic animals and so to their own livelihood. The primeval history in Genesis portrays this state of enmity between humans and wild animals as the result of the development of violence in the world after the fall of Adam and Eve. Originally, humans and all animals were herbivores (Gen. 1:29–30 and 9:3). (The difficulty this poses for modern readers will be discussed below.) But this in itself need not preclude violence, as becomes clear in the human case with the stories of Cain and Abel (Gen. 4:1–16) and of Cain's descendant Lamech (Gen. 4:19–24). Competition for resources could set humans against animals and animals against animals. Perhaps this is the reason why the Earth became 'filled with violence' in the period before the Flood (Gen. 6:11, 13). The violence is blamed on 'all flesh', including animals (at least, land animals and birds) as well as humans. The Flood is not really a solution to this problem. Violence has become too endemic in the lives of humans and animals. So God's covenant with Noah after the Flood is designed to regulate a violent situation rather than to extirpate the violence. The human dominion over other living creatures is reformulated as a form of protection of humans from dangerous animals (Gen. 9:2), and humans are permitted to kill and eat animals, with the proviso that the sacredness of all life be acknowledged by abstention from blood (Gen. 9:3–4).

Despite this permission, it is worth noting, the Israelites did not in fact hunt and eat wild animals, and certainly not the dangerous ones. The animals permitted in the dietary laws of the Torah were almost all domestic ones (deer, gazelle and some wild birds are the only exceptions), so that Ellen Davis is able to see these laws as 'the Bible's method of taming the killer instinct in humans'.[42] Since Israelites did not hunt or eat the dangerous wild animals,[43] it was natural for them to think of wild animals as a threat to themselves, but not of themselves as a threat to wild animals. (We, on the other hand, know that we are responsible for the rapid extinction of species.)

Therefore, in Ezekiel's ecotopia, the people are assured that they will no longer have to suffer the oppression of enemy nations or the predation of wild animals (Ezek. 34:28) because God 'will make with them [Israel] a covenant of peace and banish wild animals from the land, so that they may live in the wild and sleep in the woods securely' (Ezek. 34:25).[44] Here the ideal is for people to inhabit the forests again, as Adam did, but it entails ridding the land of Israel of the dangerous wild animals (which need not mean these cease to exist elsewhere). Once again, we see that dangerous animals are the only reason for negativity towards forest in the Hebrew Bible. The pioneer farmer's sense of competition between farmed land and forest does not come into it.

More attractive is Isaiah's famous prophecy of the peaceable Kingdom of the Messiah:

> The wolf shall live with the lamb,
>> the leopard shall lie down with the kid,
> the calf and the lion and the fatling together,
>> and a little child shall lead them.
> 7The cow and the bear shall graze,
>> their young shall lie down together;
>> and the lion shall eat straw like the ox.
> 8The nursing child shall play over the hole of the asp,
>> and the weaned child shall put its hand on the adder's den.
> 9They will not hurt or destroy
>> on all my holy mountain;
> for the land[45] will be full of the knowledge of the LORD
>> as the waters cover the sea. (Isa. 11:6–9)

This passage has sometimes been misunderstood by modern readers as a picture simply of peace between animals. In fact, it depicts peace between the human world, with its domestic animals (lamb, kid, calf, bullock, cow), and those wild animals (wolf, leopard, lion, bear, poisonous snakes) that were normally perceived as threats both to human livelihood and to human life. What is depicted is the reconciliation of the human world with wild nature. Significantly, humans and domestic animals are all represented by their young, the most vulnerable. Each of the pairs of animals in verses 6–7 is carefully chosen, so that each predator is paired with a typical example of that predator's prey.[46] Especially from verse 7, it is clear that this peaceful condition is possible because the carnivorous animals have become, like the domestic animals, herbivores. No doubt, this also includes humans. None of the wild prey of the predatory animals are mentioned, but it would seem to follow (especially from v 9a) that they also can now live safely alongside them. However, this is not the interest of the passage, whose concern is with the reconciliation of the human sphere of life with the wild. The pairing of the snakes and the children (v 8) differs from the other pairs in that the child is not the prey of the snake, but its poison is nonetheless dangerous to a child who ignorantly interferes with its hiding-place.[47]

The cessation of *human* violence is probably considered dealt with by the activities of the Messiah earlier in the chapter, which depicts a scion of David, exceptionally endowed with the Spirit, exercising just rule, especially on behalf of the poor (11:1–5). As we have already seen in Isaiah 32:15–20, the establishment of right relationships in human society accompanies the reconciliation of human society with wild nature.[48] There may be a thematic link between the Messiah's concern to give the poor safety from their human oppressors (11:4) and the protection of the more vulnerable animals from their predators. However, these links between verses 3–5 and 6–9 do not make the depiction of the animals merely an allegory of peace between nations.[49] There is too much evidence elsewhere in the Hebrew Bible that the relationships between humans and wild animals were a real concern, especially in portrayals of an ideal future, for this to be plausible. As we have seen in Ezekiel 34:25 and Leviticus 26:6, the promise of protection from predation by imperial armies and the promise of protection from predation by dangerous animals are two distinct, though parallel, concerns, and the ecotopias address both.

Isaiah 11 itself does address the problem of Israel's enemies among the nations, but not until verses 9–10:

> They will not hurt or destroy
> > on all my holy mountain;
> for the land will be full of the knowledge of the LORD
> > as the waters cover the sea.
> [10]On that day the root of Jesse shall stand as a signal to the peoples; the nations shall inquire of him, and his dwelling shall be glorious.

The reference to the root of Jesse in verse 10 forms an *inclusio* with verse 1 (making these two verses the corresponding 'bookends' of the passage) and enables us to see that the overall structure of the passage is a 'chiastic' or concentric pattern:[50]

A. A shoot will come up from the stump of Jesse (v 1)

B. The knowledge of the LORD will rest on him (v 2)

C. The ideal age: right relationships in human society (vv 3–5)

C^1. The ideal age: right relationships between human society and wild animals (vv 6–9)

B^1. The knowledge of the LORD will fill the land (v 9)

A^1. A root of Jesse will stand as a signal (v 10)

Given this structure, we can see that just as the knowledge of the Lord enables the Messiah to establish justice in human society, so it is the knowledge of the Lord that enables peace with wild animals. The result is the abolition of all violence on the Lord's 'holy mountain', which, especially in view of Isaiah 2:2–3, seems to be Mount Zion, the temple mount,[51] though it may also allude to the fact that the Garden of Eden was located on a mountain, according to Ezekiel 28:13–14. Things are put right first among the Messiah's own people and in the Lord's own land, but with a view to spreading this knowledge of the Lord and its consequences to the nations. The nations are drawn by the Messiah's reputation to enquire of the Lord, just as they are in Isaiah 2:1–4. In that oracle, parallel and complementary to this one, the effect is universal peace among the nations.

By comparison with Ezekiel's ecotopia (Ezek. 34:25–30), where the threat from both animals and nations is removed but nothing is said about the transformation of either, in Isaiah's ecotopia there is a transformative positive effect on both. The nations live at peace with each other (2:4) and the wild animals live at peace with humans and their domestic animals (11:6–9). The substitution of peace for violence is the overall theme, summarised in 11:9: 'They shall not hurt or destroy in all my holy mountain.'

This focus on violence and its supersession by peace constitutes a key thematic link back to the primeval history of Genesis 1—11.[52]

The Isaianic ecotopia alludes to the originally vegetarian practice of all the creatures of Earth (Gen. 1:29–30),[53] to the violence on the part of 'all flesh' before the Flood (Gen. 6:11–13), and to the continuing inimical relationship of humans and wild animals, in consequence of which God permitted the consumption of meat (Gen. 9:2–6). In the passage in Isaiah, special emphasis is given to the friendly relations to be established between humans and poisonous snakes. This surely reflects the curse on the snake in Genesis 3:15: God 'will put enmity between you [the snake] and the woman, and between your offspring and hers.' The woman's offspring are represented in the ecotopia by the 'nursing child' and the 'weaned child' who may safely play near the dens of the snakes.[54]

There is probably also an allusion to the human dominion over other living creatures (Gen. 1:26 and 28). The first depiction of animals at peace (Isa. 11:6) concludes: 'a little child shall lead them'. This must be an allusion to shepherding practice,[55] in which the domestic animals willingly follow the shepherd who leads them to pasture. Even a small child can lead a flock of sheep or herd of goats, because no force or violence is required.[56] In the ecotopia the little child will be able to lead also the wolf, the leopard and the lion. It is a picture of gentle and beneficial service to wild animals, which the latter now willingly receive. This is the prophet's view of what the original dominion was meant to be and therefore in the messianic age will be. It is a clear indication that the way the dominion was expounded to Noah after the Flood (Gen. 9:2) is not what it was meant to be, but a version much adapted to a situation of violence between humans and wild animals. In Isaiah's ecotopian future, as John Olley puts it, the references to the children 'highlight a joyous interaction, without harm or dominance'.[57]

Some scholars deny that Isaiah 11:6–9 is a return to Eden. For example, Brevard Childs writes:

> The prophetic picture is not a return to an ideal past, but
> the restoration of creation by a new act of God through the

vehicle of a righteous ruler ... What Isaiah envisioned was
not a return to a mythical age of primordial innocence, but
the sovereign execution of a new act of creation in which
the righteous will of God is embraced ...[58]

That a new creative act of God is envisaged is certainly right. The
new creation surpasses Eden, but one could also say that it realises
the potential of Eden. The original innocence of humans and
animals does provide the prophet with a model for what the future
will be like. It relates the future to what has been God's will for his
creatures from the beginning, and it sees that divine intention
achieving its goal fully in the future, after which there cannot be
another fall into violence.

We now know that, while bears, as omnivores, could survive on
a vegetarian diet, this is biologically impossible for lions. A vegetarian lion would be so different as to be another species. This
creates difficulties for modern readers of the primeval history in
Genesis and also of the ecotopian future envisaged by Isaiah. (In
the former case, there is the additional difficulty that we know,
from fossil remains, that there were carnivorous animals long
before there were humans.) The difficulty with Genesis can be met
by seeing the vegetarianism of Genesis 1:29–30 as one of the
utopian aspects of the seven-day creation account. It is after giving
humans and land animals a vegetarian diet that God looks at all the
work of his hands and pronounces it 'very good' (Gen. 1:31).
Creation is actually not yet 'very good', and so the account here
looks forward to the time when it will be, at the eschaton. What
concerns both the authors or editors of Genesis 1—11 and the
prophet Isaiah, is the presence of violence in God's good creation.
Violence, whether among humans, among animals, or between
humans and animals, cannot be part of God's ultimate intention
for his creatures. It cannot be present when God pronounces his
work 'very good'. As far as the eschatological future goes, we
should expect a new creation in which animals and humans relate
to each other in peaceable, companionable ways that are mutually
enriching. We cannot say how this will be possible, but there is a

Where the Wild Things Are

great deal about the new creation of which we have to say the same. (Andrew Linzey aptly comments that Isaiah's vision of the peaceable Kingdom 'invites us to the *imaginative recognition* that God's transforming love is not determined even by what we think we know of elementary biology'.[59]) New creation refers to a transformation of this world by a newly creative act of God comparable only with the original creation. What we can know from the Bible's prophetic visions is that it is a new future for the whole of creation, not just for humans. Even from an anthropo-centric perspective, animals are so closely related to human life in this world that a human future without them would be a diminish-ment of human nature in the new world, not a fulfilment of it. But they are also indispensable to the world that God pronounced, in anticipation, 'very good'.

Biblical prophecy is not merely predictive but calls its readers to appropriate action now in the light of the future it outlines. Sibley Towner writes:

> The biblical pictures of nature in the future function as incitements toward a style of ethical living in the present that is holistic, interdependent, non-hierarchical, and one that does not reject flesh and matter as corrupt because God does not reject them.[60]

With Isaiah's vision of the peaceable Kingdom in view, we cannot simply acquiesce in violence between humans and animals, any more than we can renounce attempts to promote peace, rather than war, in human society. In both cases, peace is God's promise, but in both cases we can live in ways that correspond to the promise and hope that God gives us. This does not mean pre-empting God's eschatological action, which alone will establish his Kingdom in its universal fullness. To do so would be disastrous, because we are not capable of creating utopia or ecotopia, and attempts to do so have always proved damaging. We can anticipate God's Kingdom, but only in ways that are realistic and appropriate to our human limits. Sibley Towner concludes his discussion of this matter:

Our proper relationship to nature is not to twist it into a perfection of our own imagining, which would only turn out to be another form of oppression, but rather humbly seek to live in harmony with it in a way that prefigures the covenant of peace that only the Creator can bestow.[61]

JESUS IN ECOTOPIA

In view of what we have learned about wilderness in the Hebrew Bible, it will no doubt seem paradoxical to refer to Jesus' sojourn in the wilderness, in this case the Judaean desert, as 'Jesus in ecotopia'. In the two major Gospel accounts of Jesus' temptations in the wilderness (Matt. 4:1–11 and Luke 4:1–13), the place especially evokes the wilderness wanderings of Israel after the Exodus, where they were tested. Jesus, as it were, relives the experience of Israel, overcoming temptation where Israel had succumbed. But in the case of Mark's much briefer account of Jesus in the wilderness, I see Isaiah 11 as prominent in the background to the scene.

Mark alone mentions the wild animals:

> [Jesus] was in the wilderness forty days, tempted by Satan; and he was with the wild animals; and the angels ministered to him. (Mark 1:13, NRSV altered)

This account of Jesus in the wilderness follows Mark's account of Jesus' baptism, when he was designated the messianic Son of God, and was anointed with the Spirit like the Messiah of Isaiah 11:1–2. Then the Spirit takes Jesus into the wilderness for a task he must fulfil before he embarks on his preaching of the Kingdom of God, which follows our passage. Why must Jesus go into the wilderness? Because, as we have seen, the wilderness is the non-human sphere. It is there that Jesus will meet three categories of non-human being: Satan, the wild animals and the angels. He has to establish his relationship as Messiah to all three before he can embark on his mission in the human world, which fills the rest of the Gospel.

Brief as Mark's account of Jesus in the wilderness is, each part of it is of importance. The order of the three beings he encounters – Satan, the wild animals, the angels – is not accidental. Satan is the natural enemy of the righteous person and can only be resisted. Angels are the natural friends of the righteous person: they minister to Jesus. But between Satan and the angels the wild animals are more ambiguous. On the basis of the common perception of wild animals as a threat to humans, we might expect them to be dangerous enemies, especially when located in the wilderness, the habitat that belongs to them and not to humans. But, on the other hand, since Jesus is the messianic king, inaugurating his Kingdom, might we not expect his relationship to the wild animals to be appropriate to that Kingdom, the return to Eden we find in Isaiah 11?

Whereas Satan is simply an enemy of Jesus and the angels simply his friends, the wild animals, placed by Mark between those two, are enemies of whom Jesus makes friends. Jesus in the wilderness enacts, in an anticipatory way, the peace between the human world and wild nature that is Isaiah's ecotopia. Mark's simple but effective phrase ('he was with the wild animals') has no suggestion of hostility or resistance about it. It indicates Jesus' peaceable presence with the animals. The expression 'to be with someone' frequently has, in Mark's usage (3:14; 5:18; and 14:67; cf. 4:36) and elsewhere, the sense of close, friendly association. (It may also be relevant that Genesis describes the animals in the ark as those who were 'with' Noah: Gen. 7:23; 8:1 and 17; and 9:12.) Mark could have thought of the ideal relationship between wild animals and humans, here represented by their messianic king, as domination over them or as recruiting them to the ranks of the domestic animals who are useful to humans. But the simple 'with them' can have no such implication. Jesus befriends them. He is peaceably 'with' them.[62]

Douglas Hall has called attention to the significance of the preposition 'with' in the Bible. Its prominence relates to the facts that 'with' is the language of love, and that 'being' in the biblical tradition is relational: it implies *with-being, being-with*.[63] Hall states that in

> their better expressions, Christian theology and ethics have known how to express all this with respect to two of the dimensions of our human relatedness: God, and our human partners (the neighbour). But Christian theology has rarely explored the meaning of this fundamental ontological assumption [that being is being-with] for the third major dimension of our threefold relatedness as creatures, namely, our relation to the extra-human world.[64]

Noah in the ark and Jesus in the wilderness would be good starting points for such reflection on humanity's essential 'being-with' other creatures.

The context to which Mark 1:13 originally spoke was one in which wild animals threatened humanity. The messianic peace with wild animals promised, by healing the alienation and enmity between humans and animals, to liberate humans from that threat. Christians who read Mark 1:13 today do so in a very different context, one in which it is now clearly we who threaten the survival of wild animals, encroach on their habitat, threaten to turn their wilderness into a wasteland they cannot inhabit. To make the point one need only notice how many of the animals Jesus could have encountered in the Judaean wilderness have become extinct in Palestine during the past century: the wild ass, the desert oryx, the addax, the ostrich and no doubt many others. But Mark's image of Jesus' peaceable companionship with the animals in the wilderness can survive this reversal of situation. For us, Jesus' companionable presence with the wild animals affirms their independent value for themselves and for God. Jesus does not adopt the animals into the human world, but lets them be themselves in peace, leaving them their wilderness, affirming them as creatures who share the world with us in the community of God's creation. Mark's image of Jesus with the animals provides a biblical symbol of the human possibility of living fraternally with

Where the Wild Things Are

other living creatures. Like all aspects of Jesus' inauguration of the Kingdom of God, its fullness will be realised only in the eschatological future, but it can be significantly anticipated in the present by respecting wild animals and preserving their habitat.

THE VALUE OF OTHERNESS

We return once more to the original Garden of Eden:

Genesis 2:18–24

> Then the LORD God said, 'It is not good that the man should be alone; I will make him a helper as his partner.' [19]So out of the ground the LORD God formed every animal of the field and every bird of the air, and brought them to the man to see what he would call them; and whatever the man called every living creature, that was its name. [20]The man gave names to all cattle, and to the birds of the air, and to every animal of the field; but for the man there was not found a helper as his partner. [21]So the LORD God caused a deep sleep to fall upon the man, and he slept; then he took one of his ribs and closed up its place with flesh. [22]And the rib that the LORD God had taken from the man he made into a woman and brought her to the man. [23]Then the man said,
>
> > 'This at last is bone of my bones
> > and flesh of my flesh;
> > this one shall be called Woman,
> > for out of Man this one was taken.'
>
> [24]Therefore a man leaves his father and his mother and clings to his wife, and they become one flesh.

The first thing to notice about this passage is that the order of events – the creation of the man, then the animals, then the woman – is a storytelling device that the author has used to say something about the relationship between the sexes and the relationship of humans to other animals. After all, the order is different from that in Genesis 1, where the animals are created before the simultaneous creation of men and women. The editor who compiled this part of Genesis was evidently not bothered about the contradiction, no doubt because he took neither of the sequences literally. If we were to take this part of Genesis 2 literally it might appear that the animals were a mistake: God made them thinking, wrongly as it turned out, that they could be the helper Adam needed.[65] But, in fact, the animals have their own importance in the narrative: they are not introduced simply to make the point that only a human of the opposite sex could adequately remedy the single human's loneliness.

The key point is that Adam gives them names. This has often been taken to express Adam's power over them,[66] but there is no good reason to give it this meaning and most exegetes have now abandoned it.[67] (Moreover, if we did read it this way, we should have to take Adam's naming of Eve (Gen. 2:23 and 3:20) as an expression of his power over her.[68]) Naming is fundamentally about recognition.[69] Adam acknowledges the animals' place in the world. He takes an interest in them and distinguishes each from others, recognising the similarities and differences that belong to them by virtue of their creation by God. We might say that Adam is the first naturalist, classifying the species and giving them names, as Charles Pinches suggests:

> Adam is given the task of naming the animals, not according to their use for him, but as he, being in God's image, can see them in and for themselves. When we name and study species, we continue Adam's work.[70]

Alternatively, Adam has been seen as the first poet, since the human impulse to put things into words is the root of poetry.[71]

But naming is also the presupposition for relationship. Parents naming children are recognising them as persons in their own right and giving them the wherewithall to be identified as persons by other persons and thus to enter interpersonal relationships. The contrast between the animals and Eve in the Genesis story does not mean that Adam could not have significant relationships with the animals, only that they could not fill the special need that humans

Where the Wild Things Are

have for others who are different while also belonging to the same species. Adam's exclamation on first seeing the woman – 'This at last is bone of my bones and flesh of my flesh' (v 23) – recognises an other of the same species. It is not merely because the animals do not, for example, have language that they cannot meet Adam's greatest need, but because their 'otherness' is of a different order from Eve's. Yet this greater 'otherness' has a distinctive value of its own, even for Adam.

Otherness is not the same as alienation. Alienation from wild animals is the consequence of the loss of Eden. But the otherness of animals, as of wild nature more generally, is a good. Human experience of pleasure or delight in the otherness of other creatures is a sign that these creatures have value in themselves and for God. When we delight in the otherness of other creatures we recognise the independent value they have quite apart from us. It is part of the experience God gives to Job in Job 38—39. Our positive experience of otherness is not only a delight in the beauty of nature. We do not find all of nature beautiful. Many insects are not beautiful to many people. We sometimes find nature very strange, even repulsive. But we encounter a reality other than the human, something that we have not made our own, marked with our own preferences and values, turned into a human creation. In wild nature, we see something other than the reflection of ourselves. The effect that true wilderness has on us depends on its being a world in which we do not belong, and the good it does us depends, paradoxically, on the inherent value we recognise it to have entirely independently of us.

Commenting on the progressive loss of any nature independent of human control, McKibben says: 'the monster of our own egos is going to be reflected in everything around us.'[72] This is the route that bioengineering, to take only one example, is offering to take us. In a world where nothing is untouched by human interference and modification, we shall see only ourselves in everything and feel only pride or disgust, never humility or awe.[73]

This is not at all to denigrate human art and technology, or to forget that much of the nature we enjoy – in Britain, most of nature – has been modified by human presence and activity in ways we may not even notice. The endless variety of humanly modified forms of nature have their own value, but it is different from the special value that wild nature has precisely by being independent of us. Some forms of human art, such as painting, nature poetry or wildlife documentary films, may help us appreciate nature in itself, but they do so precisely not by attempting to replace it.

Encounter with the otherness of nature can be a sacrament of encounter with the greater otherness of God, and, conversely, the common loss of a sense of God in much of modern western society may not be unconnected with the fact that urban life now isolates most people from wild nature, and even from nature only moderately affected by human presence. In a city in the ancient world one was never far from nature, but to live in a city today is to live in a wholly humanised world that can seem even a human creation. Even the night sky, so familiar to all humans before modern forms of artificial light, is not easy to see in a city.

The way that encounter with the otherness of non-human nature can mediate an encounter with the otherness of God is not, in the biblical and Christian tradition, through a pantheistic sense of nature as divine, but through recognition of the otherness of other *creatures*, created by God. This is the experience of Job and the writer of Psalm 104. In the humanly created world it is easy to think ourselves gods; in encounter with the otherness of wild nature it is not. We find ourselves to be creatures in some kind of connection with other *creatures,* all of us creatures of God. The otherness of the creatures can evoke for us the qualitatively different otherness of God.

OUR FAMILY AND OTHER ANIMALS

Although this chapter is devoted to the Bible's portrayal of wild nature, it is convenient to add here some account of domestic animals in the biblical literature. Discussion of the Bible and the non-human creation rarely pays much attention to domestic animals. Yet these were a constant and irreplaceable feature of biblical people's lives and they appear frequently in the Bible, probably more often than wild animals do, for the obvious reason that people had far more contact with them than with most wild creatures. The Hebrew Bible regularly distinguishes the two classes of large land mammals: domestic animals (*behemah*, often translated 'cattle') and wild animals (*hayyah*)[74] or 'beasts of the earth' (*hayyah ha'aretz*). The occurrence of this distinction in programmatic catalogues of kinds of creatures with reference to creation, the Flood and the Noahic covenant (e.g. Gen. 1:24–25; 7:14 and 21; 8:1; and 9:10; cf. also Ps. 148:10) is especially significant, suggesting that the distinction belongs to the Creator's intentions. (Conversely there is no hint in the Bible that domestication of animals was other than a good thing for both the animals and humans.[75]) It is also significant that the domestic animals are absent from the otherwise complete list in Genesis 9:2, where the dominion is reformulated in the light of violent enmity between humans and other living creatures. Domestic animals are not to share 'the fear and dread' of humans that will protect humans from the danger posed by other creatures. They are assumed to be partners with humans, not even potential enemies.

Domestic animals are seen virtually as members of the extended human household, as we can see most clearly in the Sabbath commandment: 'you shall not do any work – you, or your son or your daughter, your male or female slave, or your ox or your donkey, or any of your livestock (*behemah*), or the resident alien in your towns' (Deut. 5:14; cf. Exod. 20:10). The real beneficiaries, of course, are the draft and pack animals, such as donkeys, mules and oxen, rather than sheep and goats. These working animals are considered helpers in the work of the farm, who, like human helpers, benefited from the produce that they helped to produce. In the laws of the Torah, such animals have 'owners' or 'lords' (*ba'al*), a word that also describes a woman's husband, and they can be treated very much as property with a monetary value (Exod. 21:33–36). But there are also laws designed to ensure their welfare, such as: 'You shall not muzzle an ox while it is treading out the grain' (Deut. 25:4).[76] The point is that 'an ox engaged in threshing is not to be prevented from feeding itself from the grain its hooves had beaten out'.[77] The animal is entitled to a share of the product of its work. Other laws are designed to prevent domestic animals from suffering, though they also benefit their owners (Deut. 22:14 and Exod. 23:4–5).

The biblical writers did not, of course, know that their domestic animals descended from wild ancestors. In most cases, the process of becoming domestic had taken place a very long time before biblical Israel existed.[78] Yet, at least in the book of Job, their resemblance to their wild equivalents is well recognised. When God's interrogation of Job arrives at the wild ass and the wild ox (Job 39:5–12), the message that these animals are quite beyond Job's capacity in any way to control them is reinforced by the contrast with their domestic opposite numbers. By contrast with these wild creatures, who cannot be put to work for humans or constrained to live in the human sphere, the domestic animals are, implicitly, understood to be docile and willing to take human direction. At first sight, it is surprising that the horse (39:19–25) is included with the wild animals in this catalogue, but probably the point is that the horse has wild characteristics that are evident when it is ridden into battle. It is fierce, aggressive, courageous and, crucially, has a will of its own. It shows that, even though the Bible often makes a clear distinction between wild and domestic animals, the difference is not absolute. Some domestic animals are 'wilder' than others.

A reason why domestic animals have been neglected in discussion of the Bible's portrayal of non-human nature may be that the justification for humans having domestic animals has become very controversial among many of those likely to be interested in this aspect of the Bible. For deep ecology, domestic animals are unnatural: humans have removed them from their native ecospheres and, by rearing and keeping them in artificial environments, disrupt the balance of nature. For advocates of animal rights, domestication is a kind of enslavement.[79] Clearly, neither of these approaches can be found in the Bible. The biblical writers assume that there just are domestic animals, different from the wild

Where the Wild Things Are

animals and by nature adapted to living in reciprocal relations with humans.[80] They belong to the created order of the world. Humans have not conquered them or removed them from their natural habitats. The human world is where they belong.

What we now know or can speculate about the domestication process is perhaps not too divergent from this biblical view. However it was that domestic animals became domestic, there is no doubt that, as they now exist, they are physically and mentally adapted to living in symbiosis with humans. Though some will seek the wild and adapt to conditions in the wild more readily than most, generally speaking, domestic animals are by nature dependent on human society and would not voluntarily leave it. Dogs, though descended from wolves, are not wolves and cannot 'revert' to being wolves. It is by no means clear how the process of domestication happened, but recent studies have discredited the idea that humans deliberately and knowingly turned wild animals into domestic ones. To say that they 'domesticated' animals is misleading because it suggests a one-sided process, something humans did to animals. More plausibly, domestication should be seen as a process of co-evolution, in which humans and animals developed relationships of mutual advantage.[81] Such relationships between species are common in nature, and humans are remarkable, not for the fact of such relationships, but in the number of them and the way they relate to agriculture and other, fairly distinctive, human ways of exploiting their environment.

Some animals, such as dogs and cats and perhaps pigs, seem to have more or less domesticated themselves, attaching themselves to human settlements for their own advantage and coming to be tolerated and then encouraged as humans found uses for them. Quite what happened in other cases is more debatable, but the phenomenon of domestication seems to have happened differently with different animals and in different places. It was not a strategy that ancient humans pursued in an attempt to put as many species to human use as possible. Deliberate strategy became a factor only when breeding, with the aim of developing certain characteristics and minimising others, took place, but this does not seem to have been a feature of the original processes that brought humans and other animals into symbiosis. Moreover, the actual relationships between humans and the various species of domestic animals vary quite widely in character, and the character and value of the associations can change over time. In the modern period, for example, pets (or 'companion animals') and livestock are usually quite distinct categories, but in earlier periods, including that of biblical Israel, animals kept purely as pets were uncommon (Job 41:5 is a rare biblical example), but affective relationships with farm animals and animals that people rode could easily develop and surely often did (a touching example is 2 Sam. 12:3). A shepherd's flock, for example, was small enough and the shepherd spent so much time with them (far more than with humans) that he or she knew their individual faces and gave them names (John 10:3).[82]

Thus domestication was not 'unnatural' (which implies an overly static idea of nature's good) or an exercise in human domination akin to slavery. This does not, of course, mean that humans cannot abuse their relationships with domestic animals. In fact, in the modern West, animal husbandry has largely been replaced by systematised brutality and exploitation quite unlike good farming practice in the past and in a different league of evil even from bad farming practice in the past. It cannot possibly be justified by reference to the Bible. Crucially, the Bible does not regard domestic animals as mere objects for people to use, but, like wild animals, as subjects of their own lives (e.g. Gen. 9:9 and 16; Num. 22:23–30; and Isa. 1:3).

Very instructive as to the biblical writers' views of the proper relationship between humans and their domestic animals is the frequent metaphorical use of the relationship between a shepherd and his or her sheep. It was a common metaphor for a king's relationship to his people, for which the Bible sometimes uses it, but it was therefore also an apt metaphor for God's relationship with his people. What the relationship demanded, however, was evidently not domination but caring responsibility. The shepherd becomes a model of selfless concern and activity for the welfare of

Where the Wild Things Are

the sheep. Famously, in Psalm 23, he leads the sheep to pasture and water, and he protects the sheep from harm. Even more vividly, in Ezekiel 34, God denounces the human 'shepherds' of his people for exploiting the sheep, not caring for them:

> Should not shepherds feed the sheep? ³You eat the fat, you clothe yourselves with the wool, you slaughter the fatlings; but you do not feed the sheep. ⁴You have not strengthened the weak, you have not healed the sick, you have not bound up the injured, you have not brought back the strayed, you have not sought the lost, but with force and harshness you have ruled them. (Ezek. 34:2b-4)

God then promises, as the true Shepherd of his flock, to do for them what the wicked shepherds have neglected to do (Ezek. 34:11–16). Jesus' understanding of himself as the Good Shepherd in John 10 is very much in the tradition of Ezekiel 34.[83]

Of course, shepherds care for sheep because they are useful to humans. As Proverbs 27:23–27 indicates, sheep and goats were valued primarily as a living resource supplying wool and milk (made into cheese), rather than for slaughtering and eating, though the latter was certainly not excluded.[84] The usefulness of the sheep for the human community (not, of course, for the shepherd alone) is entirely neglected when the shepherd's care for the sheep becomes a metaphorical ideal. In Ezekiel 34, it looks as though only the bad shepherds shear and eat the sheep. But this isolation of the benefit for the sheep from the benefit for humans is possible, in metaphorical use, because the real relationship is perceived as reciprocal. Sheep and humans both benefit. The wild animals, who would eat the sheep if the shepherd did not protect them and go in search of the strayed, do not benefit the sheep in any way. Moreover, when the humans do slaughter a lamb or a sheep, at least they could do so with respect and reverence for a life that, like all life, is precious and sacred to God.

Veterinary surgeon David Williams has an interesting comment on Psalm 23. He first cites the 'five freedoms' proposed by the

(British) Farm Animal Welfare Council (FAWC) as the key ingredients of welfare for farm animals:

(1) Freedom from thirst, hunger and malnutrition;
(2) Freedom from discomfort;
(3) Freedom from pain, injury and disease;
(4) Freedom to express normal behaviour;
(5) Freedom from fear and distress.[85]

Then he comments:

> Psalm 23 reads just like a poetic version of the FAWC freedoms ... needs met, appropriate environment, sufficient food and water, even protection at the hour of death. The shepherd's rod and staff (which could quite easily be seen [as] agents of domination) are comforting guides showing how dominion, properly executed, is beneficial for the animal. Surely goodness and mercy will follow the animal properly cared for throughout its life. Here is a paradigm of good animal welfare practice in Old Testament times, in Jesus' day and today.[86]

Proverbs 12:10

> The righteous person knows (*yada'*) the *nephesh* of their
>   domestic animal,
> but the compassion (*rahamim*) of the wicked person is cruel.
>   (my translation)[87]

Sometimes, a short text can pack a hefty punch. Biblical aphorisms, like those in Proverbs or in the teaching of Jesus, are designed to do so by provoking thought. In this case, the general sense of the first line is clear enough: a righteous person is considerate of their animal and attends to its needs for food or rest. But the precise meaning is more difficult, because the verb *yada'* (to know) and the noun *nephesh* (life, desire, feeling, person, soul) both have a wide range of meaning. But the occurrence of the same phrase in Exodus 23:9 is suggestive:

You shall not oppress a resident alien; you know (*yada'*) the heart (*nephesh*) of an alien, for you were aliens in the land of Egypt. (NRSV)

We might translate the phrase in this context as: 'you know what it's like to be an alien'. The Israelites knew what it was like because they'd been there themselves. Clearly, the owner of the animal does not know from experience what it is like to be an animal. But if we translate the phrase in Exodus in a more general way as: 'you can empathize with an alien', we may be closer to the meaning in Proverbs. What an alien feels is not obvious on the surface, but the Israelites can tell what he or she must be feeling inside. The animal's feelings are not obvious from the outside and it cannot voice them to its owner, but the good owner can tell how it's feeling.[88] We might say: 'The righteous person is attentive to the feelings of their animal.'[89] The statement refers to rather more than good will towards the animal. It portrays the farmer who has got to know the animal well enough to tell when it is needing to rest or gasping for a drink, and feels for the animal as one might for a human friend in such a case. Traditional farmers, unlike those who now practise intensive farming, could do this, as could people like Balaam, who rode the same donkey for years.[90] Such knowledge is available only through compassion.

The second line of the aphorism presumably means that, by comparison with the compassion of the righteous person, what the wicked consider their compassion is no better than cruelty. Bruce Waltke offers an example: 'today some farmers abuse chickens and livestock by reducing them to efficient machines and consider it a mercy to feed them the best grain to increase their production and/or fatten them for market!'[91] Compassion (*rahamim*) is a striking word in this context. It has an overtone of tenderness (cf. KJV: 'tender mercies'). It is a key attribute of God (Exod. 34:6), and both the noun and, especially, its cognate verb, are used in the Hebrew Bible very predominantly to refer to God's compassion. Most relevant is Psalm 145:9:

> The LORD is good to all,
> and his compassion is over all that he has made.

The righteous person's compassion for their animal is a reflection of God's own compassion for all his creatures. Robert Murray is correct to say that, by this aphorism, 'animals are brought within the sphere of human ethics',[92] but 'compassion' expresses more than this. It refers to a fundamental aspect of God's character, to which Jesus also referred when he said: 'Be merciful, just as your Father is merciful' (Luke 6:36). In the light of its Old Testament background, we can infer that Jesus here requires compassion for all our fellow creatures, animals as well as for humans.

FROM ALPHA TO OMEGA

In the first four chapters of this book, we have focused almost exclusively on the Old Testament, with just a few excursions into the New Testament at points where the New Testament picks up a theme from the Old. (See the sections on Matthew 6:25–33 and Romans 8:18–23 in Chapter 3, and the section on Mark 1:13 in Chapter 4.) There is a good reason for this: the Bible's theology of creation is to a large extent developed in the Old Testament and then presupposed in the New. We should never forget that the New Testament was never meant to be an independent collection of Christian Scriptures. The New Testament writers themselves assume the Old Testament as given, and the process of collecting and authorising their writings to form the New Testament canon was understood by the Church as a matter of supplementing the Old Testament, which already formed a canon of Scriptures recognised as authoritative for the Church. So it is not surprising that what is already well established in the Old Testament is not repeated in the New. The New Testament writings concentrate on the difference made by the fulfilment of the expectations of Old Testament prophecy through the coming of Jesus the Messiah. So what we find with regard to the non-human creation is a christological rendering of the Old Testament's understanding of creation. From the point of view of a sequential reading of the whole Bible, we might say that, in the New Testament, Jesus Christ joins the community of creation. But the New Testament writers do not themselves see it that way. In the light of the life, death and resurrection of Jesus, they perceive that there never was a time when he was not related to the whole of God's creation. The New

Testament does not replace the Old Testament's theology of creation, but it does reread it retrospectively in the light of Jesus Christ.

One result of the way the New Testament assumes the Old is that, whereas the Old Testament often depicts in some detail the huge variety of creatures who fill the earth, the sea and the sky, the New Testament mostly deploys only shorthand references to 'all things' or 'the whole creation'. It is easy for readers who do not have the non-human creation in mind to miss the fact that such general references are fully inclusive of all creatures. While it is true that the term 'world' (*kosmos*) often refers, at least primarily, to the human world (e.g. Col. 1:6, and the frequent use in John's Gospel), and this is occasionally true also of 'the whole creation' (*pasa ktisis*: Mark 16:15 and Col. 1:23), the frequently occurring phrase 'all things' (*ta panta*)[1] is certainly designed to include all creatures, as is the phrase 'heaven and earth' (e.g. Matt. 28:18). One difference from the Old Testament is that such references in the New Testament often rather clearly include the heavenly world of the angels, whereas this is less common in the Old Testament.

While it is understandable that some readers of the New Testament get the impression that it is much less interested in the non-human creation than the Old Testament (or parts of it) is, this impression is at least partly the result of not giving sufficient weight to the inclusive references, such as 'all things'. While it is not common for the New Testament to show interest *distinctively* in non-human creatures, it regularly *includes* them in the general category of the creation, which God made, for which God cares and provides, and for which God intends an eternal future. In the New Testament, faith in Jesus Christ and salvation through Jesus Christ do not separate humans from the rest of creation, as they have sometimes been held to do in later Christian thinking. On the contrary, they unite humans even more closely with other creatures, since the New Testament, as we shall see, depicts Jesus Christ as himself closely related to all creatures.

THE BIBLICAL META-NARRATIVE

In order to appreciate the way the New Testament relates Jesus Christ to the whole creation, we need to consider the biblical meta-narrative. For the Bible tells what is now often called a meta-narrative (an alternative term, with the same meaning, is 'grand narrative'). A meta-narrative is a story we tell about the meaning of everything. It is a comprehensive sketch of the total narrative that encompasses all the other stories we tell about ourselves or the world. Marxism, for example, in its classical form, as a scheme of necessary historical stages of different economic structures of class relationship, issuing in a future classless society, was a meta-narrative. The idea of progress that has dominated the modern age in the West is a meta-narrative. Despite the rejection of all meta-narratives by postmodernists, the idea of progress is not yet dead. Its current metamorphosis into a narrative of economic globalisation, technological salvation and the global triumph of liberal democracy is the most powerful of current meta-narratives. A self-conscious alternative to it is the Islamic meta-narrative, especially as understood by radical Islamists who use it to oppose western domination.

The Bible's meta-narrative is a very ambitious one, since it runs from eternity to eternity, more especially from creation to new creation. The beginning of the Bible's great story and the future end of that story are, necessarily, told in symbolic, mythical or parabolic form, since they fall outside the kind of reality about which we can have literal knowledge, and so these biblical beginnings and endings need not compete with our developing scientific knowledge of the universe. The beginning and the end of the Bible's meta-narrative are recounted in theologically meaningful images, while the historical story that takes place between them is given us in the Bible in a variety of different sorts of historical writing and related material. The meta-narrative has some prominent stages: there is the story of the human race and all the nations that comprise it; there is the eventful story of God's special people Israel, whose calling is to model, for the sake of all nations, what it means to be a people of God; then, within Israel's story, there is the story of Jesus, his birth, ministry, death, resurrection and exaltation to heaven; and there is the story of how, through Jesus and the mission of his Church, Israel's story expands to include all the nations and the whole world; this story is leading to the goal that has been in view from the beginning, when God, in an act of new creation, will take his whole creation into his own eternity.

In that short summary of the meta-narrative, I have included the Gospel story of Jesus as one of the key stages of the narrative. This does less than justice to its key importance for the whole narrative. We could call it the master story, the story that holds the key to the meaning and course of the rest. But, in a sense, the story of Jesus is even more than that, because, when we view the whole meta-narrative from the point of view of the story of Jesus, as the New Testament writers do, then we see that the whole story of the world is also Jesus' own story. We can only adequately tell the story of Jesus by bringing in the whole creation and the whole of its trans-historical story, and conversely, we can only fully and adequately tell the story of the whole world by relating it to Jesus. Of course, because neither story – neither the story of the world nor the story of Jesus – is yet complete, even the Bible can tell the story of the world and the story of Jesus only in a provisional form. Only at the future consummation of all things, what the New Testament calls the coming of Christ in glory to judgement, will we see the final meaning of the world in its relationship to Jesus Christ, and the fullest significance of Jesus Christ when his relationship to all reality is laid before us by God.

In the book of Revelation, Jesus Christ says: 'I am the Alpha and the Omega, the first and the last, the beginning and the end' (22:13). Since alpha and omega are the first and last letters of the Greek alphabet, the three phrases are equivalent in meaning. They are divine titles (cf. Rev. 1:8 and 21:6) that stem originally from Isaiah, where God declares himself 'the First and the Last' (Isa. 41:4; 44:6; and 48:12), meaning that he is the sole Creator of all things, sovereign Lord of all history, and the goal of all things and all history. He encompasses, as it were, the whole meta-narrative of the created world. As its origin and goal, the whole story is his.

From the perspective of the New Testament and, in this case, the book of Revelation in particular, the historical human Jesus, the Messiah, shares the divine identity of the one God. He too is 'the Alpha and the Omega, the first and the last'. He is the origin and goal of the whole history of the created world. To call him 'the Alpha and the Omega' is to summarise that history as christological meta-narrative.

THE META-NARRATIVE AS ECO-NARRATIVE

For this chapter, the christological character of the whole biblical meta-narrative is vital. But also indispensable for the theme of this chapter is this: that the biblical meta-narrative is about the relationship between God, human beings *and* the non-human creation. It has at least three key participants, each of them a figure for more than one participating subject. But, of these three participants, God, humanity and the rest of creation, so often in Christian thought the third participant has been minimised, degraded or forgotten altogether. So often, in the Christian tradition, we have thought of the non-human creation merely as a stage on which the drama of the history of God and humans is being played out – and a temporary stage, at that, due to be dismantled and removed when the story reaches its final climax. Even worse, so often, in the Christian tradition, we have thought of human embeddedness in nature as a fate from which humans need to be liberated. I hope it is already apparent to readers of this book that none of this religious disparagement of the non-human creation comes from the Bible. The Bible is full of material about the relationship of humans to the rest of creation, partly at least because for people in biblical times it was an inescapable, taken-for-granted aspect of human life lived close to the soil and to non-human creatures. The trouble is that, so often, Christian readers of Scripture have not attended seriously to such material. They have thought of it as just part of the historical context, the sort of lives people lived then, and that therefore it can be left aside when it comes to considering the message and significance of biblical texts. The message, it has so often been assumed, must be about humans and God. Alternatively, such biblical material has been considered no more than poetic imagery deployed to tell us about humans and God. Now that contemporary human society has once again woken up to the absolute seriousness of the way humans relate to the rest of nature, we must read the Bible with our eyes retrained to see that the Bible also takes our relationship to the non-human creation with absolute seriousness.

We could imagine the threefold relationship between God, humans and the rest of creation as a triangle, with these three key participants in the meta-narrative occupying the three corners, and the sides of the triangle standing for the relationship of each to the others.[2] For some purposes, it might be better to think of a four-sided figure, crossed by lines that link opposite corners. The four corners would represent God, humans, other living creatures, and the inanimate creation, each of which has its own relationships with the other three. This representation would do justice to the fact that Genesis 1 and many other passages (e.g. Gen. 2:19–20; 6:7; and 9:2, 5, 10, 15 and 16) draw a significant distinction between living creatures and inanimate nature (including plants), attributing to humans much more commonality with the former than with the latter. Genesis 1 and Psalm 104 treat inanimate nature as the environment or (better) habitat of living creatures. This differs significantly from the modern tendency in 'environmental' discourse to treat the whole of nature, including wildlife and inanimate nature, as 'the environment' – i.e. the human environment. The Bible recognises living creatures as subjects of their own lives in a way that is not true of plants or mountains. This is certainly not to deny that plants and mountains have value in themselves. In Genesis 1, where God pronounces good the creations of each of the first three days, before the appearance of animate creatures, and in Psalm 148, where animate and inanimate creatures are all called, indiscriminately, to worship God, it is clear that inanimate creatures do have value for God in themselves, not only as the habitats of living creatures. Nor should we lose sight of the inter-connections and interdependence of all sorts of creatures which modern ecology reveals in scientific detail, but which the

Bible also recognises in a general way. Nevertheless, living creatures are distinctive and should be treated as such. The modern objectifying and instrumentalising of them in such practices as factory farming are hideous crimes against God's creatures which we could not tolerate if we recognised them as, for example, partners in God's covenant with Noah and the animals.

Of course, the Bible is a book for humans. As far as the line(s) in our diagrams (triangular or quadrilateral) that connect God with the non-human creation are concerned, the Bible focuses on the extent to which God's relationship to the non-human creation is relevant to humans. We need to know enough about it to understand and to live our own relationships to God and to other creatures and the way they converge. But, so long as we avoid the anthropocentric fantasy that God relates to the rest of creation only via humans, it is easy to realise that there must be a great deal about God's relationship to other creatures that we shall never know – at least, this side of the end of history. There are questions about which we can only speculate: are other creatures conscious of God, perhaps in quite different ways from humans? Are there forces of evil at work in the non-human creation quite apart from our relationship to it? Why is there suffering and death in the animal world? What is going on, from the point of view of God's purposes for creation, in those vast reaches of the universe beyond this Earth? Intelligent speculation, deploying all that we do know (including our ever-expanding scientific understanding of the universe), is not to be excluded, but we need to retain a reverent tentativeness about any provisional conclusions we reach. In thinking biblically and theologically about the non-human creation, we tread the edge of mystery, as we do when we think of God. It will not be surprising if, like Job, we often find ourselves both awestruck and baffled.

What we can know is that the rest of creation matters to God and matters to our own relationship with God. These tenets are intrinsic to the Christian meta-narrative as the Bible tells it. Why then has the Christian tradition so often lost sight of that? A large part of the answer must be that it has been influenced by other current meta-narratives, other worldviews, other cultural perceptions, which in one way or another have downgraded the non-human creation. In the early centuries of Christianity, Platonism (especially the later versions known as Middle Platonism and Neoplatonism) offered both advantages and dangers for Christian appropriation of its intellectual resources. Platonism understood the world in terms of a strong matter/spirit dualism, in which matter was not seen as evil (as in Gnosticism), but certainly as radically inferior to spirit. Spirit was eternal, matter transient. Humans straddled the dualism, having both a physical body and an immaterial mind (or soul or spirit). But the real person was the immaterial part. The desire and destiny of the human mind (spirit, soul) was to be free of the body and to join or to rejoin the world of pure Being, which was the world of God and the gods. Thus humans were encumbered with a physical connection to the rest of the material world only in this life. They were in essence quite different from it. In the early centuries of the Church, Christian theologians struggled with this aspect of Platonism, and their strong bulwark against an unacceptable degree of Platonising of Christianity was the belief in bodily resurrection, both that of Jesus and that of humans in the eschatological future. God made humans to be bodily persons, an integral unity of spirit and body, and the bodily resurrection of Jesus demonstrated beyond Christian doubt that human destiny is not to be pure spirits liberated from matter, but to be bodily persons, transformed, of course, but transformed as whole persons, body, soul and spirit. In principle, this point was secured for the mainstream Christian tradition, but in practice the influence of the Platonic notion that our destiny is to leave aside the body, and with it the rest of the material creation, has remained very influential. It received a modern boost from nineteenth-century idealism, which argued in its own way that mind or spirit is the true reality of the world.

However, in the modern period this kind of matter/spirit dualism has probably been exceeded in influence by a peculiarly modern phenomenon: the modern scientific-technological project to subjugate the whole of nature to human use, and thereby engineer utopia. The project was born theoretically in the mind of Francis Bacon at the beginning of the seventeenth century and has produced, as we know, not only much that we value but also the contemporary ecological crisis. It has produced, in fact, a complex muddle in which much of what we value is actually responsible for our ecological woes.[3] As Thomas Berry puts it, 'our supposed progress towards an ever-improving human situation is bringing us a wasteworld instead of a wonderworld'.[4] That this was not anticipated was due to a certain sort of meta-narrative or worldview.

The modern project of technological domination of nature worked with a different kind of dualism from the Platonic one: a dualism of nature and human history. Nature was there to be transformed into something of human use, something that, from the point of view of human benefit, would be much better than nature untouched by humans. Further, what the modern project was to achieve was the progressive liberation of humans from nature and the progressive sovereignty of humans over nature. Our crippling dependence on nature would be replaced by a free supremacy founded on our subjection of nature wholly to our designs. So, in a sense, the modern project, like Platonism, thought of human destiny as freedom from the material world, but in the modern project nature would be abolished by serving as the resource from which humans would fashion a purely human world. Of course, nature has hit back with a vengeance. But the dream of technological re-creation of the world continues in the minds of the technophiles who now work with bioengineering and artificial intelligence for a world in which there will no longer be any nature independent of us. In these dreams, the Platonic dualism returns in a new form, for the future belongs not to human beings, in their bodily wholeness, but to pure intelligence, minds transferred into machines, minds that can remake their own material encasement and achieve intellectual immortality. We should be deploying the Christian belief in the resurrection of the body against these anti-human technological aspirations, just as the Fathers did against Platonic dualism.

Christian theology in the modern period frequently colluded with the technological project of domination, largely because it was committed to human betterment. What is particularly relevant to this book is the effect on modern interpretation of the Bible. The modern dualism of nature and human history was read into the Bible. In the Old Testament, it was salvation history that mattered, not creation theology, which acquired the stigma of nature religion. The God of Israel was not a nature god, but a God who acted and was known in Israel's history. Creation and history were (strangely, as it now seems to many scholars) played off against each other, to the detriment of creation.[5] The same dichotomy carried over into New Testament interpretation, where salvation was seen as a purely anthropological matter impacting human history or, in some versions, only the human individual. In its own way, New Testament interpretation reflected and tacitly endorsed the modern meta-narrative of human emancipation from nature.

Of course, biblical interpretation never takes place in a cultural vacuum, and often it is a cultural transition that makes it possible to recognise, with hindsight, the mistakes that previous interpreters made. The more holistic, integrated and ecological view of the world that has become available to us in recent decades (which is not to say that it has triumphed over the modern dichotomy of nature and history) helps us to read the Bible differently. It becomes clear that the Bible's meta-narrative assumes that humans live in mutuality with the natural world, not domination, and especially not with the aim of emancipation from nature, but in complex mutuality. The mandate of human dominion in Genesis 1 plays a part only within this reciprocity between humans and other creatures. For the biblical meta-narrative, history is the story of humans in relationship with the rest of creation. Salvation is not the replacement but the renewal of creation. God's purpose in history and in the eschatological future does not abstract humans from nature, but heals the human relationship with nature. Only after fully appreciating that human embeddedness in, and solidarity with, the rest of creation, can we then understand rightly the

From Alpha to Omega

sense in which humanity is in certain ways highly distinctive by comparison with the rest of creation on this Earth. The unparalleled diversity of human habitats and forms of life has given humans an understanding of the world as a whole that enables us to take appropriate responsibility – not by any means total responsibility, but appropriate responsibility, under God, for the world as a whole. The unparalleled power that humans have to affect the rest of creation on this Earth makes that responsibility momentous.

This is by way of summarising much that has been our concern in previous chapters. The purpose of the summary is to help us envisage the New Testament's meta-narrative as a story about Jesus Christ that encompasses humanity and other creatures in reciprocal relationship – a christological eco-narrative. We shall focus on a series of major New Testament passages and themes in which the relationship of Jesus Christ to the whole creation is in view. The one with which we begin offers the fullest overview of such a christological eco-narrative.

THE COSMIC CHRIST IN COLOSSIANS

Colossians 1:15–20

He is the image of the invisible God,
the firstborn over all creation;
[16]for *in him all things in heaven and on earth* were created,
things visible and invisible,
whether thrones or dominions
or rulers or powers –
all things have been created *through him* and *for him*.
[17]He himself is before *all things*,
and *in him all things* hold together.

[18]He is the head of the body, the church;
he is the beginning,
the firstborn from the dead,
so that he might be pre-eminent in *all things*.
[19]For *in him* all the fullness (of God)[6] was pleased to dwell,

²⁰and *through him* to reconcile *to him all things,*
whether *on earth or in heaven,*
by making peace through the blood of his cross. (NRSV adapted)

EXEGETICAL COMMENTS ON THE COLOSSIAN HYMN

This passage is usually called a hymn, and it certainly has a poetic quality that invites us to read it as a structured and concentrated embodiment of meaning, while its pervasive focus on Jesus Christ makes it almost doxological in character. Whether, as many scholars think, it already existed before Paul[7] took it over for use in this letter, at the same time making some editorial adaptations, is of little relevance to us now (I am inclined to think that poetic passages like this in Paul's letters were composed by Paul for other purposes and then inserted into the letters). But we do need to notice that the passage is structured as two strophes,[8] dealing respectively with the creation of all things in Christ and the reconciliation of all things in Christ. In the text above, I have italicised the obvious verbal parallels between the two strophes:

> in both Christ is the firstborn;
> the phrase 'all things' recurs (four times in strophe 1, twice in strophe 2);
> both strophes refer to all things in heaven and on Earth (or vice versa);
> in both strophes Christ's relation to all things is described by use of the three prepositions 'in' (*en*), 'through' (*dia*) and 'for'/'to' (*eis*).

One of the things that the hymn impresses on us is the cosmic scope of both creation and reconciliation – through the phrases 'all creation', 'all things' (6 times) and the further specification of all things as both visible and invisible, both in heaven and on Earth. The inclusion of the whole created world in both creation and reconciliation could hardly be more emphatically stated. The scope of reconciliation is as wide as the scope of creation.

Equally impressive is the emphasis on Jesus Christ (whereas God is explicitly mentioned only to define Christ's relationship to him at the outset of the hymn). Joseph Sittler writes: 'These verses sing out their triumphant music between two huge and steady poles – "Christ" and "all things".'[9] The passage is the most thoroughly christological summary of the biblical meta-narrative to be found in the New Testament. It attributes 'pan-temporal and pan-cosmic significance to the person of Christ'.[10] We need to be clear that it is the human Jesus Christ, the incarnate Son, who is the subject of the whole passage. Only in his humanity is Christ 'the image of the invisible God', as the first line of the hymn describes him.[11] In other words, although the Christ of the first strophe is undoubtedly the pre-existent Christ, he is perceived as, in effect, already incarnate. This is in fact the way that Paul usually speaks of the pre-existent Christ.[12] Here the identification of the pre-existent Christ as Jesus has to be taken very seriously, because Paul does not merely call the pre-existent one Jesus, but describes him as 'the image of the invisible God'. Even before creation, the pre-existent Christ was already destined to be the one who would make God visibly present in his world by entering creaturely existence as Jesus. In fact, if we take the second strophe into account, it is not simply Jesus who is the icon of the invisible God, but the *crucified* Jesus. Jesus' sacrificial and shameful death[13] illuminates, more than anything else, his significance for the whole creation.

Therefore the hymn is not an invitation to think of a cosmic Christ who is 'bigger than Jesus'[14] but to recognise the universal significance precisely of Jesus Christ, the man in whom the fullness of God was pleased to dwell. The hymn is a very remarkable instance of the recurrent relationship between universality and particularity in biblical theology. Particularity is not dissolved in universality, but remains, as it were, the essential focus of universal significance. What the first strophe says about the created world concerns its relationship to the man Jesus Christ, because the agent of its creation was the one destined to be, and so already identifiable as, Jesus Christ.

That Christ was 'the firstborn of all creation' cannot, in view of what follows, mean that he was the first creature to be created, but rather that he precedes all creation, and yet has such a close relationship to it that he has the status of the firstborn in relation to all creatures, the supremacy of the firstborn over them (cf. Ps. 89:28). He is 'the firstborn from the dead' in a somewhat different sense, as the one who, risen from the dead, has pioneered resurrection and new creation for the whole of creation. The parallel between his relationship to creation and his relationship to new creation is assisted by calling him 'the beginning', a term usually associated with the beginning of creation (Gen. 1:1; Ps. 102:25; Prov. 8:22; John 1:1; Heb. 1:10; and Rev. 3:14). Finally, the parallel is encoded in the prepositional phrases: in him, through him, for/to him. Such sets of prepositions were standardly used to speak of God's relationship to the world. God himself is the origin, agent and goal of his creation (cf. Rom. 11:36). Here it is Jesus Christ who is included in the whole of the divine relationship to the world. He shares God's relation to the world, both in its creation and in its reconciliation, just as he is also the creaturely icon and dwelling of God within creation.

The effect of all this is to relate Jesus Christ intimately to the whole creation, and thereby to underline most emphatically the continuity between creation and new creation, especially in scope. The Christ who created all things and for whom they were created, the Christ who holds everything together, is the Christ who can and does reconcile all things. For the first readers of Colossians it was evidently 'the powers' who were of special concern, that is the creatures, so enigmatic to us, who are described as 'thrones or dominions or rulers or powers'. The first strophe is so constructed as to make absolutely unambiguous that they were created, along with everything else, in, through and for Jesus Christ:

> in him *all things* in heaven and on earth *were created*,
>> things visible and invisible,
>>> whether thrones or dominions
>>> or rulers or powers –
> *all things have been created* through him and for him.

The repetition of the statement that all things were created encloses the list of the powers, who are probably all classified as 'things invisible', although some scholars think they should be divided between 'things visible' and 'things invisible', and so understood to include both spiritual powers and earthly powers.[15] Whether or not that is the case, the hymn is concerned to stress that, whatever powers there may be in the world, none are independent of Christ, all were created by him, and therefore also all have been 'reconciled' by and to him. The Colossian Christians who feared such powers are assured that Christ is supreme over them all (cf. also 2:10 and 15), both as their Creator and as their Reconciler.

The unstated implication must be that these powers (or some of them), have, in the interval, as it were, between the two strophes, strayed from or exceeded their God-given role in the creation. Perhaps Paul is unwilling to be too specific about this. About the origins of evil the Bible is characteristically reticent. In some sense, however, the powers need to be pacified (something that is described in a more military image in 2:15). The second strophe's statement that all things have been reconciled must presumably be understood in accordance with the 'inaugurated eschatology' of Paul and other New Testament writers. The cross has achieved this result in principle, but it has yet to be fully implemented. The new creation is far from complete as yet. But the Colossian Christians need have no doubt that they themselves are no longer subject to hostile powers (1:13).

The whole meta-narrative thus summarised is presented by the hymn as both the story of the whole creation and the story of Jesus Christ. The two are intrinsically related. Because Christ is the creator of all things, the destiny of all things is bound up with his. Because all things were made 'for him', he will ensure that they reach that goal. This means that the Gospel story – the story of the life, death and resurrection of Jesus – is focal and decisive for all creation. As Marianne Meye Thompson puts it, 'what happens to Christ in microcosm is what happens to the whole world in macrocosm'.[16] The fullness of God in him is the intensive presence of the God who fills heaven and earth. His sacrificial death identifies him with the whole of the suffering and perishing creation. His resurrection inaugurates the renewal of all creation. The whole narrative is thus highly particular in its focus on the story of Jesus Christ and at the same time holistic in its embrace of the whole creation. Any Christian attempt to understand creation as a whole must likewise see all in the light of Jesus Christ and the Gospel story.

Through Christ, 'all things, whether on earth or in heaven', are reconciled to Christ.[17] This general statement need not imply that every creature is in a state of enmity with Christ and needs to be individually reconciled. This can hardly be true of the faithful angels in heaven, and it is hard to see how it could be true of, for example, trees. The meaning is rather that the whole creation, whose harmony has been disrupted by the violence of those who are alienated from their Creator, is brought into a state of peace by the reconciliation of those creatures. However, the 'powers', so prominent in the hymn's account of creation, must be among the objects of reconciliation. The four terms for the powers – thrones, dominions, rulers, powers – all refer to political entities, and it is therefore appropriate that reconciliation is also primarily a political metaphor.[18] It alludes to a process whereby political powers that are at enmity are brought into a relationship of peace. The reference to the *cross* (rather than simply death) is also, of course, political, in that Jesus was executed by the political authorities (cf. 1 Cor. 8:6, where it is debatable whether 'the rulers of this age' are human or invisible authorities). Whether or not the powers in Colossians are entirely superhuman, they certainly made themselves felt in the human political process that led to Jesus' death. Paradoxically, through precisely his submission to such a death, Jesus reconciled the powers to himself. The hymn refers both to reconciliation to Christ and to making peace. It may be that while the former is the reconciliation of the creation to Christ himself, overcoming its alienation from him, the latter is the resulting relationship among and between creatures. Peace is here not merely the absence of conflict, but the wholeness, harmony and well-being of the whole creation that transpires when the creatures are in right relationship with each other.

The relevance of the hymn to its first readers in Colossae is therefore not simply that Christ shares the supremacy of God over all things, even the powers. It also says something about the implication of this supremacy for the created order and goodness of the world. In their fear of the hostile powers, in their sense of domination by unfriendly fate, the Colossians lack confidence in the ultimate goodness of the created order. The hymn tells them that Christ is God's guarantee of this. The powers are ultimately subject to the wise and good purpose of God for his creation. Against the rebellious powers this purpose has reasserted itself conclusively in the death and resurrection of Jesus. The cross may appear a success for the forces of chaos that derange and destroy the good order of creation, but in the mystery of God's purpose the cross is the sacrifice that makes peace, restoring the good order of the world, making creation whole again. Rather than resorting to other means of warding off the enmity of the powers, the Colossian Christians can have confidence that Christ himself is the wisdom of God restoring the wholeness of creation.

ECOLOGICAL REFLECTIONS ON THE COLOSSIANS HYMN

(1) The hymn offers a holistic vision of the whole creation integrated in Jesus Christ. It is he who 'holds it all together'. He is intimately related to the whole, and the meaning of the whole creation consists in having Jesus Christ as its source, its focus, its healer and its goal. Conversely, Jesus Christ is to be understood most fully in his relationship to God and to the whole creation, not only to humans. This is the sense in which 'the cosmic Christ is bigger than Jesus' – not that the cosmic Christ is anyone or anything other than Jesus, but that Jesus' full significance is found in his relationship to all creation. The prepositional phrases ('in him', 'through him', 'for him') are all about relationality. So as well as the interconnectedness of all creatures among themselves, they are all also intimately connected to Jesus Christ. He is their goal in

the sense that this relationship to Christ is what will in the end constitute the peace of the whole creation. To see creation whole we must see it in relation to the crucified and risen Jesus.

(2) This holism does not, however, mean that Christ is in any obvious way revealed in the cosmic order as it is. There is cosmic order, but there is also cosmic disorder that puts a question mark against Christ's lordship over the world. To recognise the world as Christ's, we have to recognise the reconciliation of all things through his cross, which presupposes pre-existing disharmony. Contextualising this approach in the contemporary world, Jürgen Moltmann writes:

> Today a cosmic christology has to confront Christ the redeemer with a nature which human beings have plunged into chaos, infected with poisonous waste and condemned to universal death; for it is only this Christ who can save men and women from their despair and preserve nature from annihilation.[19]

In such a context, Jesus Christ is related to the world as the one who, through his cross, reconciles all things and also as the one who, through his resurrection (as 'the firstborn from the dead'), renews all things. Thus to see creation whole we must see it in relation to the *crucified and risen* Jesus.

(3) We may therefore understand the crucified and risen Christ to be that hidden mystery of the world which is revealed in the Gospel. God's secret purpose at work in the whole creation took visible shape in Jesus Christ.[20] From the creation itself alone we could not tell that its destiny is peace and especially not that the way to that peace is not through violent conquest but through self-giving love. Modern science and especially Darwinian evolution have revealed, far more than most ancient people realised, the extent to which violence is part and parcel of the whole process of the world:

> The universe, earth, life and consciousness are all violent processes. The basic terms in cosmology, geology, biology

and anthropology all carry a heavy charge of tension and violence. Neither the universe as a whole nor any part of the universe is especially powerful ... Life emerges and advances by the struggle of species for more complete life expression. Humans have made their way amid the harshness of the natural world and have imposed their violence on the natural world. Among themselves humans have experienced unending conflict.[21]

This is one-sided. In evolution, for example, species collaborate as well as conflict. But there is no denying that violence is integral to the process. That God has definitively transcended that violence through the self-giving love of God in Christ is what the Gospel reveals about the whole creation.[22]

(4) The enmity and violence in the created world certainly have something to do with 'the powers'. It seems very likely that Paul is referring to unseen spiritual forces, of a kind that the Colossian Christians felt determined their fate and was responsible for the evils in their lives. But of course these unseen forces had very tangible dimensions: natural disasters, sickness, death, oppressive political and social structures. Paul is not necessarily endorsing the ways in which the Colossians thought about such powers, but affirming that, whatever hostile powers there might be, in heaven or on earth, Christ has pacified them, at least in the sense of having definitively established the peace that is to prevail throughout the creation. In our contemporary context, we might appropriately apply this insight to the forces at work in the current destruction of nature: the global economic system, consumerism with the addiction to excess that it promotes, the seemingly unavoidable 'short-termism' of even the most democratic political systems. Such realities of our world may seem out of human control, subjecting us to their fateful direction rather than implementing some collective will. Their hostility to God's purpose is more than the sum of human intentions to despoil and destroy God's world. In such a context, we may understand Christ's pacification of such powers as taking effect through us, as we confront them and seek peace

between humans and the rest of creation despite their seeming supremacy.

(5) Yet the issue of 'the powers' also raises the most difficult question in ecotheology: as well as the damage that humans have done to creation, is there also something wrong in the natural world itself, irrespective of our human presence in it, something that was wrong long before there were humans at all? In traditional theological terminology the question is: is nature fallen?[23] At one time it was possible to suppose that suffering and death in the non-human world were a consequence of the fall of Adam and Eve. Our scientific understanding of the history of life on the planet makes this approach impossible for us, since if there is something wrong in nature it was wrong long before humans appeared on the scene. Some would therefore see suffering and death in the non-human creation as the work of malign spiritual powers, who, like the powers in the Colossians hymn, were created good but chose to oppose God and spoil his creation. Against this, it has to be recognised that anything remotely like the development of life on this planet over millions of years is inconceivable without animal death (and, of course, plant death), while the violence and suffering of the evolutionary process (the aspect of the matter that seems most unequivocally an evil)[24] seem to be indivisible from the value the process produces in 'complexity, diversity, excellence of adaptation'.[25] It does not seem possible to have the good of this creative process without the evil. If this is attributed to the intervention of malign powers, then it would seem that these powers are so extensively responsible for the character of life on the planet as to be virtually its creators. This is in effect the Gnostic solution: the creation of the material world is the work of an evil and incompetent lesser god. These points belong in the present discussion because they illustrate how difficult it would be to cast 'the powers' of the Colossian hymn in such a role. After all, the overall effect of the hymn is to establish the fundamental goodness of the world that Christ himself has created, as well as reconciled. My own impression, from considering the very real problem that animal suffering raises for the

goodness of God and his creation, is that the Bible offers very few hints of a solution other than the eschatological one: that the whole creation will be liberated from the evils it now suffers, both humanly inflicted and otherwise.[26] We may have to be content to say simply that creation is not yet perfect.

THE COSMIC CHRIST IN THE PROLOGUE TO THE GOSPEL OF JOHN

In the beginning was the Word,
and the Word was with God,
and the Word was God.
[2]He was in the beginning with God.
[3]All things came into being through him,
and without him not one thing came into being.
What has come into being [4]in him was life,
and the life was the light of all people.
[5]The light shines in the darkness,
and the darkness did not overcome it ...
[9]The true light, which enlightens everyone, was coming into
the world.
[10]He was in the world, and the world came into being
through him;
yet the world did not know him ...
[14]And the Word became flesh and lived among us,
and we have seen his glory,
the glory as of a father's only son, full of grace and truth.
(John 1:1–5, 9–10 and 14)

All four of the Gospels begin their story of Jesus by in some way connecting it with the Old Testament narrative, indicating that it should be read as a continuation and climax of that narrative. Matthew begins by tracing Jesus' genealogy from Abraham, thereby resuming the whole biblical story from Genesis 12 onwards. Mark begins with a prophecy of Isaiah, while Luke sets his opening narrative in the Jerusalem Temple. But John's Gospel alone begins by evoking the fully cosmic scope of the biblical meta-narrative. He begins again where Genesis began, with the phrase 'in the beginning'. Any reader or hearer of John's Gospel who knew the Hebrew Scriptures, even a little, would immediately recognise the famous opening words of Genesis, while a well-informed reader might remember that another biblical creation account (Prov. 8:22–31) also begins at 'the beginning'. But the Gospel's starting point is not even the initial act of creation. It takes 'the beginning' in Genesis to refer to the divine eternity 'before' creation. John's narrative starts as far back as it is conceivably possible to start, the eternity in which God already intended creation, but before he spoke his word to bring the world into existence.

The echoes of Genesis continue in the images of life, light and darkness (John 1:4–5 and 7–9). But we should not imagine that John intends to replace the creation account in Genesis. He presupposes it. Therefore he gives no detail about what God created, but refers to the whole creation simply as 'all things' (1:3), which was in Jewish literature a frequent way of referring summarily to the whole of God's creation. All the rich detail of Genesis 1 is thereby summed up. The non-human creation, not only humanity, is in view in verse 3. John is not replacing Genesis 1, but he is offering his readers or hearers a way of reading the Genesis account in the light of his Gospel's story of Jesus. By introducing Jesus Christ at the earliest point at which one could possibly begin any narrative, God's eternity, John reads the whole biblical meta-narrative as also the story of Jesus, just as the Colossians hymn does. The pre-incarnate Christ, whom John calls the Word, belonged to the eternal being of God, and it was this Word who created all things. Already in Genesis 1 it is by his word that God creates, i.e. he brings things into existence by speaking. Hidden in this feature of the Genesis text, John discovers the eternal, divine Word, who – we discover later in the Prologue – became incarnate in the world as the man Jesus Christ. In this way, John situates his story of Jesus on Earth in the widest possible temporal and spatial context.

While 'all things' is the most comprehensive term for creation, 'the world' (*kosmos*: 1:9–10) is probably limited to the world

From Alpha to Omega

beneath the sky, excluding the heavens where God dwells. It has a peculiarly varying usage in John's Gospel, where it occurs no less than seventy-eight times. Already in verse 10 of the Prologue we can see it move from being the whole terrestrial creation, which the Word created and, in incarnation, entered, to meaning the human inhabitants of the world, who are the ones who 'did not know' their Creator when he came into the world. Mostly in the Gospel, the *kosmos* has this sense of humans in the world, but the wider sense also recurs (17:5 and 24). Verse 10 of the Prologue also illustrates how easily the reference to humans can gain a strongly negative connotation, whereby often in the Gospel 'the world' refers to the system of human life in its hostility to God (e.g. 8:23 and 15:18–19). This is its most common significance in John, but the more neutral sense is not entirely excluded. The Gospel is overwhelmingly concerned with the salvation of humans, but the predominance of the term *kosmos* in the Gospel does retain at least a reminder that humans are part of the wider creation. In non-biblical usage, the word normally refers to the whole natural world, only occasionally to its human inhabitants exclusively. When John sums up the Gospel's story in the famous words that begin, 'God so loved the world' (3:16), the focus is undoubtedly on humanity, but an awareness that humanity belongs to a wider created reality whose Creator loves it should not be excluded. We may say the same of the passage in which Jesus identifies himself as 'the bread of life' that 'came down from heaven and gives life to the world' (6:33; cf. also 3:17 and 12:47).[27]

What that coming down from heaven entailed is stated in the Prologue thus: 'The Word became flesh and lived among us' (1:14). With the word 'flesh', John emphasises the materiality of being human (cf. this Johannine use of 'flesh' in 3:6 and 6:63). Flesh is human nature in its vulnerability, weakness and mortality.[28] It is therefore also human nature in its commonality and kinship with the rest of creation; human nature made out of the dust of the Earth, utterly dependent on all the physical conditions of life on this planet and interconnected with other life in diverse and complex ways.[29] Jesus in incarnation is not just one of us humans but part of this worldly creation, a member of the whole community of creation. Again, this is not John's focus, but it is what his understanding of incarnation must imply.

Johannine 'dualism' has been much discussed, and it is necessary to distinguish different kinds of dualisms or dualities in John. There is a dualism of good and evil, God and 'this world' (meaning humanity in its alienation from and hostility to God), but there is also a different kind of duality of God and his good creation, which is 'the world' in the wider and non-derogatory sense. With this latter duality John correlates the duality of Spirit and flesh (3:6 and 6:63), which the Gospel presents especially in terms of forms of life. Flesh is mortal; its purely natural life lacks the power to counter death. Spirit is God's own eternal life that comes from God to give life to the world. The Word 'became flesh', the mortal nature humans share with all living things, in order to give the eternal life of God to all flesh. Creation finds its fulfilment in thus being taken into the divine life.

If we think in this way of the non-human as well as the human creation, John's Gospel does not, as Norman Habel suggests,[30] devalue the non-human creation, but opens up an eternal destiny for it as it does for humans.

THE KINGDOM OF GOD AS THE RENEWAL OF CREATION

We move now from the cosmic Christ to the ministry of Jesus on Earth as the Synoptic Gospels recount it. The theme that they see as the overriding concern of Jesus' preaching and actions is the Kingdom of God.[31] From a cursory reading of the Gospels, it would not be difficult to get the impression that the Kingdom is about the relation between God and humans, and has nothing to do with the rest of creation. But this would be to neglect two things. First, there is quite enough in the Gospels to show that Jesus presupposed the rich creation theology of the Hebrew Bible,[32] which taught, not only that God created all things, but also that God cares generously and tenderly for all his creatures (Job 12:10 and 38:41; Ps. 36:6; 104:29–30; and 145:9), not only for humans. So, too, the Father of Jesus feeds the birds and clothes the wild flowers (Matt. 6:26 and 28–30; Luke 12:24 and 27–28). Jesus is unlikely to have isolated humans from their relationships with other creatures, especially as his parables show him to be a man of the countryside rather than the city. This makes it also unlikely that Jesus saw the Kingdom of God he proclaimed as coming to abolish and replace creation.

But the second point is that the term 'Kingdom of God', which Jesus used without explanation, as though his hearers would have some idea of what it meant, has, of course, its own background in the Hebrew Bible. This can certainly be found in Isaiah (52:7, which is also the source of the word 'gospel' in the Gospels) and in Daniel (chapter 7), but the biblical book in which the kingship and rule of God are most prominent is actually the Psalms, and it is with the usage in the Psalms that we might expect Jesus' hearers to have been most familiar.[33]

In the Psalms, the kingship and rule of God are closely related to creation. It is as Creator that God rules his whole creation (Ps. 103:19–22). His rule is over all that he has made, human and otherwise (Pss. 95:4–5 and 96:11–13), and it is expressed in caring responsibility for all creatures (Ps. 145). All non-human creatures acclaim his rule now (Pss. 103:19–22 and 148) and all nations must come to do so in the future (Ps. 97:1), for God is coming to judge the world, that is, both to condemn and to save (Pss. 96:13 and 98:9). His own people Israel's role is to declare his kingship to the nations (Pss 96:3 and 10; 145:10–12). When God does come to judge and to rule, all creation will rejoice at his advent (Pss. 96:11–12 and 98:7–8).

The kingship and rule of God in the Psalms have both a spatial and a temporal dimension. They are cosmic in scope, encompassing all creation, by no means confined to human society. They are also eternal, established at creation and set to last forever (Pss. 93; 145:13; and 146:10). Yet God's rule is widely flouted and rejected by the nations, and so it is still to come in the fullness of power and in manifest glory. The God who rules from his heavenly throne (Pss. 11:4 and 103:19) is coming to establish his rule on Earth. It is this coming that Jesus proclaims. His distinctive phrase, 'the King-dom of God comes', stands for the expectation of the psalms and the prophets that God himself is coming to reign.[34] In the light of the Psalms in particular, we can see that this reign is not some kind of replacement of creation, but the renewal of the creation itself, and as cosmic in scope as creation.

The cosmic scope of the Kingdom can be clearly seen in the opening three petitions of the Lord's Prayer in Matthew's version:

> Our Father in heaven,
> hallowed be your name,
> your kingdom come,
> your will be done,
> on earth as it is in heaven. (Matt. 6:9–10)

The phrase 'on earth as it is in heaven' should probably be understood to qualify all three of the petitions. Presently, God's name is perfectly hallowed, his rule perfectly obeyed, and his will absolutely done in heaven, but all are neglected or contested on Earth. Probably the emphasis is on humans coming to hallow God's name, to acknowledge God's rule and to do his will, but we should recall that in the Hebrew Bible non-human creatures also do these things, often when humans fail to do so (e.g. praising God's name: Ps. 145:5 and 13; acclaiming his rule: Pss. 103:19–22 and 145:10–11; and doing his will: Jer. 8:7). Moreover, the coupling of 'heaven' and 'earth' cannot fail to evoke the whole creation, everything God created at the beginning (Gen. 1:1; 2:1 and 4). God, it was standardly said, is the Creator of heaven and Earth, and this is the basis on which his Kingdom must come on Earth as it is in heaven. The Kingdom does not come in order to extract people from the rest of creation, but to renew the whole creation in accordance with God's perfect will for it.

As well as proclaiming and explaining the Kingdom of God, Jesus instantiated it in the many activities of his ministry. These included the miracles of healing, exorcisms and the so-called 'nature' miracles. They also included significant acts such as his demonstration in the Temple, sharing meals with sinners, blessing children, washing the disciples' feet, and riding a donkey into Jerusalem. All these activities are to be understood as proleptic instances of the coming of the Kingdom, helping to define how Jesus understood the rule of God, but as more than just symbols of its coming. In such activities the Kingdom was actually coming, but in anticipatory fashion, in small-scale instances. Their small-scale nature comports with the way most of the parables represent the Kingdom by events set in the ordinary world of Jesus' hearers. Just as a mustard plant, in the parable, grows to the dimensions of the mythical world tree, so, when Jesus stills the storm, a squall on the lake evokes the vast destructive power of the mythical abyss. Just as the extraordinary generosity of God in his coming Kingdom is figured, in the parable, when a master serves dinner to his slaves, so it takes place when Jesus pronounces the forgiveness of a notorious sinner who washed his feet.[35]

The activities of Jesus were small-scale anticipations of the Kingdom that heralded its universal coming in the future. What is notable about them, for our purposes, is the way that their holistic character points to the coming of the Kingdom in all creation. Jesus brought wholeness to the lives of the people he healed and delivered: reconciling them to God, driving the power of evil from their lives, healing diseased bodies, making good crippling disabilities and restoring social relationships to those isolated by their misfortune. Jesus does not isolate their relationship with God from their bodily and social existence. Something of the same kind of holistic vision of the world appears in the so-called nature miracles. At least some of these anticipate the transformation of human relationships with the non-human world in the renewed creation. In the feeding miracles, God's generous provision for his people through the gifts of creation takes place even in the barren wilderness (Mark 6:30–44), as had happened in the first exodus (Ps. 78:15–16 and 23–25) and was expected for the new exodus (Isa. 35:1 and 6–7; 41:18–19; and 51:3; cf. Ezek. 34:26–39). When Jesus walks on the water and stills the storm (Mark 6:47–52 and 4:35–42), God's unique sovereignty over the waters of chaos is evoked, with the expectation that in the renewed creation the destructive powers of nature will be finally quelled. While most of Jesus' activities focused on humans and human society in relation to God, there are sufficient indications that Jesus and the evangelists also embraced the fully inclusive understanding of God's rule over all creation that is so prominent in the Psalms. As Andrew Linzey puts it, the nature miracles 'are signs among many that in Jesus is a birth of new possibilities for all creation'.[36]

So it is not enough to say that the Kingdom of God is the renewal of all creation. We must also say that it is the renewal of all the creatures in their interrelationship and interdependence, what we could call an ecological renewal because it relates to the biblical writers' sense of the interconnectedness and interdependence of God's creatures. The bodily-ness of humans makes them inextricably part of the rest of the material creation, bound up with other creatures, for good or ill, in all sorts of ways. The nature miracles are important indications that Jesus did not envisage the extrication of purely spiritual persons from those material entanglements, but rather the healing and perfecting of such relationships among the creatures. As an example, we shall look more closely at one of these miracles.

JESUS PACIFIES THE FORCES OF CHAOS IN CREATION (MARK 4:35–41)

In a story told in all three Synoptic Gospels, Jesus and the disciples are in a fishing boat on the lake of Galilee when a storm gets up and puts them in serious danger. The disciples wake Jesus up. Mark's version of the story then reads: Jesus 'rebuked the wind, and said to the sea, "Peace! Be still!" Then the wind ceased, and there was a dead calm.' The disciples' fear of the storm gives place to awe of Jesus, and they say to one another, 'Who then is this, that even the wind and the sea obey him?' (Mark 4:37–41).

The key to understanding this story is to recognise its combination of, on the one hand, a realistic situation, and, on the other hand, mythical overtones. The situation is a quite realistic description of the hazards of sailing on the lake of Galilee, and also stands for the kind of quite frequent situations in which first-century people might find themselves in danger from the forces of nature. The mythical overtones of the story do not cancel the realism but say something of religious significance about such a realistic situation.

The myth is one to which the Old Testament refers on a number of occasions.[37] It speaks of the primeval waters of chaos, the destructive powers of nature imaged as a vast tempestuous ocean, which God in creation reduced to calm and confined within limits so that the world could be a stable environment for living creatures. These waters of chaos were not abolished by creation, only confined, always ready to break out and endanger creation, needing to be constantly restrained by the Creator. For Israelites, the waters of the mythical abyss were not simply a metaphysical idea. In an event like a storm at sea, the real waters of the sea became the waters of chaos, threatening life and controllable only by God.[38] In the case of this story, a squall on the lake of Galilee (notice that Mark calls it 'the sea') is enough to raise the spectre of elemental chaos.

When Mark relates that Jesus 'rebuked the wind and said to the sea, "Peace! Be still!" ', he recalls the most characteristic ways in which the Hebrew Bible speaks of God's subduing the waters of chaos. The 'rebuke' is God's powerful word of command, as in Psalm 104:7: 'at your rebuke the waters flee' (see also Isa. 17:13). The word that silences the storm occurs, among other places, in Job 26:12: 'By his power he stills the sea', again referring to the creation myth (see also Ps. 89:9). It is the Creator's rebuke to chaos, then, that Jesus utters, and the peace of the creation secured against chaos that Jesus restores. This is why the disciples ask, 'Who is this, that even the wind and the sea obey him?' Only God fits that description.[39]

By telling the story with these mythical overtones, therefore, Mark invites us to see the event as a small-scale enactment by Jesus of God's final elimination of chaos from the natural world, when, as the book of Revelation has it, there will be no more sea (21:1),[40] and God will finally establish the harmony of his creation. Jesus' miracle presages one of the key distinctions between the present creation and the new or renewed creation, and this is how the event functions in the Gospel story as a sign of Jesus' inauguration of the Kingdom of God. It goes to the heart of the hostility between humans and nature, promising that the destructive power of the forces of chaos, still active in the natural world against living creatures, will in the end be pacified by God.[41] It is notable that, even in this image of God's renewal of creation, he does not meet the destructive violence of nature with destructive violence of his own. He pacifies, he brings peace to a disordered world. For the forces of destruction in nature – the earthquakes, the tsunamis, the volcanoes, the hurricanes and the hidden forces of climate change, to name only some of the most fearful – are not, as we now know from science, intrinsically evil. They are manifestations of funda- mental forces, without which this planet could not be the home to living creatures that it is, but which from time to time, sometimes with human connivance, act with destructive force against living creatures.[42]

When we reflect on this story in contemporary context, it is important to keep in mind the lesson that this sort of control over the forces of nature is intrinsically divine and not human. The great scientific-technological project of the modern world went wrong to the extent that it over-reached itself and imagined that modern humanity could accomplish what belongs only to the omnipotence of God. The project of attempting to harness and control nature, as though we could grasp the Creator's tools and remodel creation to our own design, achieved much, but often at the price of unexpected consequences that have proved increas- ingly disastrous for the rest of creation as well as ourselves. Climate change is the latest instance of the way our attempts to master nature can so easily end up releasing powers of nature inimical to human life. In this case it is we who have unwittingly unleashed chaos.

The story of Jesus' pacification of the storm reminds us that control of nature is godlike and humans may rightly participate in it only as creatures, dependent on God, not making themselves gods. Its limits in the givenness of the world as God's creation must be respected. Insofar as the project of modern civilization has sought for humans divine omnipotence to recreate the world at will, it has been a usurpation of divinity, fired by greed and the will to power, inevitably producing the opposite of true divine creativity: chaos, not cosmos. In order to exercise such control of nature as we have in such a way as to restrain chaos and to promote the harmony of God's creation, the pacification of the human heart, the recognition of our creatureliness in the community of creation, is first required.

THE UNIVERSAL SOLIDARITY OF THE RISEN CHRIST

In discussing the Prologue to John's Gospel, I said that incarnation needs to be understood as participation not only in common humanity, but also in the common creatureliness of all creation. Since the mortal bodies of humans are their solidarity with the rest of the material creation, when the Word of God 'became flesh', he too entered into the physical, mortal and transient life of the whole earthly creation. In dying, he shared the fate of all living creatures on this Earth, and we cannot think that in rising to new life beyond death he abandoned this solidarity with the whole community of creation. His resurrection was the beginning of the new creation. With respect to the human world, it is the common New Testament understanding that, as he died for others, so also he rose for others, pioneering the way into the life of the new creation that believers will fully share when they too rise from death. If the new creation is the transformation of the whole of this material creation so that all creatures may share in the life of the divine eternity, then Jesus' resurrection must lead the way to new creation for the whole community of creation, not just humans.[43]

For this understanding of Jesus' resurrection it is important that it was *bodily* resurrection. It constitutes the redemption of human life in its psychosomatic wholeness, not some sort of Platonist deliverance of spirit from matter. This holistic salvation of humans retains the solidarity of human physicality with the whole material creation, and cannot be conceived apart from the salvation of the latter too. In the modern period of New Testament interpretation, there was a good deal of hesitation about affirming the really bodily character either of Jesus' resurrection or of the expected resurrection of believers. Among the Gospel resurrection narratives, the strong emphasis on the bodily nature of the risen Jesus in both Luke's and John's Gospels was often seen as a late apologetic accretion to the traditions of the risen Jesus' appearances. Paul's understanding of resurrection was understood to be of a much more 'spiritual' kind. In retrospect, this line of interpretation looks much at home in the context of nineteenth-century idealistic philosophy for which mind was the true reality behind matter. It also has much more in common with the Platonist anthropology that the early Church Fathers and the theological tradition rejected by insisting on belief in bodily resurrection.

The cosmic dimension of Jesus' resurrection is apparent in the Colossians hymn, which we have already discussed, when Jesus is said to be 'the firstborn from the dead, so that he might be pre-eminent in all things' (Col. 1:18). This parallels the statement in the first strophe that Jesus is 'the firstborn of all creation'. In the latter case, as we saw, the meaning cannot be that Jesus was the first to be created, but rather that he has the pre-eminent position in creation. As 'firstborn from the dead', Jesus actually was the first to rise from death, ahead of all others, but this is of much more than chronological significance. It makes him pre-eminent in the new creation of all things.

THE UNIVERSAL WORSHIP OF THE TRIUMPHANT CHRIST

The cosmic pre-eminence of the risen Christ appears in another way in passages where the New Testament takes up from the Old Testament the important theme of the worship of God by all creatures, which we studied in Chapter 3. We noted there that there is a sense in which this worship, portrayed in imperative mode in Psalm 148, is eschatological. Psalm 148, with its cosmic choir of all the creatures, including humans, betrays no hint of anything lacking or awry in creation. That many humans so far refuse to join the choir is a fact not allowed to intrude on the unqualified positivity of praise as this psalm portrays it. Nor is there a hint that there are features of the world for which one cannot wholeheartedly praise the Creator, since they contest his good will for his creation. In that sense, Psalm 148 is an invitation to praise the Creator that will not find universal response until the time when God's Kingdom comes in its fullness. (An indication of this can be seen in other psalms, such as 96:10–13.)

In the christological 'hymn' (as it is often called) in Philippians 2:6–11, we find that the story of Jesus culminates in universal worship of God expressed as submission to the lordship of Jesus Christ:

> Therefore God also highly exalted him
> and gave him the name
> that is above every name,
> [10]so that at the name of Jesus
> every knee should bend,
> in heaven and on earth and under the earth,
> [11]and every tongue should confess
> that Jesus Christ is Lord,
> to the glory of God the Father.

This is not the place to develop the christological implications of this passage,[44] but we should note that it alludes to Isaiah 45:22–23, where God declares on oath that his sole sovereignty will in the future come to be universally acknowledged: 'To me every knee shall bow, every tongue shall swear' (Isa. 45:23). Not only does Paul expect this to be fulfilled in universal acknowledgement of Jesus Christ as Lord 'to the glory of God the Father', he also takes Isaiah's 'every knee' and 'every tongue' to indicate not just universal human worship, but fully universal worship by all creatures. The phrase 'in heaven and on earth and under the earth' is a way of summing up the whole cosmos, and we should not suppose that Paul refers only to creatures who can literally bow the knee and speak with the tongue. The passage is in the tradition of the Old Testament descriptions of trees clapping their hands and mountains skipping like lambs. All creatures – whether angelic, human, animate or inanimate – will in their own ways glorify the one who has brought God's purposes for his whole creation to triumphant conclusion.

Another New Testament passage, different in idiom but remarkably similar in substance, occurs in the book of Revelation. In the prophet John's vision of God's throne in heaven, he portrays the way in which the heavenly worshippers continually bow down and praise God as the Creator of all things (Rev. 4:9–11). But then something new happens. John sees the figure of a lamb enthroned on the cosmic throne of God (5:6). The Lamb still looks like a sacrificial animal that has been slaughtered, much as the risen Christ retained the marks of crucifixion on his body, but the Lamb is also seen to be victorious. It is through this victory of the slaughtered Lamb that the book of Revelation sees the Kingdom of God finally coming in its full reality to all creation. Vision after vision in the rest of the book configure, in rich symbolic imagery, the way this is to come. But the final result is already anticipated in chapter 5, when it describes the cosmic worship of the Lamb. Initially the Lamb's victory is celebrated in heaven by the circle of heavenly worshippers John has already seen worshipping God around the throne (5:8–10). But then the circle expands to include 'the myriads of myriads, and thousands of thousands' of angels in all the heavens praising the slaughtered and victorious Lamb (5:11–12). Then again this vast choir expands even further, becoming fully universal, when 'every creature in heaven and on earth and under the earth and in the sea, and all that is in them' praise God and the Lamb together (5:13).

Here the rhetoric of cosmic inclusiveness is even fuller than Paul's 'in heaven and on earth and under the earth'. After 'every creature in heaven and on earth and under the earth and in the sea',[45] the additional phrase, 'and all that is in them',[46] is actually redundant, but the author wants to leave no doubt that he is encompassing the whole creation in all its vast plenitude and diversity. He goes out of his way, as it were, to prevent us from thinking only of creatures able to think and verbalise their praise.

Here the heavenly praise of God, the Creator of all things (in chapter 4), has become also the cosmic praise of Jesus Christ, the Redeemer of all things.[47]

THE NEW CREATION AS ECOTOPIA

In the final vision of the book of Revelation, John sees 'a new heaven and a new earth; for the first heaven and the first earth had passed away, and the sea was no more' (Rev. 21:1). The resemblance between this text and Paul's statement about new creation in 2 Corinthians 5:17 has rarely been noticed, no doubt because exegetes think of Paul and Revelation as too different to be worth setting in parallel. Paul says: 'So if anyone is in Christ – new creation! The old things have passed away; behold, all things have become new!'[48] Paul's use of 'behold' even gives his exclamatory words a visionary quality (cf. Rev. 21:3 and 5). When someone becomes a Christian, new creation happens. The new creation that is the future of all things comes about already in this instance at this instant, as it were. The references to 'old things' and 'all things', along with new creation, make it quite clear that Paul has the expected cosmic transformation in view. In that case, it may be that when Paul proceeds to say that 'in Christ God was reconciling the world to himself' (2 Cor. 5:19), he is using the term 'world' (*kosmos*) to refer not only to humanity but to the whole creation.[49]

What is especially significant for our present purpose is that Paul plainly does not regard new creation as the replacement of the present creation by a quite different, new one. If he did, he would have to suppose that in Christian conversion one human being is replaced by a brand new one. He evidently sees new creation as the eschatological renewal of creation. The vivid language of old things passing away and all things becoming new refers to a transfiguration of reality into a new form. It is radical transformation, but not replacement.[50]

Paul here shows us that there is no difficulty in understanding Revelation 21:1 in the same way. It does not foresee the replacement of an old creation by a new one, but the renewal of the whole creation.[51] The renewal is a radical transformation, as it must be if the new creation is no longer to be governed by death and transience (cf. 21:4), but to live from the eternal life of God (21:6). It is a kind of transposition into eternity. But it takes up into eternity whatever is valuable and fit for eternity. God's new creative act (21:5: 'Behold I am making all things new') surely corresponds to his verdict of 'good' and 'very good' on the things he made in the beginning (Gen. 1). The whole of that 'very good' creation becomes for the first time truly 'very good' when it is rescued from all that threatens it, but it is surely the whole of creation – teeming with all the diverse creatures that Genesis 1 depicts – that God is going to make eschatologically new.

This point has been made several times in this book, but I have developed it more fully here, because it is the essential key to an ecological eschatology, i.e. a living hope, not for the abolition of other creatures, but for the healing and perfecting of human relationships with all other creatures. Such an eschatological hope can be an inspiration for seeking such healing of these relationships as is possible here and now, a peaceable living with other creatures that will be of a quality fit for transposition into the new creation.

Revelation's vision of the new creation focuses on the image of the New Jerusalem that comes down from heaven to be the home of God and humans for eternity. There are beautiful images of intimacy between God and his peoples (21:3),[52] when God will 'wipe away every tear from every eye' (21:4), and when they will dwell together in a manner reminiscent of Eden, when God walked in the garden in the cool of the evening. There will be no need of a temple, because God and the Lamb will be present throughout the city (21:22), which as a whole is depicted as a kind of holy of holies for all people to enter. The redeemed will see the face of God and the Lamb, worshipping in face-to-face presence (22:34). But our present interest is in the ecotopian aspect of the vision.[53]

The New Jerusalem is in some sense a return to Eden – its river and its trees of life (21:2) recall the garden, but they also recall Ezekiel's vision of the river of life that flows from the new temple of the future, turning lifeless waters into habitats swarming with

abundant life (Ezek. 47:6–12): 'everything will live w
goes' (47:9). Ezekiel's vision is of ecological renewa
tures the vision of the original creation, in whicl
creatures of the waters were to multiply and fill l
1:21–22), as well as surpassing the original in its depiction of the
marvellous fruitfulness of the trees that are nourished by the river.
The key to all this life-giving vitality is, of course, the fact that the
river flows from the Temple, that is, from the presence of God. Life
is renewed from its source in God. So it is too in Revelation
(22:1–2), but it is worth recalling the ecological detail of Ezekiel's
vision when reading the more allusive summary in Revelation,
because Ezekiel's detail facilitates our recognition of the ecological
character of the water of life and the trees of life in Revelation.
They are not just symbols of eternal life for humans, though they
are that. They conjure a vision of the natural world renewed with
new life from the divine source of all life. The healing of the
nations (22:4) and the gift of eternal life for all are given by God
not solely and directly to humans, but in the form of a living
relationship with a living environment for human life.

The New Jerusalem surpasses Eden because the tree of life, from
which Adam and Eve did not eat, is now available – multiplied, in
fact, as twelve species of tree, whose leaves heal the scars of this
world and whose fruit nourishes with eternal sustenance (22:2).
But the New Jerusalem also surpasses Eden in being a city. Where
Eden was a temple-garden, the New Jerusalem is a temple-city.
The New Jerusalem is the transposition into the new creation of all
that is good in human culture, all that human beings since Eden
have well made of the resources given them by the other creatures
of Earth. The kings of the Earth are welcomed into it, bringing the
glory and honour of the nations to contribute to the glory of God
with which the city is illuminated (21:24–26). The New Jerusalem
fulfils humanity's desire to build out of nature a human home, a
place of human culture and community. Yet the paradise garden,
Eden unspoiled, also lives within it. It is a garden city of a kind to
which humans have often aspired, a place where human culture
does not replace nature but lives in harmony and reciprocity with

. It represents the final reconciliation of culture and nature, of the human world and the other creatures of Earth. It lives from the vitality of the natural world without plundering and exhausting its resources.

The new creation lives from the life of God and the Lamb, the river of life that flows from their throne in the New Jerusalem (21:1–2). Early in the book, the risen and exalted Christ had said: 'I am the first and the last, and the living one. I was dead, and see, I am alive forever and ever; and I have the keys of Death and of Hades' (1:17–18). The life of the new creation is the resurrection life of Jesus Christ. It is the life that sprang up beyond death and so can vivify the whole of this dying creation. Whereas mortal life comes from God but runs out in death, eternal life is inseparable from its source in God. Such life is available to all creation because the one who calls himself 'the living one' attained it for the whole creation through his dying solidarity with all creation. Thus the story of the whole creation reaches its goal as it joins irrevocably and forever the story of Jesus Christ.

That goal, which is not imaginable in literal terms, is sketched for us by the prophets and configured supremely by the prophet John at the end of the whole Bible, in order to give hope and inspiration for the present. Paul's vision of new creation in Christ, which we quoted at the beginning of this section, goes on to speak of our reconciliation to God and of his own 'ministry of reconcili-ation' (2 Cor. 5:18–20). John's vision of the New Jerusalem likewise pictures our reconciliation to God – along with all creation. Reconciliation with God and reconciliation with the rest of God's creation are not alternatives but natural partners. In the end they are inseparable, as John's vision shows, and in the crises of our contemporary world both are urgent needs. The Church's 'ministry of reconciliation' today must surely embrace both. And finding our place in the biblical meta-narrative – reconciled in Christ, on the way to the reconciliation of all things in Christ – will help to sustain hope in dark times.

NOTES

Chapter 1 STEWARDSHIP IN QUESTION

1 Christopher Southgate, 'Stewardship and its Competitors: A Spectrum of Relationships between Humans and the Non-Human Creation', in R. J. Berry ed., *Environmental Stewardship: Critical Perspectives – Past and Present* (London/New York: T. & T. Clark International, 2006), pp 185–195, here p 185.

2 Quoted by Robin Attfield, 'Environmental Sensitivity and Critiques of Stewardship', in Berry ed., *Environmental Stewardship*, pp 76–91, here pp 78–79.

3 Larry Rasmussen, 'Symbols to Live By', in Berry ed., *Environmental Stewardship*, pp 174–184, here pp 178–179, having registered criticisms of the idea of stewardship, finds agreement in one important implication of stewardship: accountability to God for what humans do not own.

4 Interview in *Third Way*, June 2005, p 20.

5 James Lovelock, *The Revenge of Gaia: Why the Earth is Fighting Back – and How We Can Still Save Humanity* (London: Allen Lane [Penguin], 2006).

6 Lovelock, *The Revenge,* pp 146–147. Cf. also Michael Allaby, *A Guide to Gaia: A Survey of the New Science of Our Living Earth* (New York: Dutton, 1990), chapter 9 ('The Earth is Not a God'), though his argument is limited to showing that Gaia is not an intelligent personal being. This is not the only way in which Gaia could be granted divine value. On 'Gaian pantheism', see Michael Northcott, *The Environment and Christian Ethics* (New Studies in Christian Ethics; Cambridge: Cambridge University Press, 1996), pp 112–113.

7 Lovelock, *The Revenge*, 148; cf. James Lovelock, *The Ages of Gaia: A Biography of our Living Earth* (Oxford: Oxford University Press, 1988), chapter 9.

8 This is evidently Lovelock's meaning when he sometimes speaks of Gaia, the Earth system, as 'alive'. This is probably a misleading usage, which has been much criticised, and which has certainly been misused in popular, especially New Age, contexts. Colin A. Russell, *The Earth, Humanity and God* (London: UCL Press, 1994), p 121, complains: 'The organismic belief that the Earth really is "alive" is a pre-scientific hangover, and the hypothesis reverts to myth. It cannot even be metaphor, since no new characteristics of life are added to the model [of a self-regulating system]; Earth does not, for instance, reproduce itself.' On the other hand, Lovelock, *Revenge*, p 16, in his most recent statement on the subject, says: 'I am continuing to use the metaphor of "the

living Earth" for Gaia; but do not assume that I am thinking of the Earth as alive in a sentient way, or even alive like an animal or a bacterium.'

9 For some of the scientific arguments against Lovelock's Gaia hypothesis, see Celia Deane-Drummond, 'God and Gaia: Myth or Reality?', *Theology* 95 (1992), pp 277–285, and Russell, *The Earth*, pp 119–121. Russell considers that 'the Gaia hypothesis may be properly described at present as a scientific theory, *but only in the form of a "conceptual model"* ' (p 121: italics original). He uses Mary Hesse's term, 'conceptual model', because there is as yet no way of knowing how the full mechanism of Gaia works.

10 Lovelock, *The Revenge*, p 137.

11 James Lovelock, 'The Fallible Concept of Stewardship of the Earth', in Berry ed., *Environmental Stewardship*, pp 106–111, here p 108.

12 Clare Palmer, 'Stewardship: A Case Study in Environmental Ethics', in Berry ed., *Environmental Stewardship*, pp 63–75, here p 72.

13 See also Northcott, *The Environment*, p 129.

14 Lovelock, 'The Fallible Concept', p 109.

15 Lovelock, *The Revenge*, p 152; cf. Lovelock, 'The Fallible Concept', p 109.

16 This paragraph summarises a detailed historical argument in Richard Bauckham, *God and the Crisis of Freedom* (Louisville: Westminster John Knox, 2002), chapter 7 ('Human Authority in Creation'). Developments in the early modern period are treated more briefly in Richard Bauckham, 'Modern Domination of Nature – Historical Origins and Biblical Critique', in Berry ed., *Environmental Stewardship*, pp 32–50. See also Peter Harrison, 'Subduing the Earth: Genesis 1, Early Modern Science and the Exploitation of Nature', *JR* 79 (1999), pp 86–109, reprinted (with revisions) in Berry ed., *Environmental Stewardship*, pp 17–31.

17 Russell, *The Earth*, p 125, has difficulty with this because Lovelock's Gaia is geared to the continuance of life, but not to human life in particular. But a Christian theological interpretation of Gaia could well suppose that the continuance of human life is contingent on respect for the given order of creation within which we must live.

18 Hale's view is taken over with full approval by John Black, 'The Dominion of Man', in Berry ed., *Environmental Stewardship*, pp 92–96, here pp 95–96. This passage was originally published in 1970, and, when compared with more recent treatments, shows how the tenor and emphasis in Christian thinking about environmental stewardship have shifted in that time from improvement to preservation.

19 Bauckham, *God*, pp 169–170.

20 See, for example, the *Evangelical Declaration on the Care of Creation*, in R. J. Berry ed., *The Care of Creation* (Leicester: InterVarsity Press, 2000), pp 18–22.

21 See the criticism of this understanding of stewardship by Palmer, 'Stewardship', in Berry ed., *Environmental Stewardship*, p 73.

22 Cf. David E. Noble, *The Religion of Technology: The Divinity of Man and the Spirit of Invention* (New York: Penguin, 1999), pp 194–200.

23 Southgate, 'A Spectrum', p 194; more detail in Christopher Southgate, *The Groaning of Creation: God, Evolution, and the Problem of Evil* (Louisville: West-

minster John Knox, 2008), pp 124–132. He sees this as human partnership with Christ in his role of 'redeeming evolution', but this is to see extinction as a failing of evolution, whereas in our time it is overwhelmingly the result of human activity.

24 Cf. Stephen Jay Gould, quoted by Bruce R. Reichenbach and V. Elving Anderson, 'Tensions in a Stewardship Paradigm', in Berry ed., *Environmental Stewardship*, pp 112–125, here p 120.

25 Reichenbach and Anderson, 'Tensions', p 123.

26 For these concepts and their recent advocates, see Southgate, 'A Spectrum', pp 186–187 and 193–195. Cf. Arthur R. Peacocke, *Creation and the World of Science* (Oxford: Clarendon Press, 1979), p 305: 'man [*sic*] now has, at his present stage of intellectual, cultural, and social evolution, the possibility of consciously becoming *co-creator* and *co-worker* with God in his work on Earth, and perhaps even a little beyond Earth'; Andrew Linzey, *Animal Theology* (London: SCM Press, 1984), p 71: 'we ourselves achieve redemption by becoming redeemers'; Loren Wilkinson ed., *Earthkeeping in the Nineties: Stewardship of Creation* (Grand Rapids: Eerdmans, 1991), p 298: 'Humans are to become saviors of nature, as Christ is the savior of humanity (and hence, through humans, of those parts of creation placed under their care).'

27 For the interpretation of dominion as priesthood, see my discussion in Chapter 3.

28 Bauckham, *God*, chapter 7.

29 This is also argued by Ruth Page, 'The Fellowship of All Creation', in Berry ed., *Environmental Stewardship*, p 97–105. Douglas J. Hall, 'Stewardship as a Key to a Theology of Nature', in Berry ed., *Environmental Stewardship*, pp 129–144, here especially pp 139–143, finds in stewardship precisely the combination of horizontal and vertical relationships missing in other models. On the other hand, Huw Spanner, 'Tyrants, Stewards – or Just Kings?', in Andrew Linzey and Dorothy Yamamoto eds., *Animals on the Agenda: Questions about Animals for Theology and Ethics* (London: SCM Press, 1998), pp 216–224, here pp 222–223, says that, 'we think of a steward as other than and superior to the property he or she manages', whereas a king is 'essentially of the same kind as' his subjects. There is an ambiguity here in the notion of stewardship: Hall thinks of the steward put in charge of his fellow-servants in a household (as in Luke 12:42), whereas Spanner thinks of the steward as manager of an estate or other kinds of non-human property.

30 The reason for this omission is unclear, but that these creatures also have the task of procreating and multiplying seems to be assumed.

31 William P. Brown, *The Ethos of the Cosmos: The Genesis of Moral Imagination in the Bible* (Grand Rapids: Eerdmans, 1999), p 52.

32 There are six occurrences of 'God saw that it was good', and this distinctive variation is therefore the climactic seventh.

33 'the wild animals' does not occur in MT, LXX or Vulgate, and therefore not in English versions until recently. The NRSV, JB, REB and NIV margin supply it from the Syriac. This correction of the MT seems very likely to be right, since 'all the land/Earth' in the middle of a list that is otherwise of animals is

odd, and out of line with the similar lists in vv 24, 25 and 28 (of which vv 24 and 25 specifically mention 'the wild animals'). The correction is accepted by Claus Westermann, *Genesis 1–11* (trans. John J. Scullion; London: SPCK, 1974), p 79, n 26b, although his translation (p 77) unaccountably omits the whole of v 26 after 'image'.

34 The confusion must be largely due to the text of v 26 in MT, LXX and Vulgate: see previous note.

35 Brown, *The Ethos*, p 46, speaks of 'an ethos of order that requires effort but no weaponry'. On the other hand, Norman Habel, 'Geophany: The Earth Story in Genesis 1', in Norman C. Habel and Shirley Wurst eds., *The Earth Story in Genesis* (Earth Bible 2; Sheffield: Sheffield Academic Press, 2000), pp 34–48, here p 46, thinks of 'harsh control'; similarly Norman Habel, *An Inconvenient Text: Is a Green Reading of the Bible Possible?* (Adelaide: ATF Press, 2009), pp 66–68.

36 Ps. 8:7 does not speak of a more extensive dominion. The 'all' of this verse comprises the creatures specified in the following two verses. Inanimate nature is not in view.

37 The only exception is Joel 4:13 [3:13], where the word may be from a different root. See Norbert Lohfink, *Theology of the Pentateuch: Themes of the Priestly Narrative and Deuteronomy* (trans. Linda M. Malony; Edinburgh: T. & T. Clark, 1994), pp 11–12. But Lohfink's suggestion that the dominion refers to the domestication of animals is implausible because 1:26, as well as referring to birds and sea creatures, distinguishes 'wild animals' from 'cattle' (domestic animals).

38 E.g. Simkins, *Creator*; J. Baird Callicott, 'Genesis and John Muir', in Carol S. Robb and Carl J. Casebolt eds., *Covenant for a New Creation* (Maryknoll, New York: Orbis, 1991), pp 116–118; Theodore Hiebert, 'The Human Vocation: Origins and Transformations in Christian Traditions', in Dieter T. Hessel and Rosemary Radford Ruether eds., *Christianity and Ecology: Seeking the Well-Being of Earth and Humans* (Cambridge, Massachusetts: Harvard University Press, 2000), pp 135–154.

39 For *'adamah* as 'arable land, fertile soil that can be cultivated', see Theodore Hiebert, *The Yahwist's Landscape: Nature and Religion in Early Israel* (New York/Oxford: Oxford University Press, 1996), pp 34–35.

40 Quoted in Attfield, 'Environmental Sensitivity', p 13; Theodore Hiebert, *The Yahwist's Landscape: Nature and Religion in Early Israel* (New York/Oxford: Oxford University Press, 1996). This English pun is also cited by Norman Wirzba, *The Paradise of God: Renewing Religion in an Ecological Age* (New York/Oxford: Oxford University Press, 2003), p 29.

41 Carol A. Newsom, 'Common Ground: An Ecological Reading of Genesis 2–3', in Norman C. Habel and Shirley Wurst eds., *The Earth Story in Genesis* (The Earth Bible 2; Sheffield: Sheffield Academic Press, 2000), pp 60–72, here p 73.

42 This point was made by John Muir (Callicott, 'Genesis', pp 115–116) in strong opposition to the idea, normal in the Christianity of his time, that the rest of creation was made for humanity.

43 The quotation is from Ernst M. Conradie, 'Towards an Agenda for Ecological Theology: An Intercontinental Dialogue', *Ecotheology* 10 (2005), pp 281–343, here p 292, reporting the argument of John F. Haught, *The Promise of Nature: Ecology and Cosmic Purpose* (Mahwah: Paulist Press, 1993), p 101.

44 I say 'associate it with', rather than 'locate it in' Mesopotamia, because it may be that the geography is intentionally obscure, suggesting that Eden cannot be geographically located in the ordinary sense (Batto, *Slaying*, p 49).

45 Brown, *The Ethos*, p 139.

46 According to Ronald A. Simkins, *Creator and Creation: Nature in the Worldview of Ancient Israel* (Peabody: Hendrickson, 1994), p 180, humans are placed only temporarily in the garden, until they reach maturity and can be sent out to farm the land elsewhere.

47 The relationship between Adam and the soil in Genesis 2 is discussed further in Chapter 4.

48 E.g. Hiebert, *The Yahwist's Landscape*, p 157; Steven Bouma-Prediger, *For the Beauty of the Earth: A Christian Vision for Creation Care* (Grand Rapids: Baker Academic, 2001), p 74; Wirzba, *The Paradise of God*, p 31; Habel, *An Inconvenient Text*, p 69.

49 See George W. Ramsey, 'Is Name-Giving an Act of Domination in Genesis 2:23 and Elsewhere?', *CBQ* 50 (1988), pp 24–35. According to Mark G. Brett, 'Earthing the Human in Genesis 1–3', in Habel and Wurst eds., *The Earth Story in Genesis*, pp 73–86, here p 81, the naming is 'a celebration of diversity'. I see no basis for Brown's claim (*The Ethos*, p 141) that Adam determines the roles of the animals.

50 This passage is discussed more fully in Chapter 4.

51 Walter Houston, 'Justice and Violence in the Priestly Utopia' (forthcoming in *Genesis and Christian Theology*, papers from the 2009 St Andrews conference on Scripture and Theology), considers this the majority view, although many scholars take the view that, in 6:12, 'all flesh' refers only to humans. Bernhard W. Anderson, *From Creation to New Creation* (OBT; Minneapolis: Fortress, 1994), pp 142–146, thinks that the animals are involved in the violence, though humans were responsible for introducing it into creation.

52 For the parallels between Gen. 1 and Gen. 6–8, see Ellen van Wolde, *Stories of the Beginning: Genesis 1–11 and Other Creation Stories* (trans. John Bowden; London: SCM Press, 1996), pp 121–122.

53 Simkins, *Creator*, pp 192 and 202–205, while making other important points about the significance of the flood narrative(s), oddly neglects Noah's task of preserving the animal species. It is recognised by, e.g., Bernhard Lang, *The Hebrew God: Portrait of an Ancient Deity* (New Haven/London: Yale University Press, 2002), p 99 ('Noah is the savior of the animals'); Odil H. Steck, *World and Environment* (Biblical Encounters Series; Nashville: Abingdon, 1980), p 106; Michael Northcott, *A Moral Climate: The Ethics of Global Warming* (London: Darton, Longman & Todd, 2007), pp 71–75; Rowan Williams, 'The Climate Crisis: the Christian Response' (Operation Noah's Annual Address, 2009): http://www.operationnoah.org/calendars/campaigncalendar/13-october-

hear-dr-rowan-williams-wisdom-noah (accessed 23.10.09); and, especially, Wirzba, *The Paradise of God*, pp 33–34 and 141–143.

54 I do not think the relationship between humans and animals in these verses can be described merely as mutual respect, as van Wolde, *Stories*, pp 128–129, suggests. It envisages potential violence. The expression 'fear and dread' recurs in Deut. 11:25. Both there and in Gen. 9:2, its significance is that people will be protected from violence by the fear that their potential attackers will have of them.

55 Simkins, *Creator*, p 204.

56 Israel's dietary laws, distinguishing animals that are permitted to be eaten from others that are not (Lev. 11), extend this restraint. See Ellen Davis, *Scripture, Culture, and Agriculture: An Agrarian Reading of the Bible* (Cambridge: Cambridge University Press, 2009), pp 94–97, where she follows Jacob Milgrom in seeing these laws as 'the Bible's method of taming the killer instinct in humans' (p 95); also Walter J. Houston, *Purity and Monotheism* (*JSOTS* 140; Sheffield: Sheffield Academic Press, 1993), pp 253–258. Note how these laws are already anticipated in the classification of the animals Noah took with him in the ark (Gen. 7:2).

57 Robert Murray, *The Cosmic Covenant* (Heythrop Monographs 7; London: Sheed & Ward, 1992), p 34.

58 I borrow this term from Bill Devall, *Simple in Means, Deep in Ends: Practising Deep Ecology* (London: Green Print, 1990), p 34.

59 Christopher J. H. Wright, *Old Testament Ethics for the People of God* (Leicester: InterVarsity Press, 2004), pp 81–96.

60 On this aspect, see Aloys Hüttermann, *The Ecological Message of the Torah: Knowledge, Concepts, and Laws which Made Survival in a Land of 'Milk and Honey' Possible* (South Florida Studies in the History of Judaism 199; Atlanta: Scholars Press, 1999), pp 88–90.

61 Stephen R. L. Clark, 'Is Nature God's Will?', in Linzey and Yamamoto eds., *Animals*, pp 123–136, here p 133.

62 For this point and further discussion of domestic animals, see Chapter 4.

63 I am deliberately abstaining from that debate here, since my scope is limited.

64 Temple Grandin and Catherine Johnson, *Animals in Translation: Using the Mysteries of Autism to Decode Animal Behaviour* (London: Bloomsbury, 2006), make this point in an easily accessible way.

65 For the possibility that some animals have some moral sense, see Grandin and Johnson, *Animals*, pp 258–259; Marc Bekoff, *Animal Passions and Beastly Virtues: Reflections on Redecorating Nature* (Philadelphia: Temple University Press, 2006), pp 127–129 and 144–176.

66 For the possibility that some animals may be conscious of God, see Grandin and Johnson, *Animals*, p 260.

67 Edmond Jacob, *Theology of the Old Testament*, (trans. Arthur W. Heathcote and Philip J. Allcock; London: Hodder & Stoughton, 1958), p 171.

68 E.g. Walter Brueggemann, *Genesis* (Interpretation; Atlanta: John Knox Press, 1982), p 32; Spanner, 'Tyrants', p 222.

69 Cf. also other passages cited by Spanner, 'Tyrants', p 223.

70 Rowan Williams, 'The Climate Crisis'.

71 E.g. René Dubos, *The Wooing of Earth* (London: Athlone Press, 1980), p 80. But much of what Dubos says in this book about human 'improvement' of nature could be relabelled 'enhancement' in my sense.

72 Gen. 4:20 probably does not refer to the domestication of cattle, of which Genesis knows nothing, but merely to the herding and use of suitable animals.

73 So Claus Westermann, *Genesis 1–11: A Commentary* (trans. John J. Scullion; London: SPCK, 1984), p 337; but, for a different assessment, see van Wolde, *Stories,* pp 97–98.

Chapter 2 PUTTING US IN OUR PLACE

1 Bill McKibben, The Comforting Whirlwind: God, Job, and the Scale of Creation (Grand Rapids: Eerdmans, 1994), pp 57–58.

2 For a brief survey of the interpretations, see Donald E. Gowan, 'God's Answer to Job: How Is It an Answer?', *Horizons of Biblical Theology* 8 (1986), pp 85–102, here pp 86–89. My discussion is indebted especially to Robert Gordis, *The Book of God and Man: A Study of Job* (Chicago/London: University of Chicago Press, 1965); Norman C. Habel, *The Book of Job: A Commentary* (Old Testament Library; London: SCM Press, 1985); Gowan, 'God's Answer to Job, pp 85–102; Leo G. Perdue, *Wisdom in Revolt: Metaphorical Theology in the Book of Job (JSOTSup* 112; Bible and Literature Series 29; Sheffield: Sheffield Academic Press,1991); David Strong, 'The Promise of Technology Versus God's Promise in Job', *Theology Today* 48 (1991–92), pp 170–181; Tryggve N. D. Mettinger, 'The God of Job: Avenger, Tyrant, or Victor? ', in Leo G. Perdue and W. Clark Gilpin eds., *The Voice from the Whirlwind: Interpreting the Book of Job* (Nashville: Abingdon Press, 1992), pp 39–49; Langdon Gilkey, 'Power, Order, Justice, and Redemption: Theological Comments on Job', in Perdue and Gilpin eds., *The Voice,* pp 159–171; McKibben, *The Comforting Whirlwind;* Dale Patrick, 'Divine Creative Power and the Decentering of Creation: The Subtext of the Lord's Addresses to Job', in Norman C. Habel and Shirley Wurst eds., *The Earth Story in Wisdom Traditions* (Earth Bible 3; Sheffield: Sheffield Academic Press, 2001), pp 103–115; Robert S. Fyall, *Now My Eyes Have Seen You: Images of Creation in the Book of Job* (New Studies in Biblical Theology 12; Downers Grove, Illinois: InterVarsity Press/Leicester: Apollos, 2002).

3 All the biblical quotations in this chapter are based on the NRSV, but, especially in the case of quotations from Job 38—41, they have often been considerably modified, sometimes very considerably modified. In modifying the NRSV, I have drawn on other versions: the Jerusalem Bible, the Revised English Bible, and the authors' own translations in Habel, *The Book,* and Fyall, *Now My Eyes.* Readers should note that there are many translation problems in Job 38—41, and at times it is impossible to be at all sure of the meaning.

4 There is an implicit reference in 38:23, while 38:26 refers to the absence of human life.

5 On the sirocco in the Bible, see Aloysius Fitzgerald, *The Lord of the East Wind* (CBQMS 34; Washington: Catholic Biblical Association of America, 2002).

6 The identification of the constellations in this verse is very uncertain.

7 For 'decentring', see Patrick, 'Divine Creative Power and the Decentering of Creation'.

8 Peacocke, *Creation*, 65.

9 John Maddox, *What Remains to Be Discovered* (New York/London: Free Press, 1999), quoted in Martin Rees, *Our Final Century: Will Civilisation Survive the Twenty-First Century?* (London: Random House [Arrow Books], 2004), p 152.

10 Rees, Our Final, pp 151–153.

11 John D. Barrow, *Theories of Everything: The Quest for Ultimate Explanation* (London: Vintage, 1991), p 210.

12 Rees, *Our Final*, pp 153–155.

13 On humility as an ecological virtue, see Lawrence L. Mick, *Liturgy and Ecology in Dialogue* (Collegeville, Minnesota: Liturgical Press, 1997), pp 33–34.

14 McKibben, *The Comforting Whirlwind*, p 43.

15 All modern English translations of the Bible take these verses to refer to the ostrich, and much has been written about them on the assumption that the bird in question is the ostrich (e.g. Othmar Keel, *Jahwes Entgegnung an Ijob: Eine Deutung von Ijob 38–41 vor dem Hintergrund der zeitgenösseischen Bildkunst* (FRLANT 121; Göttingen: Vandenhoeck & Ruprecht, 1978) pp 67–68 and 83–85; Yehuda Feliks, *Nature and Man in the Bible* (London: Soncino Press, 1981) pp 263–265). I have been persuaded by Arthur Walker-Jones, 'The So-Called Ostrich in the God Speeches of the Book of Job (Job 39,13–18)', *Biblica* 86 (2005), pp 494–510, that the reference is more probably to the sand grouse. I am reluctant to surrender the more glamorous and humorous figure of the ostrich, but feel obliged to give back to the more humble sand grouse her rightful six verses of scriptural fame. There is a more certain reference to the ostrich in Lam. 4:3. Other cases where English Bibles refer to the ostrich may be rather to a certain sort of owl (Feliks, *Nature*, 101; see also Virginia C. Holmgren, *Bird Walk through the Bible* (New York: Dover, 1972), pp 120–131).

16 The sand grouse is contrasted with birds that have the wisdom and skill to build nests for their young in safe places.

17 For this bird as the griffon vulture, not the eagle, as in most English translations, see Feliks, *Nature*, p 133.

18 Norman C. Habel, ' "Is the Wild Ox Willing to Serve You?": Challenging the Mandate to Dominate', in Habel and Wurst eds., *The Earth Story in Wisdom*, pp 179–189; cf. also J. Gerald Jantzen, 'Creation and the Human Predicament in Job 1:9–11 and 38–41', *Ex Auditu* 3 (1987), pp 45–53.

19 Cf. Gene M. Tucker, 'Rain on a Land Where No One Lives: The Hebrew Bible on the Environment', *JBL* 116 (1997), p 15: 'Although the first divine speech is not a direct critique of the commission to have dominion, it explicitly challenges the human instinct to control, especially to domesticate.'

20 The hawk, paired with the vulture in 39:26, is also carnivorous, but the point is not explicit in the text, which focuses rather on its habit of migrating.

21 I see no indication here that 'the cruelties and brutalities of the animal kingdom are manifestations of the power of evil' (Fyall, *Now My Eyes*, p 80).

22 Cf. McKibben, *The Comforting Whirlwind*, pp 53–54.

---

23 The phrase is used by Jay McDaniel, 'All Animals Matter: Marc Bekoff's Contribution to Constructive Christian Theology', *Zygon* 41 (2006), pp 29–57, here p 37.

24 Bekoff, *Animal Passions*, pp 25–27, 35–39 and 150–151; Marc Bekoff, 'Animal Passions and Beastly Virtues: Cognitive Ethology as the Unifying Science for Understanding the Subjective, Emotional, Empathic, and Moral Lives of Animals', *Zygon* 41 (2006), pp 71–104, here pp 89–90.

25 Some modern poems about animals, for example some by Rainer Maria Rilke and Les Murray, achieve something like this.

26 Habel, *The Book*, pp 519–520 (the exception in 38:39 is presumably an oversight).

27 McKibben, *The Comforting Whirlwind*, p 63. I like particularly the example he gives of reforming the materialistic excess of Christmas celebrations in the USA (pp 65–68).

28 Feliks, *Nature*, pp 265–269. In the case of Leviathan, he speaks of 'an admixture of the crocodile and the whale with the legendary monsters of the deep' (p 268). The identification of Behemoth with the elephant was once common, but is not maintained by any recent scholars. Against the view of B. Couroyer, 'Qui est Béhémot? Job, XL, 15–24', *RB* 82 (1975), pp 418–443, that Behemoth is the wild ox, see Keel, *Jahwes Entgegnung*, pp 127–131.

29 See especially Keel, *Jahwes Entgegnung*, pp 127–156.

30 Feliks, *Nature*, p 268, thinks this feature is borrowed from the whale, 'which, when in cold waters, breathes tall jets of warm vapour through its nostrils', but 41:19–21 clearly refer to flames of fire.

31 Gordis, *The Book*, pp 119–120. Against Gordis's argument, see Fyall, *Now my Eyes*, pp 127–128.

32 For the latter, see Fyall, *Now my Eyes*, p 133.

33 This is probably an allusion to children with pet birds.

34 On the chaos myth, see Jon D. Levenson, *Creation and the Persistence of Evil: The Jewish Drama of Divine Omnipotence* (San Francisco: HarperCollins, 1988).

35 Fyall, *Now my Eyes*, sees Behemoth as Death (Mot) and Leviathan as Satan, but the connections he finds to justify these identifications seem to me tenuous.

36 Keel, *Jahwes Entgegnung*, pp 131–156; Mettinger, 'The God of Job', p 46; Bernhard Lang, 'Job XL:18 and the "Bones of Seth"', *VT* 30 (1980), pp 360–361.

37 Unfortunately these verses are obscure and have been variously understood.

38 For the view that the description of Leviathan also portrays God as victor over evil, see, e.g., Mettinger, 'The God of Job'.

39 Habel, *The Book*, pp 557–567; cf. also Purdue, *Wisdom*, chapter 8.

40 Habel, *The Book*, p 574.

Chapter 3 THE COMMUNITY OF CREATION

1 According to J. Baird Callicott, 'The New New (Buddhist) Ecology', JSRNC 2 (2008), pp 166–182, recent ecological thinking has moved from a 'balance-

of-nature' paradigm to a 'flux-of-nature' paradigm. But he admits that flux has severe limits.

2 There are also links between Ps. 104 and Gen. 1, which have been more often observed and discussed; cf. Leslie C. Allen, *Psalms 101–150* (WBC 21; Waco: Word, 1983), pp 30–31; Adele Berlin, 'The Wisdom of Creation in Psalm 104', in Ronald L. Troxel, Kelvin G. Friebel and Dennis R. Magary eds., *Seeking Out the Wisdom of the Ancients: Essays Offered to Honor Michael V. Fox* (Winona Lake, Indiana: Eisenbrauns, 2005), pp 71–83.

3 In this verse I have modified NRSV.

4 The significance of calling the cedars of Lebanon 'YHWH's trees' that 'he planted' is not clear. It may be that these huge trees, with their massive girth and long lives, were thought to survive from the time of creation when God himself planted trees on the Earth (cf. Gen. 2:8–9).

5 According to Yehuda Feliks, *Nature and Man in the Bible* (London: Soncino Press, 1981), p 31, these are the high juniper (*Juniperus excelsa*), tall trees which grow alongside the cedar on the mountains of Lebanon.

6 'Coney' here does not refer to the rabbit (though this was the original meaning of the English word), but to the rock hyrax (also mentioned in Prov. 30:26). See George Cansdale, *All the Animals of the Bible Lands* (Grand Rapids: Zondervan, 1970), pp 129–131; Feliks, *Nature*, p 223. They are the smallest of the land animals named here.

7 The phrase is used by Walter Brueggemann, *Theology of the Old Testament* (Minneapolis: Fortress, 1997), p 156.

8 William P. Brown, *Seeing the Psalms: A Theology of Metaphor* (Louisville, Kentucky: Westminster John Knox, 2003), p 159.

9 Odil Hannes Steck, *World and Environment* (Biblical Encounters Series; Nashville: Abingdon, 1980), p 86.

10 It seems quite possible that birds really experience joy in singing: Temple Grandin and Catherine Johnson, *Animals in Translation* (London: Bloomsbury, 2006), p 280.

11 On this basis, Allen, *Psalms 101–150*, p 33, claims that humanity 'is creation's central focus', though he goes on to say that 'man shares the world' with other creatures. I doubt whether this 'central' position for humanity is really how the psalm presents things. Brown, *Seeing*, p 160, on the other hand, writes: 'The cosmos revolves not around humankind but around the Earth, the medium of divine provision.'

12 Brown, *Seeing*, p 158.

13 John Felister, *Can Poetry Save the Earth: A Field Guide to Nature Poems* (New Haven: Yale University Press, 2009), p 26.

14 However, the lions (v 21) are not vegetarian, as all the animals are in Gen. 1.

15 Brueggemann, *Theology*, p 156; similarly, Allen, *Psalms 101–150*, p 34.

16 A possible translation of v 26b is 'Leviathan whom you made to amuse you' (JB), but it seems to me less likely than the NRSV's translation, with which most other English translations agree. Unfortunately, therefore, I cannot endorse Brown's images of God and Leviathan as playmates, or of Leviathan as God's rubber duck or 'special pet' (*Seeing*, p 161). Depending on this reading of the

verse, one of the rabbis said that every day God first studies Torah, then judges, then feeds the animals, and finally relaxes by playing with Leviathan ('*Avod. Zar.* 3b)!

17 Brown, *Seeing*, p 161, says that the psalm incorporates Leviathan 'into the fold of God's life-sustaining order'. For the argument that Leviathan is not a chaos monster in this context, see Rebecca S. Watson, *Chaos Uncreated: A Reassessment of the Theme of 'Chaos' in the Hebrew Bible* (BZAW 341; Berlin: De Gruyter, 2005), pp 235–237.

18 See Scott Hoezee, *Remember Creation: God's World of Wonder and Delight* (Grand Rapids: Eerdmans, 1998), pp 26–42.

19 I have discussed this passage in more detail in Richard Bauckham, 'Reading the Sermon on the Mount in an Age of Ecological Catastrophe', *SCE* 22 (2009), pp 76–88.

20 See also Job 38:39–41; Ps. 145:15–16; Ps. 147:9. In Luke's parallel to Matt. 6:25–33, Jesus refers to the ravens (Luke 12:24) rather than to birds in general. They must constitute an allusion to Job 38:41 and/or Ps. 147:9. Ravens were a popular example of God's feeding of the creatures, presumably because their raucous cry sounds as though they are calling on God to feed them.

21 Very poor people had to use even straw as fuel for fires.

22 On humans as more valuable than animals, see also Matt. 10:31 and 12:12, and Luke 12:7 and 24, and the discussion of these passages in Richard Bauckham, 'Jesus and Animals I: What Did He Teach?', in Andrew Linzey and Dorothy Yamamoto eds., *Animals on the Agenda* (London: SCM Press, 1998), pp 33–48, here pp 44–47.

23 Cf., e.g., Matt. 5:29–30 and 42.

24 John Naish, *Enough* (London: Hodder & Stoughton, 2008), speaks of substituting 'enoughness' for 'ever more'.

25 I have discussed this theme at greater length in Richard Bauckham, 'Joining Creation's Praise of God', *Ecotheology* 7 (2002), pp 45–59; cf. also Edward P. Echlin, *The Cosmic Circle: Jesus and Ecology* (Dublin: Columba Press, 2004), pp 128–139. Terence E. Fretheim, *God and the World in the Old Testament: A Relational Theology of Creation* (Nashville: Abingdon, 2005), pp 267–278, lists fifty texts in which nature praises God. Most are in the Psalms and Isa. 35–66.

26 The Greek Additions to Daniel, found only in the Greek versions of Daniel, include a psalm attributed to the three men in the fiery furnace which develops the theme of Ps. 148 at great length (LXX Dan 3:36–90). It is found among the Apocrypha in Protestant Bibles, but among the deutero-canonical books of the Old Testament in Roman Catholic and Orthodox Bibles. In liturgical use it is known as the *Benedicite*.

27 Fretheim, *God*, p 257.

28 Fretheim, *God*, p 258.

29 Presumably for the same reasons, this theme is grossly neglected even in Old Testament scholarship and discussion of the theme of creation in the Old Testament. E.g. only one paragraph (p 150) is devoted to it by Ronald A. Simkins, *Creator and Creation: Nature in the Worldview of Ancient Israel* (Peabody, Massachusetts: Hendrickson, 1994).

30 When the biblical writers treat the cry of the young ravens (Ps. 147:9) or the roar of the young lions (Job 38:41; Ps. 104:21) as addressed to God, they are indulging in a little anthropomorphism.

31 Daniel W. Hardy and David F. Ford, *Jubilate: Theology in Praise* (London: Darton, Longman & Todd, 1984), p 82.

32 Brown *Seeing*, p 164, makes this mistake when, comparing Psalm 8 and Psalm 148, he writes that 'the author of Psalm 148 "fulfills" the exercise of dominion, not by subjugation and slaughter but by exhortation to praise. Dominion over animals is redefined as enablement to praise.' But the animals in this psalm have no special importance; they belong with angels, stars, oceans, weather, mountains and trees to the universal choir. The dominion is not redefined here but ignored.

33 There is a helpful discussion of the angels who praise God in heaven in Michael Welker, *Creation and Reality* (trans. John F. Hoffmeyer; Minneapolis: Fortress, 1999), pp 54–59.

34 Christopher Southgate, *The Groaning of Creation: God, Evolution, and the Problem of Evil* (Louisville: Westminster John Knox, 2008), p 111.

35 Brown, *Seeing*, p 164.

36 Similarly, Fretheim, *God*, pp 265–266.

37 Brian Swimme and Thomas Berry, *The Universe Story: From the Primordial Flaring Forth to the Ecozoic Era – A Celebration of the Unfolding of the Cosmos* (London: Penguin, 1994), pp 263–264.

38 I opposed it rather strongly in Bauckham, 'Joining', pp 49–51, as did Michael S. Northcott, *The Environment and Christian Ethics* (Cambridge: Cambridge University Press, 1996), pp 132–134. Elizabeth Theokritoff, 'Creation and Priesthood in Modern Orthodox Thinking', *Ecotheology* 10 (2005), pp 344–363, responds to these critiques. It is interesting to note that Swimme and Berry, *The Universe Story*, p 264, have their own non-theistic version of humanity's priesthood: 'Our own special role is to enable this entire community to reflect on and to celebrate itself and its deepest mystery in a special mode of conscious self-awareness.'

39 George Herbert, 'Providence', in John N. Wall ed., *George Herbert: The Country Parson, The Temple* (Classics of Western Spirituality; New York/Mahwah: Paulist, 1981) p 238.

40 John Zizioulas, 'Priest of Creation', in R. J. Berry ed., *Environmental Stewardship: Critical Perspectives – Past and Present* (London: T. & T. Clark 2006), pp 273–290; Theokritoff, 'Creation and Priesthood', where the contributions of several modern Orthodox theologians are surveyed and distinguished.

41 Jürgen Moltmann, *God in Creation: An Ecological Doctrine of Creation* (trans. Margaret Kohl; London: SCM Press, 1985), pp 70–71. Larry Rasmussen, 'Symbols to Live By', in Berry ed., *Environmental Stewardship*, pp 174–184, here p 181, does no more than paraphrase Moltmann.

42 Southgate, *The Groaning*, pp 110–113.

43 Zizioulas, 'Priest of Creation', p 290.

44 Theokritoff, 'Creation', especially pp 345–350.

45 Theokritoff, 'Creation', p 351.

46 I have explored this idea of reciprocity in the praise of God a little more in 'Joining', pp 51–53.

47 The terminology used is quite confusing. Also used are: de-deification, demystification, desacramentalisation, and disenchantment, with a range of connotations.

48 For a much more nuanced account of the desacralisation of nature, not in the Bible but in Christian history, see Thomas Berry, 'Christianity's Role in the Earth Project', in Dieter T. Hessel and Rosemary Radford Ruether eds., *Christianity and Ecology: Seeking the Well-Being of Earth and Humans* (Cambridge, Massachusetts: Harvard University Press, 2000), pp 127–134.

49 Fretheim, *God*, p 251; Christopher J. H. Wright, *Old Testament Ethics for the People of God* (Leicester: InterVarsity Press, 2004), pp 111–112. R. J. Berry, 'Foreword', in R. J. Berry ed., *The Care of Creation* (Leicester: InterVarsity Press, 2000) pp 7–9, here p 8, writes: 'The Christian desacralizing of nature (the recognition that it is creation, not Creator) was an indispensable prelude to the whole scientific enterprise and is essential to the development of the Earth's resources today. We *respect* nature because God made it; we do not *reverence* nature as if it were God and inviolable.' I would say that nature is *sacred because God made it* and we should treat it reverentially as something that is valued by God and helps us to worship God. See, in a little more detail, Richard Bauckham, 'Human Authority in Creation', in Bauckham, *God and the Crisis of Freedom: Biblical and Contemporary Perspectives* (Louisville: Westminster John Knox, 2002), pp 128–177, here pp 163–164.

50 My own use of this phrase probably derives originally from Moltmann, *God in Creation*, pp 31, 70 and elsewhere.

51 See especially Aldo Leopold, 'The Land Ethic', in Aldo Leopold, *A Sand County Almanac and Sketches Here and There* (New York: Oxford University Press, 1987 (1st edition, 1940)), pp 201–226; cf. also J. Baird Callicott, 'Land Ethics: Into Terra Incognita', in Curt Meine and Richard L. Knight eds., *The Essential Aldo Leopold: Quotations and Commentaries* (Madison, Wisconsin: Wisconsin University Press, 1999), pp 299–313; Norman Wirzba, *The Paradise of God: Renewing Religion in an Ecological Age* (New York: Oxford University Press, 2003), pp 100–105; Max Oeschlaeger, *The Idea of Wilderness: From Prehistory to the Age of Ecology* (New Haven: Yale University Press, 1991), chapter 7.

52 Leopold, *A Sand County Almanac*, p viii.

53 Leopold, 'The Land Ethic', p 204.

54 Robin Attfield, *The Ethics of Environmental Concern* (2nd edition; Athens, Georgia: University of Georgia Press, 1991), pp 156–160; and cf. also the critical assessment of Leopold's land ethic in Northcott, *The Environment*, pp 106–110.

55 From a Christian perspective, our obligations to other creatures rest on their being created by God and valued by God, but our interconnectedness with them and theirs with each other must affect the ways in which these obligations translate into concrete responsibilities and duties.

56 Wendell Berry, 'Christianity and the Survival of Creation', in Berry, *Sex, Economy, Freedom and Community: Eight Essays* (New York: Pantheon Books, 1993), pp 93–116, here p 106. Thomas Berry used the term 'Earth Community' (see Thomas Berry, *The Dream of the Earth* (San Francisco: Sierra Club, 1988), chapter 2), which has also been taken up by the Earth Bible Project (see Norman C. Habel, 'Introducing the Earth Bible' in Norman C. Habel ed., *Readings from the Perspective of Earth* (Sheffield: Sheffield Academic Press, 2000), pp 25–37, and the Earth Bible Team, 'Guiding Ecojustice Principles', in Habel ed., *Readings*, pp 38–53). Thomas Berry also calls the Earth community a 'sacred community' (Thomas Berry and Thomas Clarke, *Befriending the Earth: A Theology of Reconciliation Between Humans and the Earth* (Mystic, Connecticut: Twenty-Third Publications, 1991), pp 43–44). Joseph Sittler, *Evocations of Grace: Writings on Ecology, Theology and Ethics*, (ed. Steven Bouma-Prediger and Peter Bakken; Grand Rapids: Eerdmans, 2000), p 204, speaks of creation as 'a community of abounding love' and also as humanity's 'companion-world'. Richard L. Fern, *Nature, God and Humanity: Envisioning an Ethics of Nature* (Cambridge: Cambridge University Press, 2002), chapter 7, speaks of 'the fellowship of creation'.

57 Wendell Berry, 'Two Economies', in Berry, *Home Economics: Fourteen Essays* (San Francisco: North Point Press, 1987), pp 54–75, here pp 72–73.

58 Northcott, *The Environment*, pp 174–176.

59 See Alan Weisman, *The World Without Us* (London: Virgin Books, 2007).

60 Berry, 'Christianity', p 103.

61 On the meaning of *'aval* in these contexts, see Katherine M. Hayes, *'The Earth Mourns': Prophetic Metaphor and Oral Aesthetic* (SBLAB 8; Atlanta: SBL, 2002), pp 12–18; Fretheim, *God*, p 175.

62 The two words also appear in parallel in Isa. 34:3, and these three are the only occurrences of *bohu* in the Bible.

63 The fourfold 'I looked' may be used of the number four as indicating the whole Earth (which has four directions and four corners).

64 For this theme in a variety of texts in the prophets, see Hilary Marlow, *Biblical Prophets and Contemporary Environmental Ethics: Re-Reading Amos, Hosea and First Isaiah* (Oxford: Oxford University Press, 2009); Terence E. Fretheim, 'The Earth Story in Jeremiah 12', in Habel ed., *Readings from the Perspective of Earth*, pp 96–110; Melissa Tubbs Loya, ' "Therefore the Earth Mourns": The Grievance of Earth in Hosea 4:1–3', in Habel and Peter Trudinger eds., *Exploring Ecological Hermeneutics* (SBLSymS 46; Atlanta: SBL, 2008), pp 53–62; Laurie J. Braaten, 'Earth Community in Joel 1–2: A Call to Identify with the Rest of Creation', *HBT* 28 (2006), pp 113–129 (a shorter version is in Habel and Trudinger eds., *Exploring*, pp 63–74).

65 Walter Brueggemann, *A Commentary on Jeremiah: Exile and Homecoming* (Grand Rapids: Eerdmans, 1998), p 59.

66 Cf. Robert Murray, *The Cosmic Covenant* (Heythrop Monographs 7; London: Sheed & Ward, 1992), chapter 4.

67 Northcott, *The Environment*, p 173, and chapter 2.

68 Northcott, *The Environment*, pp 196–198, summarises his exposition of the created order in the Hebrew Bible in seven points that are worth close attention.

69 This is not a generally accepted view, but I have been persuaded by Laurie J. Braaten, 'All Creation Groans: Romans 8.22 in Light of the Biblical Sources', *HBT* 28 (2006), pp 131–159. In an article that came to my attention after writing this chapter, Jonathan Moo, 'Romans 8.19–22 and Isaiah's Cosmic Covenant', *NTS* 54 (2008), pp 74–89, argues that in this passage Paul was especially dependent on Isaiah 24—27.

70 I have changed the NRSV's translation at this point. In the Greek, Paul uses two verbs: *sustenazei* and *sunodinei*.

71 The metaphor does not usually imply a positive outcome, but refers only to the pain.

72 Cherryl Hunt, David G. Horrell and Christopher Southgate, 'An Environmental Mantra? Ecological Interest in Romans 8:19–23 and a Modest Proposal for its Narrative Interpretation', *JTS* 59 (2008) pp 546–579, here pp 560–563, express doubts about the common assumption that Adam and the Fall are in the background to Paul's thought in this passage. Olle Christoffersson, *The Earnest Expectation of the Creature: The Flood-Tradition as Matrix of Romans 8:18–27* (ConBNT 23; Stockholm: Almqvist & Wiksell, 1990), argues instead for the Genesis Flood narrative.

73 The reference then is not to death as a universal feature of the animal and vegetable creations (which is probably the most common interpretation), but to processes of ecological degradation and destruction that occur frequently and widely where humans live.

74 For example, in the Greek version of Ecclesiastes *mataiotes* is used frequently with the sense of 'vanity' or 'futility' or 'meaninglessness'.

75 This point has been made many times, e.g., most recently, by Christopher Southgate, *The Groaning of Creation: God, Evolution and the Problem of Evil* (Louisville: Westminster John Knox, 2008), pp 28–29.

76 These are the domestic animals, distinguished from the wild animals in v 20.

77 The rare verb *'arag* may mean 'to long for', as in Ps. 42:2. Might it be the basis for *apokaradokia* ('eager expectation') in Rom. 8:19? Hays, ' "The Earth Mourns" ', p 196, translates it as 'thirst for you', and comments: 'The distinction between the verbs *qara'*, "call", and *'arag*, "thirst for, long for", reflects the difference between the voiced appeal of the human speaker [in v 19] and the mute longing of the animals.'

78 Hunt, Horrell and Southgate, 'An Environmental Mantra?', p 572, rightly comment that 'the narrative [implied in Rom. 8:19–23] is profoundly eschatological'.

79 This is a very different view from Christopher Southgate's evolutionary interpretation of Rom. 8:19–23 (*The Groaning*, pp 92–96). He interprets the 'futility' to which creation has been subjected as the suffering and tragedy inherent in the evolutionary process, and sees humans as assisting God's healing of the evolutionary process.

---

80 Hunt, Horrell and Southgate, 'An Environmental Mantra?', take up the term from John Bolt, 'The Relation between Creation and Redemption in Romans 8:18–27', *CTJ* 30 (1995), pp 34–51, here p 34.

81 Ellen F. Davis, *Scripture, Culture, and Agriculture: An Agrarian Reading of the Bible* (Cambridge: Cambridge University Press, 2009), pp 9–10.

82 Fretheim, *God*, 163–165, is an excellent brief treatment.

83 Fretheim, *God*, 160.

84 For this eschatological dimension, see also Fretheim, *God*, p 265.

Chapter 4 WHERE THE WILD THINGS ARE

1 Roderick Frazier Nash, *Wilderness and the American Mind* (4th edition; New Haven: Yale University Press, 2001), pp 14–15.

2 Nash, *Wilderness*, p 16.

3 Nash, *Wilderness*, p 35.

4 Robert Barry Leal, 'Negativity towards Wilderness in the Biblical Record', *Ecotheology* 10 (2005), pp 364–381. See also Robert Barry Leal, *Wilderness in the Bible: Toward a Theology of Wilderness* (Studies in Biblical Literature 72; New York: Peter Lang, 2004), where he gives more attention to 'wilderness as God's good creation' (chapter 7), but where nevertheless it is the negative biblical attitudes to wilderness that receive most attention. The idea that the Hebrew Bible takes a wholly negative view of wilderness also owes much to the influence of Johannes Pedersen, *Israel: Its Life and Culture*, 2 vols. (Oxford University Press: London, 1946–1947), pp 454–460 (on 'wilderness' in the biblical sense of desert land), on which see Peter Addinall, 'The Wilderness of Pedersen's *Israel*', *JSOT* 20 (1981), pp 75–82.

5 Cf. Evan Eisenberg, *The Ecology of Eden* (London: Picador (Macmillan), 1998), p 93.

6 In Chapter 1, I rejected the suggestion that the verb *'avad* should be translated 'to serve' in this context.

7 Hiebert, *The Yahwist's Landscape*, p 52.

8 The four rivers correspond to the four directions or the four corners of the Earth.

9 Odil Hannes Steck, *World and Environment* (Biblical Encounters Series; Nashville: Abingdon, 1980), p 74; similarly Robert Murray, *The Cosmic Covenant* (Heythrop Monographs 7; London: Sheed & Ward, 1992), p 100; *contra* Claus Westermann, *Genesis 1–11: A Commentary* (trans. John J. Scullion; London: SPCK, 1984), p 221.

10 Bernhard Lang, *The Hebrew God: Portrait of an Ancient Deity* (New Haven: Yale University Press, 2000), p 157.

11 Eisenberg, *The Ecology*, p xix. A more common and perhaps more straightforward reading would focus on preserving the fertility of the soil that humans farm. Eisenberg's approach depends on his view of Eden as the quintessence of wild nature (p 93).

12 E.g. Bill McKibben, *The End of Nature* (London: Viking, 1990), p 54: 'We have deprived nature of its independence, and that is fatal to its meaning. Nature's

independence *is* its meaning: without it there is nothing but us. (italics original).

13 Nash, *Wilderness*, p 15.

14 The usage that emerges in Nash's discussion of the American Puritans and the early pioneers in the American West, is that 'wilderness' is all of wild nature, nature outside human control, while the human task was understood as 'conquering' such wildness and bringing all of nature under human control, which at its best would be paradise. It seems that this usage determined later use of the term wilderness in American discussion.

15 For the characteristics of 'wilderness', see S. *'midbar'* TDOT 8.87–118, here 95 and 101–2.

16 On the types of forest, see Michael Zohary, *Plants of the Bible* (Cambridge: Cambridge University Press, 1982), pp 28–30 and 33.

17 See the map in Zohary, *Plants*, p 29, but contrast Yehuda Feliks, *Nature and Man in the Bible* (London: Soncino Press, 1981), pp 26–31.

18 It is a serious problem in Leal, *Wilderness*, that in his account of the biblical material (Parts A and B) he keeps to what the Bible calls wilderness, but when he goes on to relate it to modern environmental concerns (Part C) he works with the modern sense of wilderness as including forests and oceans. Yet he is well aware of the difference between the two usages (*Wilderness*, pp 36–37).

19 Michael S. Northcott, *A Moral Climate: The Ethics of Global Warming* (London: Darton, Longman & Todd, 2007), p 234, sees the expulsion from Eden as symbolising 'the ancient move from hunter-gathering to farming'. Cf. also Max Oeschlaeger, *The Idea of Wilderness: From Prehistory to the Age of Ecology* (New Haven: Yale University Press, 1991), p 31; Daniel Hillel, *The Natural History of the Bible* (New York: Columbia University Press, 2006), p 245: 'The expulsion from Eden is a folk memory of the beginning of agriculture.' It is true that Eden precedes the distinction between the human world and wild nature, but it does not seem to me plausible to characterise Adam as a hunter-gatherer. Note that the same expression, 'to till the ground', is used of his work both within the garden and outside (2:5 and 15, and 3:23).

20 Leslie Allen, *The Books of Joel, Obadiah, Jonah and Micah* (NICOT; Grand Rapids: Eerdmans, 1976), p 224.

21 There is much humour in Jonah, but not at this point.

22 Further examples in Talmon, 'midbar' 103.

23 E.g. 2 Kings 2:24; Jer. 5:6; Mic. 5:8.

24 For opposition between the human world and the wild as characteristic of cultures practising agriculture, see Tihamer R. Kover, 'The Domestic Order and its Feral Threat: The Intellectual Heritage of the Neolithic Landscape', in S. Bergmann, P. M. Scott, M. Jansdotter Samuelsson and H. Bedford-Strohm eds, *Nature, Space and the Sacred: Transdisciplinary Perspectives* (Farnham, Surrey: Ashgate, 2009), pp 235–247.

25 As well as the examples discussed below, see Jer. 9:10–11; 49:33; 50:3 and 12–13; 51:25–26 and 43; Ezek. 29:10–12; and Zeph. 2:13–15.

26 In this passage, I have made changes to the NRSV that follow the translation of Joseph Blenkinsopp, *Isaiah 1–39* (AB 19; New York: Doubleday, 2000), p 276.

27 The flocks here are herds of wild animals, the wild asses or others. But the claim by Ronald A. Simkins, *Creator and Creation: Nature in the Worldview of Ancient Israel* (Peabody, Massachusetts: Hendrickson, 1994), p 224, that the site's 'only inhabitants will be wild animals, *demonic and symbolic of chaos*' (italics added), has no basis in the text.

28 For evidence of close observation of wild creatures, see also the four words for lions in Job 4:10–11, and the four words for locusts in Joel 1:4.

29 Blenkinsopp, *Isaiah 1–39*, pp 448–449.

30 Feliks, *Nature*, pp 100–104; cf. also pp 217–219.

31 Feliks, *Nature*, pp 102–103. See also Virginia C. Holmgren, *Bird Walk through the Bible* (New York: Dover, 1972), pp 68–73, and especially Hilary Marlow, *Biblical Prophets and Contemporary Environmental Ethics: Re-Reading Amos, Hosea and First Isaiah* (Oxford: Oxford University Press, 2009), p 230–233.

32 The idea (reflected in some of the English translations) that some of the creatures in this and other pictures of desolation may be not birds or mammals but evil spirits may well be mistaken. Feliks, *Nature*, p 103, thinks the names *sa'ir* and *lilith* were later given to demons through popular identification of the birds as evil spirits. But John D. W. Watts, *Isaiah 34–66* (WBC 25; revised edition; n.p.: Thomas Nelson, 2005), p 536, thinks that Lilith at least is unmistakably demonic, while John B. Geyer, 'Desolation and Cosmos', *VT* 49 (1999), pp 49–64, here pp 55–62, inclines to the view that some of the creatures mentioned in these passages are demons, and thinks the howling or yelling sounds implied by the onomatopoeic names of some of them was probably more important to the writers than their zoological identification. This seems implausible in Isa. 34, where so many species are distinguished.

33 Isa. 19:17 is an example of judgement portrayed as reversal of conditions; cf. 40:4.

34 Simkins, *Creator*, pp 209–211, speaks of the 'catastrophe/new-creation myth'.

35 I borrow the term from Bill Devall, *Simple in Means, Deep in Ends: Practising Deep Ecology* (London: Green Print, 1990), p 34.

36 I have omitted v 19: 'The forest will disappear completely, and the city will be utterly laid low'. This is very obscure and the translation uncertain. Commentators suggest that 'the forest' here must be a political metaphor, designating the Judaean kingdom or the empire of Assyria. Otherwise it would seem in flat contradiction to v 15. The political symbolism of trees is widespread in Isaiah.

37 Karl Löning and Erich Zenger, *To Begin With, God Created: Biblical Theologies of Creation* (Collegeville: Liturgical Press, 2000), p 181.

38 Watts, *Isaiah 34–66*, p 542.

39 The identity of this flower is uncertain.

40 Feliks, *Nature*, pp 110–112; Zohary, *Plants*, pp 106–107.

41 Cf. YHWH compared with a cypress in Hos. 14:8. The words 'glory' (*kavod*) and 'majesty' (*hadar*) are used together of God in Isa. 2:10, 19 and 21; Ps. 145:5 and 12.

42 Davis, *Scripture*, pp 95 and 103.

43 Some wild animals were hunted for their pelts: see Oded Borowski, *Every Living Thing: Daily Use of Animals in Ancient Israel* (Walton Creek, California: AltaMira Press, 1998), chapter 7.

44 Lev. 26:6 is similar but less radical, because it lacks the idea that people will live in the forest.

45 The meaning could be 'land' or 'earth' (NRSV), but the former is more plausible in the context of vv 9a and 10. So Robert Murray, *The Cosmic Covenant* (Heythrop Monographs 7; London: Sheed & Ward, 1992), p 200 n 26.

46 Feliks, *Nature*, pp 87–89.

47 For the realistic nature of the example, see Feliks, *Nature*, pp 89–90.

48 Gene M. Tucker, 'The Peaceable Kingdom and a Covenant with the Wild Animals', in William P. Brown and S. Dean McBride eds., *God Who Creates: Essays in Honor of W. Sibley Towner* (Grand Rapids: Eerdmans, 2000), pp 215–225, here p 217.

49 John W. Olley, ' "The Wolf, the Lamb, and a Little Child": Transforming the Diverse Earth Community in Isaiah', in Norman C. Habel ed., *The Earth Story in the Psalms and the Prophets* (Earth Bible 4; Sheffield: Sheffield Academic Press, 2001), pp 219–229, here p 225, argues against the allegorical reading.

50 See Marlow, *Prophets and Environmental Ethics*, p 238.

51 Olley, ' "The Wolf" ', p 227, goes so far as to say: 'The vision of the future worshipping life on the holy mountain includes animals.'

52 On this, see especially Löning and Zenger, *To Begin With,* pp 175–176.

53 In the light of Gen. 1:29–30, it is not true that the 'Bible is not concerned about violence within the animal world', but only with violence 'between the human and the animal world' (Simkins, *Creator*, p 226).

54 The summary version of Isa. 11:6–9 in Isa. 65:24–25 differs here: 'the serpent – its food shall be dust', which confirms the curse of Gen. 3:14. This makes the allusion more explicit, and also assumes the end of the enmity between humans and snakes.

55 Murray, *The Cosmic Covenant*, p 104, gives the translation: 'a little boy herding them'.

56 For children as shepherds, see Borowski, *Every Living Thing,* p 48.

57 Olley, ' "The Wolf" ', p 224.

58 Brevard S. Childs, *Isaiah* (OTL; Louisville: Westminster John Knox, 2001), p 104. However, Tucker, 'The Peaceable Kingdom', thinks the degree of transformation is too small to represent a return to Eden.

59 Andrew Linzey, *Animal Theology* (Urbana: University of Illinois Press, 1995), pp 82–83 (italics added). Christopher Southgate, *The Groaning of Creation: God, Evolution, and the Problem of Evil* (Louisville: Westminster John Knox, 2008), pp 88–89, quotes a poem by James Dickey that imagines what life in the new creation might be like for predators and prey, preserving, as Southgate says, 'the characteristics of species, but without pain or death or destruction'.

60 W. Sibley Towner, 'The Future of Nature', *Int* 50 (1996), pp 27–35, here p 33.

61 Towner, 'The Future', p 34.

62 I have argued at length for this interpretation of Mark 1:13 in Richard Bauckham, 'Jesus and the Wild Animals (Mark 1:13): A Christological Image for an Ecological Age', in J. B. Green and M. Turner eds., *Jesus of Nazareth: Lord and Christ: Essays on the Historical Jesus and New Testament Christology* (Festschrift for I. Howard Marshall; Grand Rapids: Eerdmans, 1994), pp 3–21.

Among recent studies, this view is also taken by Joel Marcus, *Mark 1–8* (AB 27; New York: Doubleday, 1999), pp 167–168.

63 Douglas Hall, 'Stewardship as Key to a Theology of Nature', in R. J. Berry ed., *Environmental Stewardship: Critical Perspectives – Past and Present* (London: T. & T. Clark, 2006), pp 129–144, here p 140 (italics original).

64 Hall, 'Stewardship', p 141.

65 Bruce Vawter, *On Genesis: A New Reading* (New York: Doubleday, 1977), p 73, speaks of 'false starts'.

66 E.g. Elijah Judah Schochet, *Animal Life in Jewish Traditions* (New York: Ktav, 1984), p 11; Vawter, *On Genesis*, p 74.

67 See especially George W. Ramsey, 'Is Name-Giving an Act of Domination in Genesis 2:23 and elsewhere?', *CBQ* 50 (1988), pp 24–35.

68 Ramsey, 'Is Name-Giving', pp 26–29, shows that variation in the verbal formula makes no difference to the meaning.

69 Westermann, *Genesis 1–11*, pp 228–229; Ramsey, 'Is Name-Giving', p 34: 'If the act of naming signifies anything about the name-giver, it is the quality of *discernment.*'

70 Charles Pinches, 'Each According to Its Kind: A Defense of Theological Speciesism', in Charles Pinches and Jay B. McDaniel eds., *Good News for Animals? Christian Approaches to Animal Well-Being* (New York: Orbis, 1993), pp 187–205, here p 200.

71 John Felsteiner, *Can Poetry Save the Earth? A Field Guide to Nature Poems* (New Haven: Yale University Press, 2009), pp 21–23. Cf. H. W. Garrod, quoted in C. Day Lewis, *The Poetic Image* (London: Jonathan Cape, 1947), p 25: 'Once upon a time the world was fresh, to speak was to be a poet, to name objects an inspiration.'

72 Bill McKibben, *The Comforting Whirlwind: God, Job, and the Scale of Creation* (Grand Rapids: Eerdmans, 1994), p 79.

73 Cf. McKibben, *The Comforting Whirlwind*, p 83.

74 Both words can be used of mammals in general (e.g. *behemah* in Gen. 6:20; 7:23; and 8:17, and *hayyah* in Gen 8:19), but most often have these distinct meanings, especially when occurring together.

75 The original vegetarianism of humans in Genesis could be seen as qualifying this point, but in Old Testament Israel all the domestic animals were useful in other ways besides providing meat.

76 Paul's rather surprising and problematic exegesis of this text in 1 Cor. 9:9–11 is discussed by Robert N. Wennberg, *God, Humans, and Other Animals* (Grand Rapids: Eerdmans, 2003), pp 297–298; Anthony C. Thiselton, *The First Epistle to the Corinthians* (NIGTC; Grand Rapids: Eerdmans, 2000), pp 685–688. It has to be seen in relation to Paul's conviction that the Torah was written for the early Christians (1 Cor. 10:6 and 11).

77 Anthony Phillips, 'Animals and the Torah', *ExpTim* 106 (1995), pp 260–265, here p 260.

78 The domestic chicken seems to have been a late arrival in Palestine.

79 Rosemary Radford Ruether, 'Men, Women, and Beasts: Relations to Animals in Western Culture', in Pinches and McDaniel eds., *Good News for Animals?*, pp

12–23, here p 14, thinks that 'organized warfare, domination of women, of conquered people and of animals' developed concurrently and encouraged the equation of all three dominated groups (women, conquered people, animals) as symbolically the same. She also suggests: 'Perhaps yoking animals to the plow and driving them with whips also suggested that such plow animals were a type of slave, and slaves, who were similarly chained and driven to pull large stones for public works, were "beasts".'

80 Though from a modern perspective, Genesis 4:20 might be thought to describe domestication, it probably means no more than that Jabal began the practice of nomadic herding. No change in the animals is implied.

81 T. P. O'Connor, 'Working at Relationships: Another Look at Animal Domestication', *Antiquity* 71 (1987), pp 149–156; Stephen Budiansky, *The Covenant of the Wild: Why Animals Chose Domestication* (London: Weidenfeld & Nicolson, 1994); Richard W. Bulliet, *Hunters, Herders, and Hamburgers: The Past and Future of Human–Animal Relationships* (New York: Columbia University Press, 2005), chapters 5–6. Some writers put this in theological terms, speaking of a 'covenant' between humans and domestic animals.

82 This seems to be the only biblical reference to individual animals having names, but the practice of naming animals has been so common with farmers in the past that it is hard not to believe that it happened more generally in biblical societies.

83 For God as caring shepherd, see also Isa. 40:11 and Jer. 50:6–7 and 17–19.

84 John W. Rogerson, 'What was the Meaning of Animal Sacrifice', in Andrew Linzey and Dorothy Yamamoto eds., *Animals on the Agenda* (London: SCM Press, 1998), pp 8–17, here pp 13–14.

85 David Williams, *Animals Rights, Human Responsibilities* (Grove Booklet E151; Cambridge, 2008), p 17.

86 Williams, *Animals Rights*, p 22.

87 There are particularly helpful comments on this verse in Murray, *The Cosmic Covenant*, p 113; Bruce K. Waltke, *The Book of Proverbs Chapters 1–15* (NICOT; Grand Rapids: Eerdmans, 2004), pp 526–527.

88 Richard J. Clifford, *Proverbs: A Commentary* (OTL; Louisville: Westminster, 1999), p 131: 'to be sympathetically aware of an animal's condition, especially if it has enough to eat'.

89 Roger Norman Whybray, *Proverbs* (NCB; London: Marshall Pickering, 1994), p 193, suggests the translation 'feelings' for *nephesh*.

90 In Num. 22:30, the donkey tells Balaam he should have known that something unusual was wrong: 'Am I not your donkey, which you have ridden all your life to this day? Have I been in the habit of treating you this way?'

91 Waltke, *The Book of Proverbs*, p 527.

92 Murray, *The Cosmic Covenant*, p 113.

Chapter 5 FROM ALPHA TO OMEGA

1 e.g. Matt. 11:27; Luke 10:22; John 3:35; 13:3; and 16:15; Acts 10:36; 1 Cor. 15:27–28; Eph. 1:22; Phil. 3:21; and Heb. 1:2 and 2:8; cf. Eph. 1:23 and 4:10.

2 Calvin B. DeWitt, 'Behemoth and Batrachians in the Eye of God: Responsibility to Other Kinds in Biblical Perspective', in Dieter T. Hessel and Rosemary Radford Ruether eds., *Christianity and Ecology: Seeking the Well-Being of Earth and Humans* (Cambridge, Massachusetts: Harvard University Press, 2000), pp 291–316, here pp 296–298, speaks of 'a three-party relationship' and offers a triangular figure of the kind I describe.

3 Cf. Terry Eagleton, *Reason, Faith, and Revolution: Reflections on the God Debate* (New Haven/London: Yale University Press, 2009), pp 84–85: 'There is indeed progress – as long as we bear in mind that the civilisation which manifests it is also one which seems bent on destroying the planet, slaughtering the innocent, and manufacturing human inequality on an unimaginable scale.'

4 Thomas Berry, *The Dream of the Earth* (San Francisco: Sierra Club Books, 1988), p 17.

5 For the shift in Old Testament scholarship away from this dichotomy of creation and history, see Walter Brueggemann, *Theology of the Old Testament* (Minneapolis: Fortress, 1997), pp 159–164.

6 That the fullness (*pleroma*) is the fullness of the divine presence is not explicit in Greek. Michael Trainor, 'The Cosmic Christology of Colossians 1:15–20 in the Light of Contemporary Ecological Issues', *ABR* 53 (2005), pp 54–69, here p 67, argues that the reference is to the fullness of creation. However, not only the parallel with 2:9 ('in him the whole fullness of deity dwells bodily'), but also the fact that in 1:19–20 the *pleroma* is the subject of 'was pleased to dwell … and to reconcile', strongly support the usual view that the divine fullness is in view.

7 My view is that Colossians is an authentic letter of Paul, but the issue of authorship is of no importance here.

8 This much is common to most scholars' view of the structure. For a somewhat more elaborate recent proposal, see Vincent A. Pizzuto, *A Cosmic Leap of Faith: An Authorial, Structural, and Theological Investigation of the Cosmic Christology in Col. 1:15–20* (CBET 41; Leuven: Peeters, 2006), pp 118–119 and 203–205.

9 Joseph Sittler, *Evocations of Grace: Writings on Ecology, Theology and Ethics* (eds. Steven Bouma-Prediger and Peter Bakken; Grand Rapids: Eerdmans, 2000), p 39.

10 Pizzuto, *A Cosmic Leap*, p 258.

11 The description of God as 'invisible' thus makes the significance of the phrase different from the otherwise parallel usages with respect to Wisdom in Wisd. 7:26 and to the pre-existent Christ in Heb. 1:3. The image of the *invisible* God must surely be visible (paradoxical though this sounds).

12 Cf. 1 Cor. 8:6; 2 Cor. 8:9; and Phil. 2:5–6.

13 As usually in Paul (though not elsewhere combined in this way), 'blood' evokes sacrifice, 'cross' debasement and shame.

14 The phrase was used by John A. T. Robinson, *The Human Face of God* (London: SCM Press, 1973), p 10. A good example of the tendency to reduce the connection between the cosmic Christ and Jesus is Matthew Fox, *The Coming of the Cosmic Christ* (San Francisco: Harper & Row, 1988), where Jesus is but one incarnation of the cosmic Christ.

15 E.g. Pizzuto, *A Cosmic Leap*, pp 190–202.

16 Marianne Meye Thompson, *Colossians and Philemon* (Two Horizons NT Commentary; Grand Rapids: Eerdmans, 2005), p 113.

17 Many interpreters take 'to him' in v 20 to refer to God, but a reference to Christ is likely in view of the parallelism between the prepositional phrases in the two strophes. In v 16, the phrase 'for him' (Christ) uses the same Greek preposition (*eis*) as 'to him' in v 20.

18 Thompson, *Colossians*, p 33.

19 Jürgen Moltmann, *The Way of Jesus Christ: Christology in Messianic Dimensions* (trans. Margaret Kohl; London: SCM Press, 1990), p 275.

20 Christ as the mystery of God is a theme in Colossians (1:27 and 2:2).

21 Thomas Berry, *The Dream of the Earth* (San Francisco: Sierra Club, 1988), pp 216–217.

22 Cf. Andrew T. Lincoln, 'The Letter to the Colossians', in *The New Interpreter's Bible,* vol. 11 (Nashville: Abingdon, 2000), pp 551–669, here pp 608–609: 'What does it mean in a world of fragmentation, suffering, and confusion to repeat [the hymn's] claim that all things cohere in Christ or that they have been reconciled in him? … [D]espite fragmenting and chaotic forces at work, we humans can trust that the pattern of Christ's death and resurrection is more fundamental and gives the power that sustains the world its distinctive character.'

23 See Michael Lloyd, 'Are Animals Fallen?', in Andrew Linzey and Dorothy Yamamoto eds., *Animals on the Agenda* (London: SCM Press, 1998), pp 147–160; Andrew Linzey, *Animal Gospel: Christian Faith as though Animals Mattered* (London: Hodder & Stoughton, 1998), pp 29–36; Jonathan Clatworthy, 'Let the Fall Down: The Environmental Implications of the Doctrine of the Fall', *Ecotheology* 4 (1998), pp 27–34; Charles Foster, *The Selfless Gene: Living with God and Darwin* (London: Hodder & Stoughton, 2009), chapter 8; Christopher Southgate, *The Groaning of Creation: God, Evolution, and the Problem of Evil* (Louisville: Westminster John Knox, 2008), pp 28–35.

24 I am much less convinced that death or even extinction of species as such is necessarily a problem if the context for understanding them is the expectation that all creatures will participate in the new creation. What some see as the wastefulness of the evolutionary process looks quite different if all of evolution's products are not just part of the temporal process of life but contributions to the new creation.

25 Southgate, *The Groaning*, pp 9–10.

26 Cf, Southgate, *The Groaning*, chapter 5. Southgate, *The Groaning*, chapter 4, also develops the idea of God's co-suffering with the whole creation, as does Niels Henrik Gregersen, 'The Cross of Christ in an Evolutionary World', *Dialog* 40 (2001), pp 192–207. According to Gregersen, 'The Cross of Christ', p 205: 'God bears the cost of evolution, the price involved in the hardship of natural selection.'

27 Vicky Balabanski, 'John 1 – the Earth Bible Challenge: An Intra-textual Approach to Reading John 1', in Norman C. Habel and Vicky Balabanski, eds., *The Earth Story in the New Testament* (Earth Bible 5; London: Sheffield Academic Press, 2002), pp 89–95, here p 92, judges that when *kosmos* is used

with 'reference to salvation – even though the primary reference is to humans – Earth is implicitly included'.

28 This Johannine use of 'flesh' should not be confused with Paul's use, in which 'flesh' is associated more with the tendency to evil in unredeemed human nature. John's usage is close to that of the Old Testament, e.g. in Gen. 6:3 and Isa. 40:6.

29 Gregersen, 'The Cross of Christ', p 205, calls this 'deep incarnation': 'an incarnation into the very tissue of biological existence, and system of nature'.

30 Norman C. Habel, 'An Ecojustice Challenge: Is Earth Valued in John 1?', in Habel and Balabanski, eds., *The Earth Story in the New Testament,* pp 76–82.

31 In John, 'eternal life' takes the place of 'kingdom of God' in the Synoptics.

32 See Matt. 5:45; 10:29–31; 11:25 and 19:9; Mark 10:6; Luke 10:21 and 12:6–7.

33 Most treatments of the background to the Kingdom of God in the Gospels give no great prominence to the Psalms, but Bruce Chilton, *Pure Kingdom: Jesus' Vision of God* (Grand Rapids: Eerdmans/London: SPCK, 1996), chapter 2, especially remedies this failure.

34 John P. Meier, *A Marginal Jew: Rethinking the Historical Jesus*, vol. 2: *Mentor, Message, and Miracles* (New York: Doubleday, 1994), pp 298–299.

35 For these examples, see Mark 4:30–32 and 4:35–42; Luke 12:37; and John 13:3–20.

36 Andrew Linzey, *Animal Theology* (Urbana/Chicago: University of Illinois Press, 1995), p 87.

37 See especially Jon D. Levenson, *Creation and the Persistence of Evil: The Jewish Drama of Divine Omnipotence* (San Francisco: HarperCollins, 1988).

38 For a passage in early Jewish literature that associates actual danger at sea with the myth of chaos and creation, see 1 Enoch 101:4–7.

39 According to 2 Macc. 9:8, it was a blasphemous pretension to divinity when king Antiochus Epiphanes thought he could command the waves of the sea.

40 Jonathan Moo, 'The Sea That is No More: Rev 21:1 and the Function of Sea Imagery in the Apocalypse of John', *NovT* 51 (2009), pp 148–167, argues, rightly in my view, that the absence of sea in the new creation marks its difference from the first creation. The forces of chaos, always a latent threat of destruction for the first creation, can no longer threaten the new creation. On the other hand, Barbara R. Rossing, 'River of Life in God's New Jerusalem: An Eschatological Vision for Earth's Future', in Hessel and Ruether eds., *Christianity and Ecology,* pp 205–224, here pp 212–213, makes an interesting case for connecting it with the critique of Rome's sea trade in Rev. 18, so that the disappearance of the sea indicates the end of trade in luxury goods.

41 The discussion of this passage by Thomas Kazen, 'Standing Helpless at the Roar and Surging of the Sea: Reading Biblical Texts in the Shadow of the Wave', *ST* 60 (2006), pp21–41, here pp 30–32, misses this theme of eschatological anticipation, and so makes the story much more difficult to reconcile with a modern understanding of the forces of nature than is necessary.

42 Kazen, 'Standing Helpless', p 28.

43 For a systematic theological development of the cosmic dimension of the resurrection of Jesus, see Jürgen Moltmann, *The Way of Jesus Christ* (trans. Margaret Kohl; London: SCM Press, 1990), pp 252–259.

44 On the Christology, see Richard Bauckham, *Jesus and the God of Israel:* God Crucified *and Other Studies on the New Testament's Christology of Divine Identity* (Milton Keynes: Paternoster/Grand Rapids: Eerdmans, 2008), pp 37–38, 41–45 and 197–210.

45 For these four realms of creation, cf. Job 11:8–9. For the oceanic abyss under the Earth, cf. Gen. 49:25; Exod. 20:4; Deut. 5:8; and Job 26:5–6.

46 There is an echo here of such texts as Exod. 20:11; Ps. 146:6; and Neh. 9:6.

47 For more on this topic, see Richard Bauckham, 'Creation's Praise of God in the Book of Revelation', *BTB* 38 (2008), pp 55–63.

48 My own literal translation.

49 Jean-Yves Thériault, 'La Portée Écologique de la Notion Paulinienne de Création', *EgT* 22 (1991), pp 295–313, here pp 306–307; Douglas J. Moo, 'Creation and New Creation: Transforming Christian Perspectives', in Robert S. White ed., *Creation in Crisis: Christian Perspectives on Sustainability* (London: SPCK, 2009), pp 241–254, here pp 250–251 (tentatively). But for an argument against this view, see Moyer V. Hubbard, *New Creation in Paul's Letters and Thought* (SNTSMS 119; Cambridge: Cambridge University Press, 2002), p 181.

50 But to press for a distinction of meaning between the two Greek words for 'new' – *kainos* and *neos* – is mistaken.

51 One other New Testament passage has been frequently understood to speak of the destruction of the present heavens and Earth and their replacement by the new creation: 2 Peter 3:10–13. On this passage, see Jonathan Moo, 'Environmental Unsustainability and a Biblical Vision of the Earth's Future', in White ed., *Creation in Crisis*, pp 255–270, here pp 261–267.

52 I think the plural ('peoples') is the correct reading in Rev. 21:3, and that it is significant and to be connected with the theme of 'the nations' throughout Revelation and in 21:24–26.

53 For a fuller discussion of the New Jerusalem in Revelation, see Richard Bauckham, *The Theology of the Book of Revelation* (Cambridge: Cambridge University Press, 1993), chapter 6. For the ecological dimension, see also Rossing, 'River of Life'.

BIBLIOGRAPHY

Addinall, Peter. 'The Wilderness of Pedersen's *Israel*'. *JSOT* 20 (1981), pp 75–82.

Allaby, Michael. *A Guide to Gaia: A Survey of the New Science of Our Living Earth*. New York: Dutton, 1990.

Allen, Leslie C. *Psalms 101–150*. WBC 21. Waco: Word, 1983.

Allen, Leslie C. *The Books of Joel, Obadiah, Jonah and Micah*. NICOT. Grand Rapids: Eerdmans, 1976.

Attfield, Robin. 'Environmental Sensitivity and Critiques of Stewardship'. In R. J. Berry ed., *Environmental Stewardship*, pp 76–91.

Attfield, Robin. *The Ethics of Environmental Concern*. 2nd edition. Athens, Georgia: University of Georgia Press, 1991.

Anderson, Bernhard W. *From Creation to New Creation*. OBT. Minneapolis: Fortress, 1994.

Balabanski, Vicky. 'John 1 – the Earth Bible Challenge: An Intra-textual Approach to Reading John 1'. In Norman C. Habel and Vicky Balabanski eds., *The Earth Story in the New Testament*, pp 89–95.

Barrow, John D. *Theories of Everything: The Quest for Ultimate Explanation*. London: Vintage, 1991.

Batto, Bernard Frank. *Slaying the Dragon: Mythmaking in the Biblical Tradition*. Louisville: Westminster John Knox, 1992.

Bauckham, Richard. 'Creation's Praise of God in the Book of Revelation'. *BTB* 38 (2008), pp 55–63.

Bauckham, Richard. *God and the Crisis of Freedom*. Louisville: Westminster John Knox, 2002.

Bauckham, Richard. 'Jesus and Animals I: What Did He Teach?' In Andrew Linzey and Dorothy Yamamoto ed., *Animals on the Agenda*, pp 33–48.

Bauckham, Richard. *Jesus and the God of Israel: God Crucified and Other Studies on the New Testament's Christology of Divine Identity*. Milton Keynes: Paternoster/ Grand Rapids: Eerdmans, 2008.

Bauckham, Richard. 'Jesus and the Wild Animals (Mark 1:13): A Christological Image for an Ecological Age'. In Joel B. Green and Max Turner eds., *Jesus of Nazareth: Lord and Christ*, pp 3–21.

Bauckham, Richard. 'Joining Creation's Praise of God'. *Ecotheology* 7 (2002), pp 45–59.

Bauckham, Richard. 'Modern Domination of Nature – Historical Origins and Biblical Critique'. In R. J. Berry ed., *Environmental Stewardship*, pp 32–50.

Bauckham, Richard. 'Reading the Sermon on the Mount in an Age of Ecological Catastrophe'. *SCE* 22 (2009), pp 76–88.

Bauckham, Richard. *The Theology of the Book of Revelation*. Cambridge: Cambridge University Press, 1993.

Bekoff, Marc. 'Animal Passions and Beastly Virtues: Cognitive Ethology as the Unifying Science for Understanding the Subjective, Emotional, Empathic, and Moral Lives of Animals'. *Zygon* 41 (2006), pp 71–104.

Bekoff, Marc. *Animal Passions and Beastly Virtues: Reflections on Redecorating Nature*. Philadelphia: Temple University Press, 2006.

Bergmann, S., P. M. Scott, M. Jansdotter Samuelsson and H. Bedford-Strohm eds. *Nature, Space and the Sacred: Transdisciplinary Perspectives*. Farnham, Surrey: Ashgate, 2009.

Berlin, Adele. 'The Wisdom of Creation in Psalm 104'. In Ronald L. Troxel, Kelvin G. Friebel and Dennis R. Magary eds., *Seeking Out the Wisdom of the Ancients*, pp 71–83.

Berry, R. J., ed. *Environmental Stewardship: Critical Perspectives – Past and Present*. London/New York: T. & T. Clark International, 2006.

Berry, R. J., ed. *The Care of Creation*. Leicester: InterVarsity Press, 2000.

Berry, Thomas, and Thomas Clarke. *Befriending the Earth: A Theology of Reconciliation Between Humans and the Earth*. Mystic, Connecticut: Twenty-Third Publications, 1991.

Berry, Thomas. 'Christianity's Role in the Earth Project'. In Dieter T. Hessel and Rosemary Radford Ruether eds., *Christianity and Ecology*, pp 127–134.

Berry, Thomas. *The Dream of the Earth*. San Francisco: Sierra Club, 1988.

Berry, Wendell. *Home Economics: Fourteen Essays*. San Francisco: North Point Press, 1987.

Berry, Wendell. *Sex, Economy, Freedom and Community: Eight Essays*. New York: Pantheon Books, 1993.

Black, John. 'The Dominion of Man'. In R. J. Berry ed., *Environmental Stewardship*, pp 92–96.

Blenkinsopp, Joseph. *Isaiah 1–39*. AB 19. New York: Doubleday, 2000.

Borowski, Oded. *Every Living Thing: Daily Use of Animals in Ancient Israel*. Walton Creek, California: AltaMira Press, 1998.

Bouma-Prediger, Steven. *For the Beauty of the Earth: A Christian Vision for Creation Care*. Grand Rapids: Baker Academic, 2001.

Braaten, Laurie J. 'All Creation Groans: Romans 8:22 in Light of the Biblical Sources'. *HBT* 28 (2006), pp 131–159.

Braaten, Laurie J. 'Earth Community in Joel 1–2: A Call to Identify with the Rest of Creation'. *HBT* 28 (2006), pp 113–129.

Brett, Mark G. 'Earthing the Human in Genesis 1–3'. In Norman C. Habel and Shirley Wurst eds., *The Earth Story in Genesis*, pp 73–86.

Brown, William P. *Seeing the Psalms: A Theology of Metaphor*. Louisville, Kentucky: Westminster John Knox, 2003.

Brown, William P. *The Ethos of the Cosmos: The Genesis of Moral Imagination in the Bible*. Grand Rapids: Eerdmans, 1999.

Brown, William P., and S. Dean McBride eds. *God Who Creates: Essays in Honor of W. Sibley Towner*. Grand Rapids: Eerdmans, 2000.

Brueggemann, Walter. *A Commentary on Jeremiah: Exile and Homecoming*. Grand Rapids: Eerdmans, 1998.

Brueggemann, Walter. *Genesis*. Interpretation; Atlanta: John Knox Press, 1982.

Brueggemann, Walter. *Theology of the Old Testament*. Minneapolis: Fortress, 1997.

Budiansky, Stephen. *The Covenant of the Wild: Why Animals Chose Domestication*. London: Weidenfeld & Nicolson, 1994.

Bulliet, Richard W. *Hunters, Herders, and Hamburgers: The Past and Future of Human–Animal Relationships*. New York: Columbia University Press, 2005.

Callicott, J. Baird. 'Genesis and John Muir'. In Carol S. Robb and Carl J. Casebolt eds., *Covenant for a New Creation*, pp 116–118.

Callicott, J. Baird. 'Land Ethics: Into Terra Incognita'. In Curt Meine and Richard L. Knight eds., *The Essential Aldo Leopold,* pp 299–313

Callicott, J. Baird. 'The New New (Buddhist) Ecology'. *JSRNC* 2 (2008), pp 166–182.

Cansdale, George. *All the Animals of the Bible Lands*. Grand Rapids: Zondervan, 1970.

Childs, Brevard S. *Isaiah*. OTL. Louisville: Westminster John Knox, 2001.

Chilton, Bruce. *Pure Kingdom: Jesus' Vision of God*. Grand Rapids: Eerdmans/ London: SPCK, 1996.

Christoffersson, Olle. *The Earnest Expectation of the Creature: The Flood-Tradition as Matrix of Romans 8:18–27*. ConBNT 23. Stockholm: Almqvist & Wiksell, 1990.

Clark, Stephen R. L. 'Is Nature God's Will?' In Andrew Linzey and Dorothy Yamamoto eds., *Animals on the Agenda*, pp 123–136.

Clatworthy, Jonathan. 'Let the Fall Down: The Environmental Implications of the Doctrine of the Fall'. *Ecotheology* 4 (1998), pp 27–34.

Clifford, Richard J. *Proverbs: A Commentary*. OTL. Louisville: Westminster, 1999.

Conradie, Ernst M. 'Towards an Agenda for Ecological Theology: An Intercontinental Dialogue'. *Ecotheology* 10 (2005), pp 281–343.

Couroyer, B. 'Qui est Béhémot? Job, XL, 15–24'. *RB* 82 (1975), pp 418–443.

Davis, Ellen. *Scripture, Culture, and Agriculture: An Agrarian Reading of the Bible*. Cambridge: Cambridge University Press, 2009.

Day Lewis, C. *The Poetic Image*. London: Jonathan Cape, 1947.

Deane-Drummond, Celia. 'God and *Gaia*: Myth or Reality?' *Theology* 95 (1992), pp 277–285.

Devall, Bill. *Simple in Means, Deep in Ends: Practising Deep Ecology*. London: Green Print, 1990.

DeWitt, Calvin B. 'Behemoth and Batrachians in the Eye of God: Responsibility to Other Kinds in Biblical Perspective'. In Dieter T. Hessel and Rosemary Radford Ruether eds., *Christianity and Ecology*, pp 291–316.

Dubos, René. *The Wooing of Earth*. London: Athlone Press, 1980.

Eagleton, Terry. *Reason, Faith, and Revolution: Reflections on the God Debate*. New Haven/London: Yale University Press, 2009.

Echlin, Edward P. *The Cosmic Circle: Jesus and Ecology*. Dublin: Columba Press, 2004.

Eisenberg, Evan. *The Ecology of Eden*. London: Picador, 1998.

Feliks, Yehuda. *Nature and Man in the Bible*. London: Soncino Press, 1981.

Felister, John. *Can Poetry Save the Earth? A Field Guide to Nature Poems*. New Haven: Yale University Press, 2009.

Fern, Richard L. *Nature, God and Humanity: Envisioning an Ethics of Nature*. Cambridge: Cambridge University Press, 2002.

Fitzgerald, Aloysius. *The Lord of the East Wind*. CBQMS 34. Washington: Catholic Biblical Association of America, 2002.

Foster, Charles. *The Selfless Gene: Living with God and Darwin*. London: Hodder & Stoughton, 2009.

Fox, Matthew. *The Coming of the Cosmic Christ*. San Francisco: Harper & Row, 1988.

Fretheim, Terence E. *God and the World in the Old Testament: A Relational Theology of Creation*. Nashville: Abingdon, 2005.

Fretheim, Terence E. 'The Earth Story in Jeremiah 12'. In Norman C. Habel ed., *Readings from the Perspective of Earth,* pp 96–110.

Fyall, Robert S. *Now My Eyes Have Seen You: Images of Creation in the Book of Job*. New Studies in Biblical Theology 12. Downers Grove, Illinois: InterVarsity Press/Leicester: Apollos, 2002.

Geyer, John B. 'Desolation and Cosmos'. *VT* 49 (1999), pp 49–64.

Gilkey, Langdon. 'Power, Order, Justice, and Redemption: Theological Comments on Job'. In Leo G. Perdue and W. Clark Gilpin eds., *The Voice from the Whirlwind*, pp 159–171.

Gordis, Robert. *The Book of God and Man: A Study of Job*. Chicago/London: University of Chicago Press, 1965.

Gowan, Donald E. 'God's Answer to Job: How Is It an Answer?' *Horizons of Biblical Theology* 8 (1986), pp 85–102.

Grandin, Temple, and Catherine Johnson. *Animals in Translation: Using the Mysteries of Autism to Decode Animal Behaviour*. London: Bloomsbury, 2006.

Green, Joel B., and Max Turner eds. *Jesus of Nazareth: Lord and Christ: Essays on the Historical Jesus and New Testament Christology*. Festschrift for I. Howard Marshall. Grand Rapids: Eerdmans, 1994.

Gregersen, Niels Henrik. 'The Cross of Christ in an Evolutionary World.' *Dialog* 40 (2001) pp 192–207.

Habel, Norman C. 'An Ecojustice Challenge: Is Earth Valued in John 1?' In Norman C. Habel and Vicky Balabanski eds., *The Earth Story in the New Testament*, pp 76–82.

Habel, Norman C. *An Inconvenient Text: Is a Green Reading of the Bible Possible?* Adelaide: ATF Press, 2009.

Habel, Norman C. 'Geophany: The Earth Story in Genesis 1'. In Norman C. Habel and Shirley Wurst eds., *The Earth Story in Genesis*, pp 34–48.

Habel, Norman C. 'Introducing the Earth Bible'. In Norman C. Habel ed., *Readings from the Perspective of Earth*, pp 25–37.

Habel, Norman C. 'Is the Wild Ox Willing to Serve You?' Challenging the Mandate to Dominate'. In Norman C. Habel and Shirley Wurst, eds., *The Earth Story in Wisdom*, pp 179–189.

Habel, Norman C., ed. *Readings from the Perspective of Earth*. Earth Bible 1. Sheffield: Sheffield Academic Press, 2000.

Habel, Norman C. *The Book of Job: A Commentary*. Old Testament Library. London: SCM Press, 1985.

Habel, Norman C. ed. *The Earth Story in the Psalms and the Prophets*. Earth Bible 4. Sheffield: Sheffield Academic Press, 2001.

Habel, Norman C., and Vicky Balabanski eds. *The Earth Story in the New Testament*. Earth Bible 5. London: Sheffield Academic Press, 2002.

Habel, Norman C., and Peter Trudinger eds., *Exploring Ecological Hermeneutics*. SBLSymS 46. Atlanta: SBL, 2008.

Habel, Norman C., and Shirley Wurst eds. *The Earth Story in Genesis*. Earth Bible 2. Sheffield: Sheffield Academic Press, 2000.

Habel, Norman C., and Shirley Wurst eds. *The Earth Story in Wisdom Traditions*. Earth Bible 3. Sheffield: Sheffield Academic Press, 2001.

Hall, Douglas J. 'Stewardship as a Key to a Theology of Nature'. In R. J. Berry ed., *Environmental Stewardship*, pp 129–144.

Hardy, Daniel W., and David F. Ford. *Jubilate: Theology in Praise*. London: Darton, Longman & Todd, 1984.

Harrison, Peter. 'Subduing the Earth: Genesis 1, Early Modern Science and the Exploitation of Nature'. *JR* 79 (1999), pp 86–109. Reprinted (with revisions) in R. J. Berry ed., *Environmental Stewardship*, pp 17–31.

Haught, John F. *The Promise of Nature: Ecology and Cosmic Purpose*. Mahwah: Paulist Press, 1993.

Hayes, Katherine M. *'The Earth Mourns': Prophetic Metaphor and Oral Aesthetic*. SBLAB 8. Atlanta: SBL, 2002.

Herbert, George. *George Herbert: The Country Parson, The Temple*. Ed. John N. Wall. Classics of Western Spirituality; New York/Mahwah: Paulist, 1981.

Hessel, Dieter T. and Rosemary Radford Ruether eds. *Christianity and Ecology: Seeking the Well-Being of Earth and Humans*. Cambridge, Massachusetts: Harvard University Press, 2000.

Hiebert, Theodore. 'The Human Vocation: Origins and Transformations in Christian Traditions'. In Dieter T. Hessel and Rosemary Radford Ruether eds., *Christianity and Ecology*, pp 135–154.

Hiebert, Theodore. *The Yahwist's Landscape: Nature and Religion in Early Israel*. New York/Oxford: Oxford University Press, 1996.

Hillel, Daniel. *The Natural History of the Bible*. New York: Columbia University Press, 2006.

Holmgren, Virginia C. *Bird Walk through the Bible*. New York: Dover, 1972.

Hoezee, Scott. *Remember Creation: God's World of Wonder and Delight*. Grand Rapids: Eerdmans, 1998.

Houston, Walter J. *Purity and Monotheism*. JSOTS 140. Sheffield: Sheffield Academic Press, 1993.

Hubbard, Moyer V. *New Creation in Paul's Letters and Thought*. SNTSMS 119. Cambridge: Cambridge University Press, 2002.

Hunt, Cherryl, David G. Horrell and Christopher Southgate. 'An Environmental Mantra? Ecological Interest in Romans 8:19–23 and a Modest Proposal for its Narrative Interpretation'. *JTS* 59 (2008), pp 546–579.

Hüttermann, Aloys. *The Ecological Message of the Torah: Knowledge, Concepts, and Laws which Made Survival in a Land of 'Milk and Honey' Possible*. South Florida Studies in the History of Judaism 199. Atlanta: Scholars Press, 1999.

Jacob, Edmond. *Theology of the Old Testament*. Trans. Arthur W. Heathcote and Philip J. Allcock. London: Hodder & Stoughton, 1958.

Jantzen, J. Gerald. 'Creation and the Human Predicament in Job 1:9–11 and 38–41'. *Ex Auditu* 3 (1987), pp 45–53.

Kazen, Thomas. 'Standing Helpless at the Roar and Surging of the Sea: Reading Biblical Texts in the Shadow of the Wave'. *ST* 60 (2006), pp 21–41.

Keel, Othmar. *Jahwes Entgegnung an Ijob: Eine Deutung von Ijob 38–41 vor dem Hintergrund der zeitgenösseischen Bildkunst*. FRLANT 121. Göttingen: Vandenhoeck & Ruprecht, 1978.

Kover, Tihamer R. 'The Domestic Order and its Feral Threat: The Intellectual Heritage of the Neolithic Landscape'. In S. Bergmann, P. M. Scott, M. Jansdotter Samuelsson and H. Bedford-Strohm eds., *Nature, Space and the Sacred*, pp 235–247.

Lang, Bernhard. 'Job XL:18 and the "Bones of Seth" '. *VT* 30 (1980), pp 360–361.

Lang, Bernhard. *The Hebrew God: Portrait of an Ancient Deity*. New Haven/London: Yale University Press, 2002.

Leal, Robert Barry. 'Negativity towards Wilderness in the Biblical Record'. *Ecotheology* 10 (2005), pp 364–381.

Leal, Robert Barry. *Wilderness in the Bible: Toward a Theology of Wilderness*. Studies in Biblical Literature 72. New York: Peter Lang, 2004.

Leopold, Aldo. *A Sand County Almanac and Sketches Here and There*. New York: Oxford University Press, 1987.

Levenson, Jon D. *Creation and the Persistence of Evil: The Jewish Drama of Divine Omnipotence*. San Francisco: HarperCollins, 1988.

Lincoln, Andrew T. 'The Letter to the Colossians'. In *The New Interpreter's Bible*, vol. 11. Nashville: Abingdon, 2000, pp 551–669.

Linzey, Andrew. *Animal Gospel: Christian Faith as though Animals Mattered*. London: Hodder & Stoughton, 1998.

Linzey, Andrew. *Animal Theology*. London: SCM Press, 1984/ Urbana: University of Illinois Press, 1995.

Linzey, Andrew, and Dorothy Yamamoto eds. *Animals on the Agenda: Questions about Animals for Theology and Ethics*. London: SCM Press, 1998.

Lloyd, Michael. 'Are Animals Fallen?' In Andrew Linzey and Dorothy Yamamoto eds., *Animals on the Agenda*, pp 147–160.

Lohfink, Norbert. *Theology of the Pentateuch: Themes of the Priestly Narrative and Deuteronomy*. Trans. Linda M. Malony. Edinburgh: T. & T. Clark, 1994.

Löning, Karl, and Erich Zenger. *To Begin With, God Created: Biblical Theologies of Creation*. Collegeville: Liturgical Press, 2000.

Lovelock, James. *The Ages of Gaia: A Biography of our Living Earth*. Oxford: Oxford University Press, 1988.

Lovelock, James. 'The Fallible Concept of Stewardship of the Earth'. In R. J. Berry ed., *Environmental Stewardship*, pp 106–111.

Lovelock, James. *The Revenge of Gaia: Why the Earth is Fighting Back – and How We Can Still Save Humanity*. London: Allen Lane, 2006.

Loya, Melissa Tubbs. ' "Therefore the Earth Mourns": The Grievance of Earth in Hosea 4:1–3'. In Norman C. Habel and Peter Trudinger eds., *Exploring Ecological Hermeneutics*, pp 53–62.

McDaniel, Jay. 'All Animals Matter: Marc Bekoff's Contribution to Constructive Christian Theology'. *Zygon* 41 (2006), pp 29–57.

McKibben, Bill. *The Comforting Whirlwind: God, Job, and the Scale of Creation*. Grand Rapids: Eerdmans, 1994.

McKibben, Bill. *The End of Nature*. London: Viking, 1990.

Marcus, Joel. *Mark 1–8*. AB 27. New York: Doubleday, 1999.

Marlow, Hilary. *Biblical Prophets and Contemporary Environmental Ethics: Re-Reading Amos, Hosea and First Isaiah*. Oxford, Oxford University Press, 2009.

Meier, John P. *A Marginal Jew: Rethinking the Historical Jesus*, vol. 2: *Mentor, Message, and Miracles*. New York: Doubleday, 1994.

Meine, Curt, and Richard L. Knight. *The Essential Aldo Leopold: Quotations and Commentaries*. Madison, Wisconsin: Wisconsin University Press, 1999.

Mettinger, Tryggve N. D. 'The God of Job: Avenger, Tyrant, or Victor?' In Leo G. Perdue and W. Clark Gilpin eds., *The Voice from the Whirlwind*, pp 39–49.

Meye Thompson, Marianne. *Colossians and Philemon*. Two Horizons NT Commentary. Grand Rapids: Eerdmans, 2005.

Mick, Lawrence L. *Liturgy and Ecology in Dialogue*. Collegeville, Minnesota: Liturgical Press, 1997.

Moltmann, Jürgen. *God in Creation: An Ecological Doctrine of Creation*. Trans. Margaret Kohl. London: SCM Press, 1985.

Moltmann, Jürgen. *The Way of Jesus Christ: Christology in Messianic Dimensions*. Trans. Margaret Kohl. London: SCM Press, 1990.

Moo, Douglas J. 'Creation and New Creation: Transforming Christian Perspectives.' In Robert S. White ed., *Creation in Crisis*, pp 241–254.

Moo, Jonathan. 'Environmental Unsustainability and a Biblical Vision of the Earth's Future'. In Robert S. White ed., *Creation in Crisis*, pp 255–270.

Moo, Jonathan. 'Romans 8.19–22 and Isaiah's Cosmic Covenant'. *NTS* 54 (2008), pp 74–89.

Moo, Jonathan. 'The Sea That is No More: Rev 21:1 and the Function of Sea Imagery in the Apocalypse of John'. *NovT* 51 (2009), pp 148–167.

Murray, Robert. *The Cosmic Covenant*. Heythrop Monographs 7. London: Sheed & Ward, 1992.

Naish, John. *Enough*. London: Hodder & Stoughton, 2008.

Nash, Roderick Frazier. *Wilderness and the American Mind*. 4th edition. New Haven: Yale University Press, 2001.

Newsom, Carol A. 'Common Ground: An Ecological Reading of Genesis 2–3'. In Norman C. Habel and Shirley Wurst eds., *The Earth Story in Genesis*, pp 60–72.

Noble, David E. *The Religion of Technology: The Divinity of Man and the Spirit of Invention*. New York: Penguin, 1999.

Northcott, Michael S. *A Moral Climate: The Ethics of Global Warming*. London: Darton, Longman & Todd, 2007.

Northcott, Michael. *The Environment and Christian Ethics*. New Studies in Christian Ethics. Cambridge: Cambridge University Press, 1996.

O'Connor, T. P. 'Working at Relationships: Another Look at Animal Domestication'. *Antiquity* 71 (1987), pp 149–156.

Oeschlaeger, Max. *The Idea of Wilderness: From Prehistory to the Age of Ecology*. New Haven: Yale University Press, 1991.

Olley, John W. ' "The Wolf, the Lamb, and a Little Child": Transforming the Diverse Earth Community in Isaiah'. In Norman C. Habel ed., *The Earth Story in the Psalms and the Prophets*, pp 219–229.

Page, Ruth. 'The Fellowship of All Creation'. In R. J. Berry ed., *Environmental Stewardship*, pp 97–105.

Palmer, Clare. 'Stewardship: A Case Study in Environmental Ethics'. In R. J. Berry ed., *Environmental Stewardship*, pp 63–75.

Patrick, Dale. 'Divine Creative Power and the Decentering of Creation: The Subtext of the Lord's Addresses to Job'. In Norman C. Habel and Shirley Wurst eds., *The Earth Story in Wisdom Traditions*, pp 103–115.

Peacocke, Arthur R. *Creation and the World of Science*. Oxford: Clarendon Press, 1979.

Pedersen, Johannes. *Israel: Its Life and Culture*. 2 vols. Oxford University Press: London, 1946–1947.

Perdue, Leo G. *Wisdom in Revolt: Metaphorical Theology in the Book of Job*. JSOTSup 112. Bible and Literature Series 29. Sheffield: Sheffield Academic Press, 1991.

Perdue, Leo G., and W. Clark Gilpin eds., *The Voice from the Whirlwind: Interpreting the Book of Job*. Nashville: Abingdon Press, 1992.

Phillips, Anthony. 'Animals and the Torah'. *ExpTim* 106 (1995), pp 260–265.

Pinches, Charles. 'Each According to Its Kind: A Defense of Theological Speciesism.' In Charles Pinches and Jay B. McDaniel eds., *Good News for Animals?*, pp 187–205.

Pinches, Charles, and Jay B. McDaniel eds., *Good News for Animals? Christian Approaches to Animal Well-Being*. New York: Orbis, 1993.

Pizzuto, Vincent A. *A Cosmic Leap of Faith: An Authorial, Structural, and Theological Investigation of the Cosmic Christology in Col 1:15–20*. CBET 41. Leuven: Peeters, 2006.

Ramsey, George W. 'Is Name-Giving an Act of Domination in Genesis 2:23 and Elsewhere?' *CBQ* 50 (1988), pp 24–35.

Rasmussen, Larry. 'Symbols to Live By'. In R. J. Berry ed., *Environmental Stewardship*, pp 174–184.

Rees, Martin. *Our Final Century: Will Civilisation Survive the Twenty-First Century?* London: Random House (Arrow Books), 2004.

Reichenbach, Bruce R. and V. Elving Anderson. 'Tensions in a Stewardship Paradigm'. In R. J. Berry ed., *Environmental Stewardship*, pp 112–125.

Robb, Carol S. and Carl J. Casebolt eds., *Covenant for a New Creation*. Maryknoll, New York: Orbis, 1991.

Robinson, John A. T. *The Human Face of God*. London: SCM Press, 1973.

Rogerson, John W. 'What was the Meaning of Animal Sacrifice'. In Andrew Linzey and Dorothy Yamamoto eds., *Animals on the Agenda*, pp 8–17.

Rossing, Barbara R. 'River of Life in God's New Jerusalem: An Eschatological Vision for Earth's Future'. In Dieter T. Hessel and Rosemary Radford Ruether eds., *Christianity and Ecology*, pp 205–224.

Ruether, Rosemary Radford. 'Men, Women, and Beasts: Relations to Animals in Western Culture'. In Charles Pinches and Jay B. McDaniel eds., *Good News for Animals?*, pp 12–23.

Russell, Colin A. *The Earth, Humanity and God*. London: UCL Press, 1994.

Schochet, Elijah Judah. *Animal Life in Jewish Traditions*. New York: Ktav, 1984.

Simkins, Ronald A. *Creator and Creation: Nature in the Worldview of Ancient Israel*. Peabody: Hendrickson, 1994.

Sittler, Joseph. *Evocations of Grace: Writings on Ecology, Theology and Ethics*. Ed. Steven Bouma-Prediger and Peter Bakken. Grand Rapids: Eerdmans, 2000.

Southgate, Christopher. 'Stewardship and its Competitors: A Spectrum of Relationships between Humans and the Non-Human Creation'. In R. J. Berry ed., *Environmental Stewardship*, pp 185–195.

Southgate, Christopher. *The Groaning of Creation: God, Evolution, and the Problem of Evil*. Louisville: Westminster John Knox, 2008.

Spanner, Huw. 'Tyrants, Stewards – or Just Kings?' In Andrew Linzey and Dorothy Yamamoto eds., *Animals on the Agenda*, pp 216–224.

Steck, Odil Hannes. *World and Environment*. Biblical Encounters Series. Nashville: Abingdon, 1980.

Strong, David. 'The Promise of Technology Versus God's Promise in Job'. *Theology Today* 48 (1991–92), pp 170–181.

Swimme, Brian, and Thomas Berry. *The Universe Story: From the Primordial Flaring Forth to the Ecozoic Era – A Celebration of the Unfolding of the Cosmos*. London: Penguin, 1994.

Theokritoff, Elizabeth. 'Creation and Priesthood in Modern Orthodox Thinking'. *Ecotheology* 10 (2005), pp 344–363.

Thériault, Jean-Yves. 'La portée écologique de la notion paulinienne de creation'. *EgT* 22 (1991), pp 295–313.

Thiselton, Anthony C. *The First Epistle to the Corinthians*. NIGTC. Grand Rapids: Eerdmans, 2000.

Towner, W. Sibley. 'The Future of Nature'. *Int* 50 (1996), pp 27–35.

Trainor, Michael. 'The Cosmic Christology of Colossians 1:15–20 in the Light of Contemporary Ecological Issues'. *ABR* 53 (2005), pp 54–69.

Troxel, Ronald L., Kelvin G. Friebel and Dennis R. Magary eds., *Seeking Out the Wisdom of the Ancients: Essays Offered to Honor Michael V. Fox*. Winona Lake, Indiana: Eisenbrauns, 2005.

Tucker, Gene M. 'Rain on a Land Where No One Lives: The Hebrew Bible on the Environment'. *JBL* 116 (1997), pp 3–17.

Tucker, Gene M. 'The Peaceable Kingdom and a Covenant with the Wild Animals'. In William P. Brown and S. Dean McBride eds., *God Who Creates,* pp 215–225.

van Wolde, Ellen. *Stories of the Beginning: Genesis 1–11 and Other Creation Stories.* Trans. John Bowden. London: SCM Press, 1996.

Vawter, Bruce. *On Genesis: A New Reading.* New York: Doubleday, 1977.

Walker-Jones, Arthur. 'The So-Called Ostrich in the God Speeches of the Book of Job (Job 39,13–18)'. *Biblica* 86 (2005), pp 494–510.

Waltke, Bruce K. *The Book of Proverbs Chapters 1–15.* NICOT. Grand Rapids: Eerdmans, 2004.

Watson, Rebecca S. *Chaos Uncreated: A Reassessment of the Theme of 'Chaos' in the Hebrew Bible.* BZAW 341. Berlin: De Gruyter, 2005.

Watts, John D. W. *Isaiah 34–66.* WBC 25. Revised edition. N.p.: Thomas Nelson, 2005.

Weisman, Alan. *The World Without Us.* London: Virgin Books, 2007.

Welker, Michael. *Creation and Reality.* Trans. John F. Hoffmeyer. Minneapolis: Fortress, 1999.

Wennberg, Robert N. *God, Humans, and Other Animals.* Grand Rapids: Eerdmans, 2003.

Westermann, Claus. *Genesis 1–11.* Trans. John J. Scullion. London: SPCK, 1974.

White, Robert S., ed. *Creation in Crisis: Christian Perspectives on Sustainability.* London: SPCK, 2009.

Whybray, Roger Norman. *Proverbs.* NCB. London: Marshall Pickering, 1994.

Wilkinson, Loren, ed. *Earthkeeping in the Nineties: Stewardship of Creation.* Grand Rapids: Eerdmans, 1991.

Williams, David. *Animals Rights, Human Responsibilities.* Grove Booklet E151. Cambridge, 2008.

Wirzba, Norman. *The Paradise of God: Renewing Religion in an Ecological Age.* New York/Oxford: Oxford University Press, 2003.

Wright, Christopher J. H. *Old Testament Ethics for the People of God.* Leicester: InterVarsity Press, 2004.

Zizioulas, John. 'Priest of Creation'. In R. J. Berry ed., *Environmental Stewardship,* pp 273–290.

Zohary, Michael. *Plants of the Bible.* Cambridge: Cambridge University Press, 1982.

INDEX OF BIBLE REFERENCES

Index of Bible References

INDEX OF SUBJECTS AND NAMES

Index of Subjects and Names

Horus 61

hubris 2, 5–7, 10, 37–8, 50–1, 65

human rights 32

human role 2

humility 44–5, 131

husbandry 136

idealism 148, 172

ideology 37

inanimate nature 91, 146

interdependence 15, 19, 28, 33, 64, 82, 87–8, 90, 146, 168

irrigation 22, 34, 106

Isaiah 161

Islam 143

Israel 26–7, 32–3, 60–1, 78, 93–4, 106, 110–11, 115, 121, 126, 143, 150, 165

Israelites 27, 71, 106, 110–11, 115, 117, 119, 139, 169

Jerusalem 108, 112, 116, 161, 167, 176–8

Jesse 121–2

Jesus Christ 26, 73–6, 126–9, 137–8, 140–5, 148, 151–70, 172–3, 175, 178

Jews 20, 73

joy 68–70, 91, 98–9, 102, 117, 123

Judea 126, 128

killer instinct 119

Kingdom of God 100, 125–6, 129, 164–8, 170, 174

kingship 32, 136, 165

kinship 20–1, 163

Lamb 174, 176, 178

Lamech 34, 119

lament 101–2, 114

land community 87, 91

land law 26–7, 33, 115

Lebanon 99, 117–18

Leviathan 54–60, 62–3, 69–71

liberal democracy 143

lifestyle 72

light 42

Lilith 112

lions 47, 51, 66, 68–9, 111, 114, 117–18, 120, 123–4

loneliness 130

Lord's Prayer 166

maquis 110

Marxism 143

master story 144

materialism 37

meat 25–6, 29, 51, 123

mercy 101, 138–40

Mesopotamia 22

Messiah 120–2, 126, 141, 145

meta-narrative 143–51, 153, 155, 162, 178

metal 34

Middle East 43, 68

Middle Platonism 148

miracles 166–9

monsters 55–61, 71, 77–8

mortality 163–4, 178

Mosaic law 26

mountain goats 47, 52, 68–9, 114

mourning 92–101

music 86

mutual advantage 135

naming 130, 136

naturalists 130

nature miracles 166–8

nature religion 86, 150

Near East 118

needs 73–5, 85, 115

Neo-Platonism 148

New Age 2, 54

new creation 175–8

New Jerusalem 176–8

New Testament 72, 115, 141–5, 150–1, 153, 155, 171–2, 174

Nineveh 110

Noah 19, 22, 32–3, 119, 123, 127–8, 133, 147

nomads 111

non-human creation 91–3, 96, 99–102, 110, 114–15, 126, 128, 133–4, 141–2, 145–7, 160, 162, 164–6

obligations 87–8

oceans 40–1, 60–1, 69, 71, 96, 100, 169

Old Testament 18, 29, 32, 50, 60, 62, 72–3, 96, 100, 103, 138, 140–2, 150, 161, 169, 172–3

ontology 92, 128

oppression 95, 119, 121, 126

orchards 103–9, 116, 118

orchestras 78

Orthodox Church 84

INDEX OF AUTHORS